MW01593243

For permission requests, write to the publisher at the address below:

Fathers and Families of Georgia, LLC. and Black Rose Mediaworks, 2394 Mt Vernon Road, Dunwoody, GA 30338

ISBN: 979-8-9988309-0-7

For permissions, bulk purchases, or special inquiries, please contact:
admin@theseasonedcollective.com

Library of Congress Control Number: 2025913735

First Edition, June 2025

TOO SEASONED TO CARE:

HOW AGING TURNS EXPERIENCE INTO WISDOM AND LIBERATION

CONTENTS

PREFACE

I didn't set out to write a memoir about aging, wisdom, or liberation. In fact, if someone had suggested to my younger self that one
day I'd write openly about the quieter vulnerabilities of becoming
seasoned, I might have laughed—or perhaps, defensively brushed
the idea aside. Yet here I am, embracing and writing from the
very space I once hesitated to enter. It's funny how life has a way
of gently nudging you toward truths you've spent years quietly
avoiding.

There is a common narrative around aging—one wrapped in
apprehension, hesitation, and loss. In my early years, I absorbed
this narrative unconsciously, believing it to be universally true.
Aging meant limitation; it implied irrelevance. It carried the quiet
suggestion that your best years were behind you and your most
valuable contributions already made. This narrative haunted me,
lurking quietly beneath my aspirations, silently shaping my fears
and decisions.

Until one day, I paused long enough to question its validity. In doing so, I discovered something extraordinary—a quiet rebellion against the very notion of limitation.

I began to view the journey of aging not as a decline, but as an evolution—an intentional movement toward freedom and clarity. It became a process of stripping away layers, leaving behind societal expectations, and finally choosing authenticity over approval. Gradually, I understood the profound meaning hidden in the everyday occurrences of my life, those seemingly mundane experiences now illuminated by seasoned eyes. Moments that had once felt ordinary now revealed their extraordinary depth, providing wisdom that only time could unlock.

I've spent decades immersed in advocacy, community building, and fatherhood programs. Through Fathers Incorporated and the countless stories of fathers and families, I've witnessed first-hand the profound intersection between life's lessons and the power of transformation. Yet, even as I advocated passionately for others, I was quietly navigating my own complexities—struggles with identity, purpose, and worth. I was outwardly assured yet inwardly questioning, projecting confidence yet often wrestling privately with doubts.

Throughout my earlier years, I chased validation as if it were oxygen. Every accolade, every nod of approval felt like confirmation of my worth. But as the years began to gather, validation from external sources gradually lost its power to sustain me. The praise felt emptier, the applause dimmer. It was not a sudden revelation, but rather a quiet shift—the gentle realization that the only true validation that mattered was my own. This newfound understanding was a subtle but monumental liberation, one that became the foundation of the narrative you now hold in your hands.

Too Seasoned to Care is more than a book title—it's a philosophy of being. It doesn't imply indifference, as some might interpret. Rather, it signifies liberation—a liberation from the heavy weight of others' opinions, expectations, and definitions. It means reaching a point in life where your identity is anchored in authenticity, your worth defined solely by your truth. It's a state of being that I arrived at slowly, through trials, triumphs, setbacks, and quiet victories. This book chronicles that journey, not as a roadmap for perfection but as a testament to the beauty and power found in imperfection, in embracing one's seasoned self fully and unconditionally.

Each chapter of this book emerged from vivid moments of reflection and realization—lessons discovered through pain, joy, laughter, loss, anger, and grace. They are insights born from the depth of personal experience and intimate encounters with countless lives I've been privileged to touch. They are stories that blend the wisdom gleaned from personal triumphs and failures with the timeless truths whispered by the voices of those who've guided me—both seen and unseen.

This book invites you into the quiet spaces of my life—moments where wisdom was born not through grand gestures but through subtle shifts in perspective. Like the moment I recognized my mother's silent strength amid life's storms, the quiet pride hidden behind my father's stoicism, or the profound vulnerability revealed during casual conversations that unexpectedly opened doors to healing. It's within these understated encounters that my understanding deepened, showing me that wisdom rarely shouts—it whispers gently in our ear, often in the quietest moments.

Reflecting on the transition into seasoned years is uniquely powerful. Age has a remarkable way of transforming experience into insight, pain into purpose, and loss into liberation. We find ourselves less hurried, more reflective, seeing connections that were invisible before. The urgency to prove oneself softens into the serenity of knowing oneself. What once felt critical—opinions, image, acclaim—slowly fades in importance, replaced by simpler, yet profoundly richer desires: peace, joy, genuine connection, meaningful legacy.

Yet, the journey toward this seasoned state isn't without discomfort. It requires courage to confront unresolved questions, past mistakes, and lingering insecurities. It demands honesty—the willingness to face uncomfortable truths about ourselves and our lives. It's in confronting these truths, however, that we find freedom. We begin to let go, realizing the strength in our vulnerability and the wisdom in our scars.

In writing Too Seasoned to Care, I've found a surprising depth of healing. Revisiting my past through seasoned eyes provided a powerful revelation: Every experience, even those filled with regret or sorrow, held purpose. Every moment contributed to the person I've become, and every lesson learned brought me closer to peace. This realization wasn't instantaneous but unfolded over time, a testament to the transformative power of reflection and patience.

This journey isn't mine alone. Each of us, in our way, navigates this winding path toward self-understanding and acceptance. My hope is that in reading these pages, you'll recognize elements of your own story. Perhaps you'll see reflections of your struggles, your triumphs, your quiet revelations. And in that recognition, you'll find comfort, courage, and perhaps a renewed sense of purpose.

Too Seasoned to Care is my humble offering to anyone who has ever doubted their worth, questioned their purpose, or felt the weight of others' expectations. It's my encouragement for you to embrace your story unapologetically and find strength in your journey. It's an invitation to step boldly into your seasoned years, discovering the peace and liberation that comes from knowing and loving who you truly are.

Ultimately, this book isn't simply my memoir—it's our shared story of becoming seasoned. It's a celebration of every gray hair, every wrinkle, every scar earned along the journey of living authentically. It's a declaration that wisdom isn't a passive state but an active choice—to see life not merely as something happening to us, but as something beautifully unfolding within us.

As you read, my hope is that you pause, reflect, and recognize the beauty of your own seasoned self. Embrace the quiet liberation found in authenticity. Claim your wisdom. Live your truth unapologetically.

Because together, we are beautifully and wonderfully seasoned.

Kenneth Braswell
Atlanta, Georgia
2025

INTRODUCTION

I stand at a moment in my life where reflection is no longer optional—it is necessary. A reckoning of sorts, the kind that comes when you realize the years ahead are fewer than the years behind. This is not a thought to mourn, but one to embrace. For the first time, I feel a firm footing beneath me, a foundation built from everything I have learned, unbothered by the things that once consumed me. I have lived long enough to recognize the patterns, to understand the cycles of joy and pain, to accept the truths that only time reveals.

In my younger years, I chased validation as though it were the air I needed to breathe. I wanted to be seen, heard, affirmed—not just by those closest to me, but by the world. I spent years crafting an image, performing for an audience that never applauded. Every decision, every word, every move felt as though it was being measured against expectations that weren't even mine to begin with. I carried the weight of perception like a burden, one I wasn't even aware I could put down.

But something happens as you age. Liberation doesn't come all at once; it is a slow unraveling, a peeling away of layers you didn't even know you were wearing. I don't remember the exact moment it happened, but one day, I woke up and realized that the whispers of judgment no longer held the weight they once did. The opinions of others, which had loomed so large in my mind, became mere background noise, fading into static on an old radio.

This book is my testament to that transformation. It is a reflection on what it means to live freely, to let go of the noise that clutters our minds, and the fears that keep us tethered to the expectations of others. It is my offering to those who find themselves at a similar crossroads, searching for a way to shed the burdens of self-doubt and embrace the person they were always meant to be.

As a Black man, my journey to this place of peace has been shaped by a unique set of challenges and triumphs. There is a weight that comes with navigating the world in this skin—a weight that is both inherited and imposed. For much of my life, I felt the need to prove myself, to be twice as good, twice as smart, twice as worthy. I wanted to defy the stereotypes, to push back against the narratives that sought to box me in. And for a time, that drive served me well. It fueled my ambition, pushing me to achieve what I once thought impossible.

But the cost of that striving was high. The pressure to be exceptional came at the expense of my peace. I was so busy trying to prove my worth that I forgot to rest in the knowledge that I was already enough. And so, slowly but surely, I began the work of letting go—letting go of the need for external validation, the desire to fit into molds that were never meant for me, the weight of other people's expectations.

Letting go is not easy. It requires courage. It demands that you confront the parts of yourself that you have hidden away, face the fears and insecurities that have been your constant companions. It forces you to ask the hard questions: Who am I without the approval of others? What do I want for my life, not because it will impress someone else, but because it will bring me joy?

These are the questions that have guided me in the later stages of my life. They have led me to clarity, to purpose, to peace. And they are the questions I hope this book will inspire you to ask yourself. As I sit here writing these words, I think about the mistakes I've made, the relationships I've nurtured, and the ones I've let go.

I think about the dreams I've pursued and the ones I've had to lay down. I think about the pain that has shaped me and the joy that has sustained me. Each of these experiences is a thread woven into the fabric of my life, intertwining to create a story that is uniquely mine.

But this book is not just about me—it is about us. It is about the journey we all take as we move through life, learning, growing, evolving. It is about the shared struggles and triumphs that connect us as human beings. It is about the liberation that comes when we realize that we are not defined by our past, our mistakes, or the opinions of others.

There is freedom in not caring—not in the sense of apathy, but in the sense of release. When you stop caring about the superficial judgments of others, you make room for what truly matters. You make room for authenticity, for connection, for joy. You make room to live a life that is true to who you are, not who the world thinks you should be.

This book is a companion for that journey. A reminder that you are not alone in your struggles, that there is beauty in imperfection, and that there is power in embracing your authentic self. It is a call to action—to shed the layers of self-doubt and societal expectation, to stand tall in your truth, to live a life that is unapologetically yours.

As I look back on my own journey, I see how far I've come. I see the boy who was afraid to speak up, the young man who worked tirelessly to prove his worth, and the seasoned man who has finally found peace. I see the moments of doubt and the moments of triumph, the times I stumbled and the times I soared. And through it all, I see the thread of resilience, the unshakable belief that I was meant for more.

This book is my way of sharing that belief with you. It is my way of saying that no matter where you are in your journey, no matter what challenges you've faced or mistakes you've made, there is always room to grow, to heal, to become. It is my way of reminding you that you are enough—just as you are.

Welcome to Too Seasoned to Care - How Aging Turns Experience Into Wisdom And Liberation. Together, we will explore what it means to live freely, to love deeply, and to face the future with a heart full of courage and a spirit unencumbered by the past. Let this journey be a testament to the power of letting go and the joy of living a life true to oneself.

CHAPTER ONE

THE JOURNEY BEGINS:
EMBRACING YOUR AUTHENTIC SELF

GROWING UP AND REALIZING A REFLECTION

I've been sitting with the question of how to start this book for a long time now. Should I begin by diving straight into why I don't care anymore about the things that once consumed me, or should I start by talking about what I cared so deeply about in the first place?

How do I take you through this journey in a way that makes sense—connecting the dots between my past and my present—so that when we get to the end, we're both clear on how I ended up here, not caring in the same way I used to?

This book didn't come from hours of research, and it isn't built on data or deep analysis. There's no stack of self-help books informing these pages. It's not that kind of book. What you're holding in your hands is a reflection of my life—my journey, my self-discovery. And the truth is, while I've been writing, I've been learning things about myself that I didn't even know. The more I sit with these memories, the more this book changes and evolves, just like I have.

When I first started writing, I thought I knew what this book would be. I had a plan. But like life itself, plans have a way of changing when you're forced to really sit with your own story.

The more I reflected, talked to people, and let myself dig into the memories that shaped me, the more I realized there were moments—moments I hadn't thought about in years—that have shaped me far more than I ever imagined. That's why I want you to know that this book is an evolution. It's not a neatly tied-up story. It's messy. It's raw. And that's the beauty of it.

There's one question that really kicked this off for me, and it's a question I hadn't asked myself in a long time: When was the first time you cared about what someone else thought of you? It sounds simple, but trust me, it's not. I sat with that question for a while, unsure of the answer. But as I started peeling back the layers, I realized how much of my life has been shaped by that need to be seen in a certain light.

We all do it, don't we? We try to impress people, change their opinions of us, mold ourselves into what we think they expect. As a boy, I thought it was mostly about how girls saw me. Then, as I got older, it became about how women viewed me as a man. But when I really started digging deeper, I found that those pressures had started much earlier. Long before I worried about how women saw me, I was worried about how the world saw me.

Let me take you back to Brooklyn. Picture this: I'm a teenager, walking the familiar streets of Crown Heights. It's a noisy neighborhood, full of life. The sounds of buses screeching to a stop, kids running down the block, and neighbors calling out to each other all blend together in a kind of chaotic harmony. The air smells like a mix of fried food from the local spots and exhaust from passing cars. My mom sends me to the grocery store with food stamps.

Now, this wasn't the kind of grocery store with shiny floors and neatly stacked shelves. This was a Brooklyn bodega, small, crowded, with a line that always seemed longer than it needed to be. The cashiers worked quickly, but there was always this tension in the air, like everyone in there was just trying to get in and out as fast as possible. And back then, food stamps weren't discreet little cards. No, they were these paper booklets, and when it was time to pay, the cashier would rip out the bills right in front of everyone.

I remember arguing with my mom. I didn't want to go. I didn't want my friends to see me using food stamps. I didn't want them to know we were poor. To me, that was like standing in front of the world with a sign that said, I'm less than you. My mom, though—she didn't have time for my pride. She worked hard, day in and day out, to keep food on the table, and she wasn't about to entertain my embarrassment.

My mom was a strong woman. She was the kind of woman who never backed down from a challenge, who found a way to make things happen, even when the odds were stacked against her. She was fierce, but there was a quiet vulnerability in her, too—one I didn't see until much later. I realize now that she probably carried that same shame I felt. I was too caught up in my own embarrassment to notice how it weighed on her to have to use food stamps in front of everyone, maybe even some of her own friends.

As I stood in line at that store, I felt the weight of a hundred eyes on me—or at least it felt like that. The cashier tore out those stamps, and each rip echoed in my mind like a loud, humiliating reminder of what I wanted to hide. But now, looking back, I see it differently. My mom was doing what she had to do to make sure we had what we needed. And I was too focused on how I thought the world saw me to understand the sacrifices she was making.

It's funny how shame works. Where did it come from, this idea that being poor was something to be ashamed of? I didn't know it back then, but that was one of the first times I realized just how much I cared about how other people saw me. And that's not an easy thing to unlearn.

Years later, I had a moment that brought it all full circle. I was in Ghana, Africa, my traveling for work, and I was taking photographs of the people and the landscape. One day, I came across a young girl standing in the doorway of a small, simple home. She couldn't have been more than seven or eight, with wide, curious eyes and skin that gleamed in the sunlight. Her clothes were worn, her shoes barely holding together.

When I raised my camera and took her picture, she didn't flinch. There was no fear, no self-consciousness. Just pure curiosity. After I snapped the photo, I walked over and showed it to her. And that's when she smiled—a wide, toothy grin that took me by surprise. She wasn't smiling because she was desperate or in need of anything. She was smiling because she was curious about the camera, about me, about the whole situation.

In that moment, I realized something. All my life, I had seen children like her in those late-night commercials asking for donations. They always looked so sad, so in need of help. But this girl? She wasn't sad. She wasn't worried about how I saw her, or how the world saw her. She was just living her life, fully and authentically.

That moment took me back to my childhood in Brooklyn. We didn't know we were poor until someone told us we were. We didn't know we were the "have-nots" until society slapped that label on us.

Before that, we were just living. That little girl in Ghana didn't care about labels, just like I didn't care as a child—until someone told me I should.

And that's what this journey is about—understanding when and how you started caring about how the world saw you, and learning to let go of that. Learning to embrace who you really are, without the weight of those labels dragging you down.

I didn't always feel this free. I didn't always care less about how people saw me. But as I've gotten older, I've learned that the things I once cared so deeply about don't matter as much anymore. What matters is how I see myself. And that's what I want to share with you.

So, let's walk through this together. Grab a notebook, jot down your own memories. Think about the times you cared too much about what others thought of you. Let's unpack these moments, and maybe, by the end of this book, we'll both find ourselves caring a little less about what the world thinks—and a little more about who we truly are.

THE GHOSTS WE CARRY: HOW CHILDHOOD ADVERSITY SHAPES WHO WE BECOME

I was sitting at my desk the other day, staring at the blinking cursor on my laptop screen, and thinking about how much of who we are is shaped long before we even know we exist. We spend so much of our lives responding—to our circumstances, to the people around us, to the stories we've been told about ourselves. And yet, we rarely pause to ask the hard questions:

Where did this all begin? Who planted these seeds? And why do I still carry them? It's a question I've wrestled with for years, especially in my work with Fathers Incorporated, where I've had the privilege of hearing thousands of stories—stories from men, women, and children who carry invisible scars from their past.

I think about those stories every time I hear the term Adverse Childhood Experiences or ACEs, and I can't help but wonder: What would happen if we stopped ignoring those ghosts?

Before I go any further, let's unpack this term. Adverse Childhood Experiences are defined as traumatic events that occur before the age of 18. These experiences can include abuse—physical, emotional, or sexual—neglect, or household dysfunction like growing up with a parent who is incarcerated, addicted, or struggling with mental illness. Divorce, witnessing domestic violence, living in poverty—all of these things fall under ACES.

The research behind ACES is extensive and undeniable. The original ACES Study, conducted in the late 1990s by the Centers for Disease Control (CDC) and Kaiser Permanente, showed a direct link between childhood trauma and negative outcomes in adulthood. People with high ACE scores—meaning they experienced multiple traumatic events as children—are more likely to suffer from chronic physical illnesses, depression, anxiety, substance abuse, and even suicide.

Here's the kicker: the trauma doesn't just sit quietly in our past. It shapes how we process the world, how we respond to stress, and how we navigate relationships. It's like carrying a backpack filled with invisible stones. No one else can see the weight, but you feel it with every step.

Adverse Childhood Experiences are the shadows cast over our childhood. They are the traumas that shape us, even when we don't know their names. Abuse. Neglect. Poverty. Violence. Loss. Addiction. The absence of a parent. They are the things that happen behind closed doors, in the darkness of a room, or out in the open where nobody chooses to see. And they have a way of following us.

You see, childhood is where the world first teaches us who we are—not who we dream of being, but who we are in its eyes. It's where we first learn whether we are safe, whether we are loved, whether we are worthy. For so many, those lessons don't come wrapped in warmth and security. They come in screams. In silence. In shame.

Let me paint the picture for you. It's a boy growing up in a house where every footstep in the hallway sounds like a warning. It's a girl watching her mother cry herself to sleep every night because her father didn't come home again. It's a child sitting at the kitchen table, stomach growling, staring at an empty plate while their parents fight in the next room. It's the weight of a secret that no one asks you to share because no one wants to hear it.

Adversity is insidious.

You don't notice it at first because it becomes normal. You adapt to it. You get used to the yelling, the hunger, the isolation. You start to think that maybe this is just how life works. And then you grow up. You carry those ghosts into adulthood without realizing it. They show up in your relationships, in your fears, in your inability to trust. They whisper to you when you're about to take a risk, when you're trying to love someone, when you're looking in the mirror and trying to believe in yourself.

And you wonder why you feel broken, why you can't seem to move past that invisible barrier in your mind, why no matter how far you run, the past feels like it's just one step behind you.

Here's what I know: ACEs are not just events. They are wounds. They are absences. They are fractures in the foundation of who we are. They are the moments when we felt unprotected, unseen, unloved. And if we don't deal with them—if we don't name them, face them, and decide to heal—they will deal with us.

There's a study that talks about how ACEs can literally rewire the brain. Early exposure to trauma disrupts the way a child's brain develops. It can compromise the nervous system, weaken the immune system, and leave the body in a constant state of fight or flight. Imagine that. A child's body, always on edge, always preparing for the worst. Now picture that same child growing up to be a man or a woman who can't relax, who can't sleep, who can't trust the people who say they love them.

The world calls it anxiety. It (the world) calls it depression. It calls it addiction. But at its core, it's just survival. The child in you is still trying to survive.

What does this look like in real life? It looks like the father who lashes out at his son because his own father used to beat him with a belt. It looks like the woman who stays in an abusive relationship because she grew up believing that love comes with pain.

It looks like the man who turns to a bottle every night because it's the only thing that drowns out the noise in his mind. It looks like the teenager who drops out of school because nobody ever told her she was smart enough to make it. These are not failures. These are symptoms. And the problem is that we've spent so much time blaming people for their symptoms instead of asking, Where does it hurt?

Hmmmm; where does it hurt?

I wish we asked that question more. I wish we asked it of ourselves. I wish we asked it of our children. Because when we don't ask, when we don't acknowledge the impact of childhood trauma, we end up raising generations of people who think pain is just part of life. And while some pain is inevitable, not all pain has to be permanent.

This brings me to something I've been thinking about for a long time now. You see, the ACEs that researchers talk about—the ones that include abuse, neglect, poverty, mental illness—they are all real and valid. But there's one that doesn't get talked about enough. Fatherlessness.

Let me be clear. When I say fatherlessness, I don't just mean a man not being physically present. I also mean a father who is emotionally absent. A father who is there but not there. A father who doesn't see his children, who doesn't nurture them, who doesn't show up when it matters most. And when a child grows up without the presence of a father—whether physically or emotionally—it leaves a mark. It's a wound that doesn't heal easily.

I see it all the time in my work. Children who crave their father's approval, even when their father is long gone. Men who try to become the fathers they never had, but don't know how because nobody showed them. Women who look for their father's love in the arms of men who don't deserve them. And it's not just emotional. Studies show that fatherlessness is linked to higher rates of poverty, lower academic achievement, and increased likelihood of substance abuse and incarceration. But you don't need a study to tell you that. You just need to sit with someone who grew up without their father and listen to their story.

I've heard those stories. I've heard the pain. I've seen grown men cry because they still feel like that little boy who was waiting at the window for his dad to come home. And what breaks my heart is that so many of those men carry shame about it. They carry shame because society tells them to "man up" and move on. But how do you move on from a hole that was never filled? How do you let go of something that shaped the way you see yourself?

The truth is, we need to talk about this more. We need to recognize that fatherlessness is not just a personal issue—it's a societal issue. It's an adverse childhood experience that ripples through families and communities. And until we name it, until we acknowledge its impact, we can't begin to heal from it.

Healing is possible, though. I believe that. I've seen it. I've seen men who grew up without fathers break the cycle and become the dads their children deserve. I've seen women who carried the weight of abandonment learn to love themselves and demand better for their lives. I've seen communities come together to fill the gaps, to provide the love and support that children need.

And it all starts with a willingness to ask the hard questions: Where does it hurt? How did this happen? What can I do to heal?

If you're reading this and you're thinking about your own child-hood, about the things you've been carrying, I want you to know this: your pain is real. Your experiences are valid. But they don't have to define you. You can name those ghosts. You can face them. And you can decide, right now, that they will not have the final say over your life.

Because you are more than what happened to you. You are more than the trauma you endured. You are more than the wounds you carry. You are still here. You are still breathing. And as long as you're here, you have the power to write a different story—for yourself, for your children, and for the generations that come after you.

That's the beautiful thing about healing. It doesn't just stop with you. When you decide to break the cycle, you give the next generation a chance to start fresh. To grow up in homes where they feel safe, seen, and loved. To know their worth from the very beginning. That's what this is all about. That's why we do this work. And that's why I'm writing this book.

So, let's face the ghosts. Let's ask the hard questions. Let's name the ACEs that shaped us, and let's decide to heal. Because we owe it to ourselves. We owe it to our children. And we owe it to the world that needs us to show up whole, healed, and ready to be who we were always meant to be.

FEAR AS A TEACHER: THE SILENT SHAPER OF HOW WE'RE SEEN

As I continue this journey of exploration, trying to pinpoint the earliest moments when I cared about how people saw me, I've come to another epiphany. It's strange because I don't have many vivid memories of my early youth. What I have are flashes of moments—specific incidents more than an overarching theme of my childhood. I piece things together by looking at old pictures, replaying conversations I've had with family, or even recalling connections to TV shows, food, or the games we played. These fragmented memories are like breadcrumbs leading me back to times that can give me insight into how I positioned myself in the world and when the opinion of others became something I held onto.

But as I sat here today, just thinking, a thought hit me. It wasn't a memory triggered by something specific, but more of an unsettling realization: fear might have been my first teacher. Fear may have been the earliest tool used to shape how I behaved, even before I started thinking about girls or worrying about embarrassment. I'm talking about the real young years—four, five, maybe six years old.

I can't recall much about that time, but I do remember the general feeling of fear being used to guide my behavior.

Even as a little boy, before I could grasp the bigger, more complex emotions, fear was something I understood. It was the go-to tactic to ensure that kids like me, kids in the sixties, would act right. Back then, teachers could hit you across the knuckles with a ruler if you stepped out of line.

That kind of punishment was normal—accepted, even. And it was designed to instill fear, a kind of controlled fear that would make sure you did what you were told. I can still remember in fourth grade—Ms. Cherry, my 4th grade teacher. She grabbed me by the ear, twisted it, and led me to the door to send me to the principal's office. I don't even remember what I did to deserve that, but I'll never forget the sting of her hand or the humiliation of being marched out in front of the class.

Fear wasn't just something that happened at school. It was at home too. Our parents, especially Black parents raising children in the 60's, used fear as a means of survival. They had to. My mother was no different.

We grew up knowing that discipline was non-negotiable. It wasn't just about us—it was about how we represented our family, our community, even our church.

Every time I stepped out of the house, it was like I carried the weight of my mother's reputation on my shoulders. She would gather us up at the door, and with that stern tone, say, "Don't go out here and embarrass me." And believe me, that wasn't a suggestion—it was a warning. The underlying message was clear: "Embarrass me, and there will be consequences."

This wasn't just about discipline for the sake of keeping kids in line; it was about survival. Our behavior as children was a reflection of our family, and how we conducted ourselves in public mattered. It shaped the way people saw us, but more importantly, it shaped the way they saw our parents. That pressure was heavy. And if you didn't conform, if you stepped out of line, fear would reel you back in—whether it came from your mother's sharp words or the whip of a switch across any available part of your body.

When I think about it, fear was always present. And it was a tool used by our parents out of necessity. They were raising children in a world that was built against us—a world where one wrong move could lead to something far more dangerous than a spanking.

My mother left North Carolina in the early 60s and moved to New York City, bringing me with her when I was just a toddler. I don't remember much from those early years, but I can imagine what kind of fear she was running from, what dangers she was trying to escape.

> *Fear wasn't just an abstract feeling for her—it was real, it was ever-present, and it was woven into every decision she made for her family.*

And that fear carried down to us, the next generation. We were taught to fear stepping out of line, to fear how people would see us if we did. But fear wasn't just about punishment—it was about survival. Black children, especially Black boys, were raised with an understanding that the world was already stacked against us. And so, our parents drilled it into us that how we were seen could mean the difference between life and death.

"Spare the rod, spoil the child." That's the scripture that was quoted to justify the spankings and the discipline. (Proverbs 13:24). The rod wasn't just about discipline—it was about ensuring that we survived in a world that saw us as a threat before we even had a chance to prove ourselves otherwise.

Now, as I look back, I see how much of my behavior was shaped by this fear, by this constant awareness of how the world saw me. We were taught, from such a young age, that everything we did mattered—how we spoke, how we dressed, how we acted—because it wasn't just about us. It was about how we represented our entire community. It's like when an influential Black figure publicly fails—the embarrassment isn't just theirs. It becomes all of ours. That failure, that moment, reflects back on every one of us.

And that's why, as kids, we were constantly reminded not to embarrass the family name. Our behavior didn't just belong to us; it belonged to the people who raised us, the people who came before us, and the people who would come after us.

But as I dig deeper into this, I'm realizing something new about fear. Yes, fear was used to keep us in line, but there's another side to it. Fear also became the foundation of how I started to care about how the world saw me. Even before I fully understood the weight of my skin color, I was being conditioned to be conscious of the way others perceived me. And that conditioning didn't stop when I left the house. It followed me into adulthood, into every room I walked into, every conversation I had.

As I continue to explore this idea, I'm starting to see that fear has been shaping me longer than I realized. Fear of embarrassment, fear of failure, fear of how the world would see me. And that's something I need to sit with for a while, to really unpack. Because as much as fear was a tool used by my mother, by my teachers, by society—it's also something that I've internalized. Something that's still shaping me, even today.

I'm sure fear has shaped you as well. Don't believe me? I know you remember this?

THE 3 O'CLOCK SHOWDOWN: FEAR, FISTS, AND SURVIVAL IN THE SCHOOLYARD

There is nothing that strikes more fear into the heart of a kid than the infamous 3 o'clock showdown. If you grew up in the 60's, 70's, maybe even the 80's, you knew what it meant. Every kid in Brooklyn—or anywhere else, really—knew that when you heard the words, "I'll see you at 3 o'clock," you were in for it. It wasn't just a challenge; it was a rite of passage, a measure of your standing in the schoolyard, and a test of how you'd show up for the world to see.

The 3 o'clock showdown wasn't something you could escape once it was set in motion. For me, that particular day in sixth grade, I didn't even know how it started. One minute I was on the handball court, and the next minute I was standing face to face with a kid named Timothy. Little, big-headed Timothy. We were bickering over something I can't even remember, but before I knew it, one of us—probably him—threw down the challenge. "I'll see you at 3 o'clock."

Now, when those words are out there, there's no taking them back. Everybody around you hears it, and just like that, your fate is sealed. If the challenge came in the morning, you had the whole day to stew in it—to feel the weight of fear and anxiety eating at your insides. If it was lunchtime, at least you only had half a day to worry about getting your face rearranged.

I was no fighter. I didn't have a dad or older brothers to rough-house with, to teach me how to throw a punch or take one. There was nobody to toughen me up or show me how to "handle my business." I was it—the oldest, the one who had to figure it out on my own. And back then, as much as we thought we could learn by watching those Chinese kung fu movies on Saturdays, and practicing my death blow, nothing ever really translated in real life. I wasn't going to be Bruce Lee or the Wu Tang Clan out there on Montgomery Street, but I sure as hell tried.

The minutes ticked by slowly, each one heavier than the last. My stomach churned as I thought about the crowd, the taunts, the fists flying—my fists, his fists, who knew whose fists would land where? But it wasn't just about the fight. The fear was bigger than that. It was about what losing meant. In that moment, you weren't just afraid of getting your ass kicked—you were terrified of what would happen next. If you got beat, you'd carry that L with you for the rest of the year, maybe even into junior high. Word would spread. The bullies would see you as an easy target. The girls—well, they wouldn't look at you the same.

When 3 o'clock hit, it wasn't the big event I had imagined. There was no massive crowd, no tickets sold, no fight card announcing the main event. Just a handful of kids standing around waiting to see what would happen. Timothy and I stood across from each other, bouncing on our feet, throwing weak insults back and forth, each of us hoping the other would back down. But then there was always that guy—the agitator. You know the one. The kid who made it his mission to get the fight going. "You gonna let him talk to you like that?" he'd say, or, "He told me to push you!" Always something to stir the pot.

Finally, we clashed. If you could call it that. There wasn't any grace to it. We tangled up in each other's limbs, kicking, shoving, slapping, anything but fighting the way we thought we would. And then it happened—my big moment.

I kicked him. Not some Bruce Lee flying kick either—just a wild, desperate kick that landed hard in his chest. He cried out and hit the ground. The kids around us went crazy, and for a split second, I felt like a king. Then Timothy got up, furious, tears streaming down his face, and charged at me. We locked into a headlock and stayed there—neither of us wanting to let go, neither of us wanting to continue. The whole thing was ridiculous.

An adult finally came over and broke us apart, sending Timothy off one way and me the other. I looked down at my pants, now smeared with dirt, and my heart sank. My mother had warned me—don't get into any fights at school. Now, I had to figure out how to explain the scuffed-up knees on my school clothes without giving away the fight. It was a whole other layer of fear—coming home to a disappointed mother who didn't want her son in trouble, who didn't want him looking a mess. I'd have to sneak those pants into the laundry and hope she wouldn't notice. But she always did.

As I think about that day now, I realize how much of it wasn't really about Timothy or the fight at all. It was about the layers of fear—fear of getting hurt, fear of looking weak, fear of how people would see me the next day at school. And that fear wasn't just in the schoolyard. It followed us everywhere. You didn't just fight to prove something to yourself. You fought to prove something to everyone else.

There was another time, later on in junior high, when Margaret—a big girl, bigger than me, a bully—called me out. "I'll get you at 3 o'clock," she said. There wasn't any back and forth, no challenge, no choice. She simply decided that I was next. And the fear hit me in a different way, because this wasn't just about getting beat up by another boy. This was a girl, and the last thing I wanted was to get my ass kicked by a girl in front of everybody.

But when 3 o'clock came, something strange happened. I walked out of the school, fully expecting to see her there, waiting to pummel me. And there she was, talking to some kids. I braced myself. She looked at me, twisted her wrist, emphasizing the thumb and forefinger; silver bracelets clanging together in that dismissive way girls did back in the 70's, simultaneously saying, "Later for you!" That was it. She turned away, and it was over. I don't know why she let me go, but she did, and I was thankful. I didn't need that kind of fight. I didn't need that smoke. Looking back, she must of liked me, cause I was the only boy I ever knew to escape a Margaret ass whompin.

The three o'clock challenge was a real thing back then, a test of your toughness, your ability to stand up for yourself. And fear—it played a major role in shaping who we were and how we moved. Fear wasn't just about the fists or the fights. It was about how you showed up in front of your peers. Fear of being seen as weak, fear of not fitting in, fear of not being respected. And as much as we thought we outgrew it, the truth is, we didn't. Those early lessons of fear, and the need to prove ourselves, stick with us—sometimes for life.

And as I reflect on those moments, it's clear that fear played a bigger part in shaping how I saw myself, and more importantly, how I thought others saw me. That fear didn't go away once the fight was over. It lingered. It grew. And it became a part of who I was and how I navigated the world. Because it was never just about Timothy, or Margaret, or the schoolyard. It was about survival—in the schoolyard and in life.

THE BLOWOUT: A LESSON IN VULNERABILITY

In the 70's, there was a hairstyle that was all the rage among Black boys and girls: the big, beautiful afro. It was more than just a hairstyle; it was a symbol of pride and identity. I remember watching the boys in my class with their perfectly round afros and the girls with their meticulously manicured hair, all standing tall and proud. My own hair, however, didn't quite have the length or volume to achieve that iconic look, and it made me feel like I was missing out on something essential.

One day, I convinced my mother to buy a hair product that promised to straighten hair and give it that full, fluffy appearance I so desired. I don't even remember the name of the product, but I do remember the excitement I felt when my mother agreed to help me use it. That night, we followed the instructions on the box to the letter. My mother applied the cream to my hair, and I waited with anticipation, imagining myself waking up with a magnificent afro that would rival any in my class.

The next morning, I rushed to the mirror with high hopes. But what I saw was far from the image on the box. My hair was straight, yes, but it was stiff and hard, nothing like the soft, bouncy afros I admired. I was disappointed but determined to make the best of it. I went to school that day, nervously hoping that maybe it wasn't as bad as I thought.

As I walked into the classroom, I felt the eyes of my classmates on me. They didn't quite know what to make of my hair. It was sort of an afro, but not really. It was bigger than my usual hair, but it lacked the form and flexibility of a true afro. Over the next few days, my hair became more brittle, and it started to break off. Each morning, I woke up to find more pieces of my hair on my pillow, my once hopeful experiment turning into a nightmare.

To hide the mess that was now my hair, I began wearing a hat—a kind of sweater hat that covered up the brittle, broken strands. I felt a deep sense of embarrassment and vulnerability. Every day, I dreaded someone asking me to take off my hat. But there was one person I dreaded seeing more than anyone else: Cindy.

Cindy was the new girl in our building, and she was beautiful in that way only a young boy could see beauty—bright eyes, a radiant smile, and a confidence that made my heart race. I was infatuated with her but terrified to talk to her. I didn't know what to say or how to act around her, so I tried to impress her from a distance, hoping she'd notice me.

My best friend, Derrick, who would later change his name to Justice, was always by my side. We had known each other since we were toddlers, and we spent our days playing jokes and fooling around. Derrick was my confidant and partner in crime, and he, too, had a crush on Cindy. We were both trying to win her attention in our own awkward, teenage ways.

One particular day, like many others, we were running around the streets of Brooklyn, specifically in our building in Crown Heights. We used to knock on people's doors, play in the hallways, and do all kinds of things that young kids did. On this day, we decided to go up to Cindy's apartment, which was on the other side of the building. I had my hat on, as usual, to cover the disaster that was my hair. I can't remember exactly why we decided to go up there or what prompted us to knock on her door, but Derrick and I found ourselves standing outside her apartment.

Her and her sister, Vicky, were home, and like many of us, they were not supposed to open the door until their parents got home. But we started talking to them through the door, chain lock and long police pole. Eventually, they opened the door just enough to have a conversation in the hallway. While I was talking to Cindy, to my utter shock and embarrassment, Derrick snatched off my hat and bolted down the stairs.

I was left standing there, my head exposed, feeling a rush of humiliation and vulnerability. I don't even remember what I said to Cindy or if I managed to cover my head quickly enough. All I remember is chasing Derrick down the stairs, my heart pounding with a mix of anger and embarrassment.

Despite this mortifying moment, Cindy and I remained friends and even dated for a time. She got over my hair mishap much faster than I did. It was a stark reminder of how much more I cared about the incident than anyone else did. This episode was a powerful lesson in how deeply concerned I was about how others perceived me.

In those early teenage years, I was acutely aware of how I presented myself to the world. From my chunky body to my light skin, from being somewhat smart and a little nerdy to not having the newest sneakers or the trendiest clothes, I placed immense value on how others saw me. Every aspect of my appearance and behavior was scrutinized through the lens of peer approval.

It was during these formative years that I began to understand just how much weight we place on others' opinions. Unfortunately, this tendency often intensifies as we grow older and we never forget how past embarrassing moments made us feel.

THE REALIZATION: CHILDHOOD MEMORIES AND THE WEIGHT OF PERCEPTION

I was surrounded by the sounds and sights of the city, the hustle and bustle of life that was all about survival. My childhood was filled with the kind of creativity that arises from necessity. We didn't have much, but we made the most of what we had, often without realizing that we were the "have-nots."

I vividly remember one particular experience that stuck with me, a moment that brought into sharp focus the power of perception and the influence of our environment on how we see ourselves. Like most kids, I was desperate to fit in, to wear what everyone else was wearing. Back then, it was all about the sneakers—Chuck Taylors, Converses, Pro-Keds. Those were the shoes that defined you, that marked you as part of the in-crowd.

But I didn't have those sneakers. What I had were worn-out shoes with holes in the soles, so bad that I had to stuff them with newspaper just to keep my feet from hitting the pavement. I begged my mother for a new pair, and after what felt like an eternity, she finally came home with a shoebox. My heart raced with anticipation, thinking she had surprised me with the coveted Converses. But when I opened the box, my excitement turned to dread.

Inside were NBA sneakers. Not the iconic brand that kids dreamed of, but something entirely unfamiliar. No logo, no stripes, nothing that resembled the shoes I had longed for. My heart sank. These weren't the sneakers that would make me feel cool or accepted; I'm sure the letters NBA on the box didn't stand for the National Basketball Association. Oh no, these were what we called "rejects." And in the world I lived in, wearing rejects was like a badge of poverty, something that made you a target for ridicule.

So what did her son do; refused to wear them. That action turned the mumbling of her voice into a shrieking; "Then don't wear nothing then! Work all day to take care of your ass and this is the thanks I get."

Fast forward to that winter, when I went to stay with my stepfather in Seneca Falls, New York. The winters there were brutal—cold, snowy, and relentless. I hated those NBA sneakers, but they were all I had. My stepfather wasn't about to buy me another pair, so I was stuck with them. I dreaded the thought of going outside and facing the judgment of kids I didn't even know, kids who didn't look like me or share my experiences.

But when I finally stepped out, I noticed something surprising. None of the kids were wearing the brand-name sneakers that were so coveted in Brooklyn. They were just out there having fun, sliding down hills, and playing in the snow. Suddenly, the label of "rejects" lost its power. These kids didn't care about brands; they cared about having a good time. And in that moment, I realized how much of my self-worth had been tied up in something as trivial as a pair of shoes.

As the day went on, I discovered that those very sneakers, with their lack of grip, allowed me to slide further and faster down the hill than anyone else. What I had initially seen as a source of shame became a tool for fun and connection. And I found myself grateful for those shoes that I had once despised.

That day, I learned a powerful lesson. I didn't know those sneakers were something to worry about until someone told me they were. I didn't care about the labels until I was conditioned to care. It was one of the first times I became aware of how the world's judgments could shape how I saw myself, how I showed up in the world.

In Brooklyn, we lived our lives without knowing we were "poor" or "disadvantaged." We were just kids, making the most of what we had, unaware that others might see us as less than. It wasn't until someone told us, until society imposed its labels on us, that we began to internalize those perceptions.

This realization is what this chapter, and ultimately this book, is about: understanding how we form our identities based on the perceptions of others, and how we can begin to shed those perceptions as we grow older. It's about recognizing the moments when we started caring about how others saw us, and learning to let go of those concerns in favor of embracing our authentic selves.

As we age, as we gain more experience, we start to see that the things we once cared so deeply about—how we're perceived, how we're judged—begin to fade in importance. Instead, we find confidence in who we truly are, shaped by all the joys, pains, struggles, and triumphs that have defined our journey.

And that's the path this book will take you on, starting with these early realizations and leading to a place of self-acceptance and freedom.

NEGOTIATING WITH MYSELF: THE COMPLEXITY OF BECOMING MY BEST SELF

Self-discovery is an ongoing negotiation. It's like sitting at a table with all the different parts of who you are—the good, the bad, the insecure, the confident, the broken, and the healed. You're trying to get them to all agree on one thing: the best version of yourself.

The problem is, these parts don't always want to cooperate. They pull you in different directions, each one insisting on its own truth. And as you get older, the conversation doesn't get any quieter. If anything, it gets louder, more urgent. Because you realize you don't have all the time in the world to figure it out anymore.

For me, this process really began in earnest when I hit my seasoned years. I was past the point of trying to impress people, past the point of trying to fit into anyone's expectations. But even when you've stopped caring about how the world sees you, there's still this inner dialogue that demands your attention. You still have to deal with yourself. And that's the hardest part.

You see, self-actualization isn't just about discovering who you are—it's about accepting who you are. And that's where the complexity comes in.

It's easy to say, "I don't care what anyone thinks of me," but do you really not care? Or have you just convinced yourself that you don't care because it's easier than confronting the parts of you that still want approval, that still need validation?

I had to ask myself that question a lot on this journey, and the answer wasn't always clear.

When I talk about negotiating with myself, I'm talking about the daily practice of looking at where I've been, where I am, and where I'm going—and finding peace with all of it. It's about reconciling the mistakes I've made, the dreams I've lost, the relationships that didn't work out. It's about owning the parts of me that still carry shame, fear, and doubt, while also celebrating the parts that have grown, evolved, and thrived.

This negotiation isn't linear. It's not like you reach a certain age and suddenly you've got it all figured out. It's messy. One day, you wake up feeling like you've conquered the world, and the next day, you're questioning everything. That's the complexity of it. It's never-ending, and it requires you to be honest with yourself in ways that aren't always comfortable.

For years, I thought self-actualization was about arriving at a place of peace, of confidence, where you've finally figured out all the answers. But the truth is, there are no final answers. There are just more questions. And I've learned that's okay. Self-actualization isn't a destination; it's a process. It's about understanding that who I am today is just as valid as who I was 20 years ago. The difference is, now I have the tools to navigate life with more wisdom, more grace, and more acceptance of my imperfections.

At this stage in life, I've come to realize that being the best version of myself isn't about being perfect. It's about being real. It's about owning my flaws, my scars, and my past without letting them define me. I don't need to prove anything to anyone, not even to myself. That's the real freedom that comes with age—the freedom to just be.

But it wasn't easy getting here. In my younger years, I spent so much time trying to be what I thought the world needed me to be. I shaped myself around the expectations of others, whether it was family, society, or my own warped perception of success. I thought if I could just hit certain milestones—make a certain amount of money, achieve certain goals, look a certain way—then I'd be happy. But every time I reached one of those milestones, the goalpost moved. There was always something more to chase, something else to become.

It took me a long time to realize that the best version of myself isn't a destination—it's a commitment. It's a commitment to growth, to learning, to evolving, even when it's uncomfortable. Especially when it's uncomfortable. It's a commitment to being better today than I was yesterday, even if that "better" looks different than what I imagined.

Part of this negotiation with myself involved letting go of the idea that I had to have it all figured out by now. There's this unspoken pressure that comes with age, this belief that once you hit a certain number, you're supposed to be wise and settled. But the reality is, I'm still figuring it out. I'm still learning, still growing, still making mistakes. And that's okay. There's beauty in the journey, even when it feels uncertain.

What I've learned is that self-actualization isn't about getting it right—it's about getting it real. It's about showing up for myself in ways that honor who I am and where I've been, while also making space for who I'm becoming. It's about accepting that I don't have all the answers, and I probably never will. But what I do have is a deeper understanding of myself and the grace to keep going, no matter what.

At this stage in life, the possibilities are endless. And that's the irony of it, isn't it? We spend our younger years believing that our options narrow as we age, that life becomes more limited. But the truth is, it's the opposite.

With age comes clarity. With clarity comes freedom. And with freedom comes possibility.

I'm not bound by the same constraints I was in my 20's or 30's. I'm not chasing anyone else's dream. I'm not trying to live up to anyone else's standard. The only person I need to impress is me. And the only thing I need to chase is the next chapter of my life— the chapter that I get to write with full authority, full agency, and full authenticity.

The best version of myself isn't some idealized version that I'm striving to become. It's the man I am right now—flawed, seasoned, learning, evolving. It's the man who has lived through enough to know that life isn't about perfection; it's about presence. It's about being fully here, fully engaged, and fully open to what's next. And that's the most powerful realization of all: that even in this seasoned stage of life, I'm still writing my story. I'm still negotiating with myself, still discovering new layers of who I am. And I wouldn't trade that for anything. The complexity, the uncertainty, the process—that's where the beauty lies.

That's where I find my true self. And that's the best version of me.

CHAPTER TWO

LESSONS FROM THE PAST: WISDOM GAINED THROUGH EXPERIENCE

A LEAP OF FAITH: THE ROAD TO THE UNKNOWN

Joining the Army wasn't part of some master plan. It wasn't the culmination of years of dreaming about honor, service, or adventure. It was, if I'm being honest, more of a Hail Mary—a last-ditch effort to find something, anything, that made sense of my life. But before I could step into that cold Texas night, before I could feel the hum of fluorescent lights and the weight of an Army-issue duffel bag on my shoulder, I had to make the decision to get there. And that journey started long before I walked into the recruitment office.

Brooklyn in the late 70's wasn't a place that nurtured soft edges. It hardened you, shaped you with its streets, its sounds, its unspoken rules. You learned to navigate it, even if you didn't always

41

understand it. For me, it was the neighborhood stoops, the crackle of double-dutch ropes slapping concrete, the bass-heavy boom of passing cars. It was home, but home wasn't always enough.

I was seventeen, a skinny, awkward kid trying to figure out my place in a world that didn't seem to have one for me. School felt like a holding pen for people who didn't fit. I showed up, sat in the back of the class, and quietly waited for the bell to ring. Teachers didn't see me, and to be honest, I didn't give them much to see. I wasn't causing trouble—I wasn't that kind of kid—but I wasn't excelling either. I just existed, drifting between expectations that weren't clear and dreams I hadn't dared to form.

My mother worked hard to hold us together, but even her relentless efforts couldn't disguise the struggle. She was a woman of quiet strength, a survivor in her own right. I can still see her, her hands calloused from long days and her voice steady even when I could tell her spirit was tired. But she never let me see her falter, even when she must have felt like crumbling.

I wanted to help her, to be something more than the boy she had to worry about. But how? Brooklyn didn't hand out answers; it handed out distractions. And I wasn't immune to them. The streets had a way of pulling at you, whispering promises of belonging and danger in the same breath. I had seen too many kids fall into that trap, and deep down, I knew I didn't want that for myself.

But what did I want? That was the question I couldn't answer. One day, a commercial came on the TV. You've seen the kind—the kind with men in crisp uniforms scaling walls, leaping from helicopters, saluting flags. The slogan was bold: "Be All You Can Be." I watched it, transfixed. It wasn't the action that caught my attention—it was the promise. The Army seemed to offer something I hadn't considered before: structure, purpose, and, most importantly, a way out of my hood; into manhood.

At first, it was just a thought, something to toy with when the monotony of my days got too heavy. But the idea grew. It started to feel like an escape hatch, a way to rewrite the story I didn't like.

I didn't tell anyone at first. How could I? It wasn't exactly a dream to share. But eventually, the thought burned too brightly to keep to myself, so I brought it to my mother.

I can still see her face when I told her. She didn't yell. She didn't protest. She just looked at me, long and hard, like she was trying to read something between the lines of my words.

"Are you sure, Kenny?" she asked. Her voice was calm, but there was something beneath it—a mix of worry and resignation.

"Yes," I said, though I wasn't sure at all.

She didn't say yes right away. She needed time to think, and I gave it to her. I could tell she was torn. Letting me go felt like losing me, I'm sure. But keeping me here, in Brooklyn, with all its lurking dangers, might have felt like losing me, too.

Eventually, she signed the papers. I wasn't old enough to enlist on my own, so her signature was my ticket out. She signed with a hand that trembled just slightly, and I don't know if it was fear, hope, or something in between.

Walking into that recruitment office felt like stepping into a different world. The recruiters were polished, their smiles practiced and their words carefully chosen. They painted pictures of what the Army could be: travel, adventure, opportunity. I listened, nodding along, but the truth was, I wasn't sold on the glamour. I just needed something—anything—that felt like a step forward.

The next few weeks were a whirlwind. Paperwork, physicals, meetings with strangers who called me "Private Braswell" before the name even felt like mine. I moved through it all with a mix of curiosity and trepidation, wondering if I was making the right choice.

The night before I left, my mom cooked a dinner that felt heavier than usual. We didn't say much—what was there to say? She hugged me tightly when I left, her arms lingering just a second too long. It was the kind of hug that tried to say everything she couldn't find the words for.

And then, I was gone.

That first night at Fort Bliss, standing under the fluorescent lights and feeling the weight of the desert air, I thought back to that hug, to the way her arms had felt around me. I thought about the boy I had been in Brooklyn, the boy who had searched for something more.

Now, I was here. And everything was about to change.

A STRANGER IN UNIFORM: BREAKING FREE OF THE OLD SELF

It was late October in Texas, and the desert's cold night air was an unexpected slap to my Brooklyn skin. I stood there, shivering, with close to 300 others, all strangers. We were all packed into neat, endless lines on the open base at Fort Bliss. The air was thick with silence broken only by the gruff orders of drill sergeants, their voices sharp enough to cut the night. They barked at us, moved us, stripped us of whatever we had brought with us from the outside world—not just our clothes, but our identities.

I had never felt so alone.

That first night in the Army was like a strange, out-of-body experience. It was as though my life before that moment—my family, my music, my city—had been wiped clean. I was no longer Kenny from the block in Brooklyn. I was a nameless recruit in a sea of shaved heads and olive drab.

The shock started earlier that evening. I don't even remember the flight to Texas. It was my first time on a plane, but the journey left no imprint, no excitement, no novelty. All I remember is arriving and feeling the ground beneath me, an unfamiliar hardness to the soil, a reminder that I wasn't in New York anymore.

The first thing they took from me was my hair. When they buzzed it down to the scalp, I felt as if they were shearing away the last piece of Brooklyn that clung to me. Here's the crazy thing; my hair was already short. Nice and and New York tight with waves, fresh with Murray's grease.

So it was more, the act of the sharp clippers against my scalp; that I felt more than the physical act of cutting my hair—it was a metaphoric stripping of my identity. My waves, my individuality, were reduced to a military standard. And just like that, I wasn't Kenneth anymore; I was a recruit. When they tossed my civilian clothes into a bin and handed me a duffel bag full of Army-issued green, it felt like I was stepping into a role I wasn't sure I wanted to play.

And then there was the line.

That first night, they lined us all up, shouting for anyone from New York City to step forward. I hesitated. My pride as a New Yorker was tangled with an unease I couldn't shake. I stepped out, along with about a dozen others, all boys who had grown up navigating the concrete jungle. The drill sergeant stared us down and then turned to the rest of the recruits.

"These," he barked, pointing at us, "are the troublemakers. Keep your eyes on them."

My stomach dropped. I had never thought of myself as a trouble-maker. Sure, I was from Brooklyn, but that didn't make me a delinquent. His words planted a seed of doubt, a question I hadn't asked myself before: Was this how the world saw me? I stood there, trying to make sense of it, the weight of my supposed reputation as a New Yorker pressing down on my chest. It wasn't the last time the Army would challenge how I saw myself.

By the time we were marched to the barracks, the night was a blur. The chill had set into my bones, but I barely noticed. Inside the barracks, the fluorescent lights buzzed overhead, and the space was filled with nothing but the scrape of boots on linoleum and the occasional shout of a drill sergeant. My duffel bag felt foreign in my hands. Everything about that moment felt foreign—except for the loneliness.

I kept thinking back to the moment my mother signed the papers that allowed me to enlist. I had to convince her—I was just 16, not yet old enough to make that decision on my own. But now, I couldn't remember what I had said to her to get her to agree. Maybe I had told her I wanted to be a man. Maybe she signed out of frustration, or maybe she believed the Army could give me what she felt she couldn't.

But in that cold barracks, standing among strangers, I wondered if I had made a mistake. I had been searching for something my whole life—for belonging, for purpose, for a tribe I could call my own. But what if this wasn't it? What if this was just another place where I didn't fit?

As the night wore on, they divided us again and again, smaller and smaller groups. Each time, I felt the loss of the tenuous connections I had begun to make. The boy next to me with the nervous laugh; gone. The guy from Philly with the same jittery energy I felt. Gone. By the end of the night, the faces around me were all new, all stripped of individuality by their matching green uniforms and buzz cuts. We were a sea of sameness, indistinguishable in the dim light.

For someone who had spent so much of his life searching for connection, for meaning, the isolation of that first night was crushing. I lay on the hard cot in the pitch-black barracks, my head spinning with questions. What had I done? Would I survive this? And most pressing of all: Who was I now?

> *That night, I felt something break inside me. The boy who had walked into the recruitment office in Brooklyn with dreams of being "all I could be" was gone. In his place was someone raw, exposed, and unsure of what came next.*

The Army didn't waste time easing you into transformation. It ripped away everything you thought you were, leaving you with nothing but questions and the cold of the night.

But even in that darkness, there was a spark of something else. I didn't recognize it at the time, but it was the beginning of a shift. Stripped of everything familiar, I had no choice but to confront the bare bones of who I was. There was no Brooklyn swagger to hide behind, no family to lean on, no music to drown out the doubts. It was just me, raw and uncertain, standing at the edge of something I couldn't yet define.

As the night dragged on, the whispers of other recruits filled the silence. Quiet conversations floated through the air—nervous jokes, murmured questions, soft reassurances. I listened, but I didn't join in. I wasn't ready to share my fear with anyone.

But their voices reminded me that I wasn't alone. We were all strangers, but we were in this together, whether we liked it or not. That first night in the Army wasn't just the start of my military career. It was the start of a journey inward, a reckoning with myself. In the weeks and months that followed, I would begin to piece together who I was and who I wanted to be.

But on that cold October night, all I knew was the weight of the questions pressing down on me, the hum of the fluorescent lights, and the ache of being a stranger; even to myself.

THE WEIGHT OF UNIFORM AND SKIN

Four months into the Army, and it felt like both an eternity and a blink of an eye. Everything had changed—the way I carried myself, the way I thought, the way I survived—but what hadn't changed, what I couldn't escape, was how the world still saw me through the lens of my skin. It was as if the uniform I wore, the sacrifices I was willing to make, didn't matter. Not to everyone. And that realization landed on me harder than any drill sergeant's bark ever could.

But before we get to that night, you need to understand how I got there—how a boy from Brooklyn ended up standing in a bathroom on a military base in Texas, facing a moment that would shape me in ways I still can't fully explain.

Joining the Army felt like the only real option back then. My life in Brooklyn wasn't going anywhere fast. I was trying to find myself, trying to figure out who I was supposed to be in a world that wasn't handing out roadmaps to kids like me. The Army promised structure, purpose, maybe even escape. I wasn't looking to become a soldier; I was looking to become someone.

The first day, they stripped everything away—your clothes, your hair, even your name. They gave you a number, a uniform, and a bunk, and they told you that this was who you were now. I went

along with it, figuring this was part of the process. I didn't realize then how deeply they would drill that concept into you. You
became a tool, a cog in their machine, and the only thing expected
of you was obedience. It wasn't about who you were or where you
came from; it was about how well you could follow orders.

And for a while, that was enough. There was a strange kind of
freedom in not having to think for yourself. They told you when to
eat, when to sleep, when to run, when to fire. And you did it. But
even in the most rigid structure, life finds a way to remind you of
who you are—or, more accurately, how others see you.

The night it happened, I was tired. Bone tired. The kind of tired
that sinks into your muscles and makes your thoughts slow and
sticky. Basic training had been grueling, and the days felt like they
stretched on forever. That night, all I wanted was to make it to my
bunk and shut the world out for a few hours. But the Army doesn't
operate on your schedule.

I was in the latrine—what we civilians would call a bathroom—
when they walked in. Two of them. White boys, clean-cut, with
that confident stride that says, This is my space, and you just
happen to be in it. I didn't know them well; the Army is a big place,
and faces blur together after a while. But their faces were sharp
that night, their eyes hard and locked onto me.

I don't remember what I was doing—washing my hands, maybe, or
just staring at myself in the mirror, trying to recognize the man I
was becoming. What I do remember is the sound of their boots on
the tile, the way they stopped just a little too close.

And then it came, that word.

"Nigger."

It wasn't whispered. It wasn't muttered under breath. It was loud, deliberate, and pointed. The kind of word that wasn't just meant to hurt—it was meant to put you in your place.

"You need to know your place, nigger."

The room shrank. My pulse quickened. I could feel the heat rising in my chest, the way my fists clenched instinctively at my sides. Brooklyn rose up in me, that fight-or-flight instinct that every kid from the block knows too well.

But this wasn't Brooklyn.

In Brooklyn, if someone stepped to you like that, you handled it. No questions asked. You didn't let disrespect slide, because letting it slide once meant you'd have to let it slide again and again. But here, in this sterile, tiled room, I wasn't just Kenny from Crown Heights. I was Private Braswell, and the stakes were different.

I had to decide, at that moment, who I was going to be.

The words kept coming, sharp and venomous, laced with spit that landed too close to my face. His friend stood there, smirking, egging him on without saying much. It was clear they were testing me, trying to see how far they could push.

Every part of me wanted to lash out. I could see it so clearly—my fist connecting with his jaw, the satisfying crunch of bone, the way his smirk would vanish in an instant. I could feel the strength in my arms, the tension in my muscles begging for release.

But I didn't move.

It wasn't fear that held me back, though. Let me be clear about that. It wasn't fear.

It was something deeper, something older. It was the prayers of my mother and grandmother, whispered into the universe long before I ever set foot in that latrine. It was the voice in my head that said, Not like this. This isn't the way.

I stood there, fists clenched, heart pounding, and I let him talk. I let him spew his hatred, his ignorance, his smallness. And when he finally ran out of words, I met his gaze. I didn't say anything. I didn't have to. My silence was louder than anything I could have said or done.

They left eventually, their footsteps echoing down the hall. I stayed behind, gripping the edge of the sink, staring at my reflection. My face was calm, but my eyes betrayed the storm raging inside me.

Was this what it meant to be a man? To endure, to hold back, to choose restraint over instinct? Or was this something else entirely?

I didn't know then. I'm not sure I even know now. But what I do know is that night changed me.

It's easy to talk about manhood in abstract terms—strength, courage, integrity. But the truth is, manhood isn't something you find in a word or a moment. It's something you build, piece by piece, choice by choice.

That night in the latrine, I started building. It wasn't the first time I'd faced racism—far from it. But it was the first time I'd had to confront it in such a raw, unfiltered way, without the safety net of familiarity. In that moment, I learned that being a man isn't just about standing your ground.

Sometimes, it's about knowing when to stand still.

Looking back, I wonder what became of those two boys. Did they ever think about that night? Did they carry it with them the way I have? I doubt it. But that's not what matters.

What matters is that I carried it. I carried it, and I learned from it, and I used it to become someone stronger, someone better.

And that's the thing about moments like this—they shape you, yes, but they don't define you. You get to decide what they mean, what you take from them, and how you use them to move forward.

That night, I chose to move forward. And I've been moving forward ever since.

THE NIGHT THE WORLD SHIFTED: A SOLDIER'S FIRST LESSONS IN GERMANY

There's a strange kind of stillness that comes over you in the moments before stepping into a completely unknown life. It's not peace—it's more like the quiet tension of a slingshot pulled all the way back, the energy so taut you're not sure if it's going to launch you forward or snap apart in your hands. That's what I felt as the cab snaked its way through the dark, winding roads of Germany, carrying me further into a life that I could barely comprehend yet.

Earlier that evening, I had landed in Frankfurt, Germany, fresh out of basic training and AIT—four months of transformation that left me raw but somehow molded into the beginnings of something new. I wasn't sure what I had become, but I knew I wasn't the same boy who'd left New York just a few months earlier.

The army had taken everything familiar, stripped it away, and replaced it with discipline, hierarchy, and a strange kind of clarity. Yet none of that had prepared me for the silence of that cab ride through the German countryside.

The driver didn't speak much, and I didn't either. It wasn't just the language barrier—it was the weight of what lay ahead. The road signs were foreign, the trees tall and shadowy, bending over the narrow lanes like silent sentinels. The only sound was the occasional swish of the windshield wipers and the hum of the engine as it carried me toward Grossenhain, a small military base perched atop a hill.

As we climbed higher, the rain started to drizzle, coating the windshield with tiny beads of water. The darkness felt heavier here, more consuming, like it could swallow the cab whole. I pressed my face against the glass, straining to catch a glimpse of anything familiar, anything that would make me feel less like I was being hurled into another dimension.

And then, just as we crested the hill, the headlights illuminated something I knew all too well: flashing red and blue lights. Police cars. The sight sent a jolt through me, my heart quickening as my mind leapt to every possible scenario. Growing up in Brooklyn, police lights always meant something was going down—usually something you didn't want to be caught up in. I hadn't come all the way to Germany to find myself back in the same chaos I'd left behind.

The cab pulled up to the gate, and the driver unceremoniously opened the trunk, pulling out my bags and placing them on the wet ground. He gave me a look that needed no translation: "You're on your own now." I handed him the travel voucher I'd been given, and he disappeared into the night, leaving me standing there, clutching my duffel bag and staring at the guardhouse.

A young soldier stepped out of the small hut, his breath visible in the freezing air. "You Braswell?" he asked, his voice a mix of boredom and authority.

"Yeah," I said, my own breath forming clouds as I spoke.

He nodded and motioned for me to step into the hut. "We've been expecting you, but the base is on lockdown. You'll have to wait here until things settle down."

Lockdown? My stomach twisted as I followed him into the cramped guardhouse. It was barely big enough for one person, let alone two, and the air inside was thick with the metallic tang of a space heater struggling against the bitter cold. My bags were left outside, a testament to just how temporary my presence here was.

"What's going on?" I asked, trying to mask the unease creeping into my voice.

"Something at the rec center," he said, shrugging. "Don't know the details. Just sit tight."

And so we waited. The minutes dragged on, each one stretching into what felt like an eternity. The guard didn't say much, and I didn't press him. Outside, the rain had turned to sleet, tapping against the tin roof in a rhythm that felt both soothing and ominous. My mind raced, trying to piece together what could possibly be happening on the other side of that gate.

The silence was occasionally broken by the crackle of his radio, a garbled voice giving updates that neither of us could fully make out. The tension was thick, but there was nothing to do but sit in that tiny space, staring at the glowing orange coil of the heater and listening to the wind howl outside.

Finally, more lights appeared in the distance, weaving their way up the hill. An ambulance this time. The guard went out to open the gate and they passed through heading straight for the rec center. The guard and I exchanged a glance after stepping over my bags, still in the rain, but said nothing. I thought to myself, whatever was happening out there, it was serious enough to need paramedics.

By the time the ambulance left, followed by the police cars, it was well past midnight. The guard finally motioned for me to grab my bags. "You're good to go," he said, pointing toward the base. "Second building on the left."

I stepped out into the freezing night, the cold cutting through my jacket like it wasn't even there. The base was eerily quiet, the kind of quiet that felt unnatural. As I trudged toward the barracks, the snow crunching under my boots, I couldn't shake the feeling that I was walking into something I wasn't prepared for.

The barracks were nothing like I'd imagined. The room I was assigned to was cramped, with just enough space for a bunk bed, a single bed, and a couple of lockers. My new roommates—Morales, a Puerto Rican from New York, and a quiet Mexican soldier whose name escapes me—greeted me with a mix of curiosity and indifference. They were friendly enough, but the tension of the night lingered in the air, making the introductions feel mechanical.

"Do you know what happened at the rec center?" I asked as I started to unpack my things.

Morales shrugged. "Not sure, but we heard someone got stabbed over a girl."

Stabbed. Over a girl. The words hung in the air, heavy and absurd. I'd left Brooklyn to escape this kind of drama, to find something better, something meaningful. Yet here I was, thousands of miles away, and the same senseless violence was playing out in front of me.

The next morning, the mess hall buzzed with the full story. Two soldiers had gotten into a fight, and one had pulled a knife, stabbing the other multiple times. The victim survived but was being sent home, while the perpetrator was on his way to Leavenworth. Over a girl!

As I sat there, picking at my breakfast, I couldn't help but feel the weight of it all pressing down on me. This wasn't what I'd signed up for. I'd come here to grow, to find purpose, to become the man I thought I was supposed to be. But the lines between the life I'd left and the life I was building were starting to blur, leaving me questioning everything.

That night, as I lay in my narrow bunk, the events of the past 24 hours played over and over in my mind. The cold, the darkness, the flashing lights, the whispers of violence—they all merged into a single, overwhelming question: What had I gotten myself into?

And yet, beneath the doubt and the fear, there was a spark of something else. Resilience, maybe. Or stubbornness. Whatever it was, it told me to keep going, to push through the discomfort and the uncertainty. This was just the beginning of my time in Germany, and I had no idea what lay ahead. But one thing was clear: I wasn't going to let this place define me. Not yet. Not ever.

I WANT TO BE LIKE

In the quiet moments when I reflect on my younger self, a phrase echoes through my mind: "I want to be like." It's a simple phrase, yet it carries the weight of countless influences and aspirations that shaped me during my teenage years and into early adulthood. It's not just about the people I admired, but also about how their lives, their choices, and their presence planted seeds of possibility within me. Looking back, it's fascinating to untangle whether these were things that actively shaped my perspective on life or results of what had already been shaping me. Perhaps it was both—a symbiotic relationship between influence and experience that defined who I was becoming.

The phrase "I want to be like" became deeply ingrained in popular culture during Michael Jordan's reign as the undisputed king of basketball. The "Be Like Mike" commercials and theme song were iconic, and even now, decades later, the sentiment still resonates.

People wanted to be like Mike because he epitomized excellence, confidence, and success. For me, though, the phrase was much broader. It wasn't confined to one person, nor was it just about sports. It was about the many people I encountered—real and fictional, near and distant—who represented what I aspired to become or who inspired traits I wanted to emulate. Some of these figures loomed large in my imagination; others made their mark in quiet, unassuming ways.

Take John Amos, for example, who played James Evans on Good Times. He wasn't just a TV dad; he was the dad. He represented strength, love, and resilience in the face of adversity. His character was the rock of his family, holding them together through tough times in a Chicago housing project. There was something magnetic about the way he carried himself—a man who was unyielding in his principles yet deeply compassionate. I wanted to be like him. I wanted to be that man who could weather life's storms while staying true to his family and his values. To me, James Evans wasn't just a character; he was a blueprint for manhood.

And then there was John Shaft. The fictional private detective brought to life by Richard Roundtree was everything I imagined a man should be: tough, fearless, and undeniably cool. He walked the streets of New York City with an air of confidence that was almost tangible. Shaft didn't take nonsense from anyone, and he fought for what was right in a way that was unapologetically bold. In a world that often seemed chaotic and unjust, Shaft was a symbol of order and righteousness—all while wearing a leather trench coat that screamed "This cat Shaft is a bad muther...shut yo mouth."

Of course, there was John Wayne. Now, as I've grown older and learned more about the man behind the cowboy hat, my feelings about him have become more complicated. Stories of his racist comments and thoughts about Black people aside. But as a child, all I saw was a hero. John Wayne's rugged individualism and his portrayal of characters who tamed the Wild West left an impression on me. He stood tall in a chaotic world and always found a way to bring order to it. At that time, I didn't know about his personal beliefs or how they conflicted with the values I've come to hold dear. What I knew was that he was the epitome of strength and resolve, and for a boy who often felt uncertain and unsure, that was enough.

Then there was John-Boy from The Waltons. He was different from the other Johns. Where James Evans, Shaft, and John Wayne represented strength and power, John-Boy represented curiosity, kindness, and a quiet determination. He wasn't flashy or commanding, but he was steadfast in his values. He was a writer, a dreamer, and a moral compass for his family. In a world that often felt unpredictable, John-Boy's steady presence was reassuring. I wanted to be like that, too—to have a core of integrity that remained unshaken no matter what life threw at me.

It's funny how these fictional characters and public figures found their way into my psyche, but they weren't the only ones. There were real people, too—people who, in their own way, left indelible marks on my soul. My cousin Al was one of those people. He was everything I aspired to be: charismatic, talented, and endlessly cool. Summers in North Carolina with him were some of the best times of my life. We'd work hard during the day, toiling in the tobacco fields and feeding the hogs, but when the evening came, he transformed. He'd lay out his clothes with meticulous care, splash on some cologne, and head out into the night, exuding confidence and style. He had a 1974 Chevy Nova that was the envy of every kid in Pinetops, North Carolina. It was sleek, powerful, and commanded attention—just like him. I wanted to be like Al. To go to an HBCU and become a brother of Omega Psi Phi. And yes, I wanted his confidence, his charm, his ability to light up a room.

But life, as it often does, had other plans. Al's life was cut tragically short when he was serving in the military. Losing him was a devastating blow, and even now, decades later, I feel his absence acutely. He was my role model, my guidepost, and his loss left a void that no one else could fill. Yet, in his absence, I've carried pieces of him with me. The lessons he taught me—about hard work, style, and the importance of living life fully—have stayed with me. They've shaped the man I've become, even as I've had to navigate a world without him.

As I moved into adulthood, the phrase "I want to be like" took on new dimensions. It wasn't just about admiration; it was about identity. Who was I? Who did I want to be? And who did I not want to be? My father loomed large in this equation. For much of my early life, I was determined not to be like him. His absence, his choices, and the pain they caused left a mark on me. I wanted to chart a different course, to build a life that was defined not by what was missing but by what was present. Yet, as I've grown older, I've come to see him through a more compassionate lens. While I still aspire to be different in many ways, I've also come to understand the complexities of his humanity.

There were others, too. Mentors, friends, and even brief encounters with strangers who left lasting impressions. Some taught me through their words; others taught me through their actions. They showed me what it meant to live with integrity, to navigate hardship with grace, and to find joy in the midst of struggle. And then there were those who taught me through their absence—who showed me, through their failures or shortcomings, the kind of person I didn't want to be. Each of these lessons, whether positive or negative, added to the makeup of my life.

Sports heroes were a big part of this, too. Growing up, I wanted to be like Julius Erving, Walt Frazier, and Muhammad Ali. These weren't just athletes; they were icons. They represented excellence, perseverance, and the power of belief. I dabbled in sports, trying my hand at basketball, football, and track. While I was decent at all of them, I lacked the mentorship and support to truly excel. Looking back, I see those moments as missed opportunities, but I also see them as stepping stones. They taught me about discipline, resilience, and the importance of showing up—lessons that have served me well in other areas of my life.

The phrase "I want to be like" isn't just about aspiration; it's about connection. It's about the people who come into our lives, whether for a moment or a lifetime, and leave us changed. It's about the ways we carry those lessons forward, shaping them into something uniquely our own. And as I sit here now, reflecting on all the people who have inspired me, I'm struck by the realization that, in some small way, I've become a composite of them all.

The strength of James Evans, the cool confidence of Shaft, the curiosity of John-Boy, and the charisma of my cousin Al—they're all part of me. And for that, I am profoundly grateful.

But of course, there were the others—the unspoken influences that came into my life quietly, unexpectedly, and left behind lessons I didn't realize I needed until much later. These weren't the famous figures, the relatives, or the neighborhood icons; they were fleeting interactions that caught me at the right moment, offering subtle, profound nudges. A stern look from a bus driver when I was about to skip my fare, the gentle admonition of a teacher who believed I could do better, even when I didn't. These moments, so small in the grand scheme of things, became some of the most significant.

I wanted to be like these people too—not necessarily in who they were, but in the way they moved through the world with a kind of grace and integrity that stayed with me long after they were gone.

And yet, woven through all of this—the people, the moments, the cultural icons—was the backdrop of my father. He was the looming contradiction, the one man I was determined not to be like, even as I unconsciously absorbed parts of him. Isn't that always the way it goes? The people we run from often find their way into our hearts and habits anyway. My father was my "not like," my anti-hero. His absence was as instructive as any presence could be, teaching me what not to do, how not to love, and yet, at the same time, his absence left questions I would spend my life answering. Who am I when I'm not defined by what I'm running from? What do I stand for when I'm no longer defined by rebellion?

It's a strange thing, realizing how much power those "I want to be like" moments hold. They're anchors and wings at the same time. They keep you steady, grounded in a sense of purpose, while also lifting you to dream bigger than you thought you could. But they also come with a burden—a kind of self-imposed pressure to live up to these ideals, to not just emulate but embody the best parts of the people and experiences that shaped you. And as I sit here, seasoned by years of learning and unlearning, I realize that the work isn't in becoming like anyone else.

> ***The work is in becoming fully yourself, taking pieces of what you've learned from others and weaving them into your own unique story.***

When I think about the Johns, my cousin Al, the athletes, the fleeting influences, and even my father, I'm struck by how they all carried a duality: they were inspirations and warnings, mirrors and shadows. They taught me to dream and to stay grounded, to push against the tide but also to find my place within it. They were my teachers, whether they meant to be or not, and for that, I am endlessly grateful.

And now, as I reflect on all of this, I realize that the phrase "I want to be like" isn't really about imitation. It's about aspiration, about seeing the potential in others and recognizing that potential in yourself. It's about honoring the lessons without being shackled by them, about taking what you need and leaving the rest behind. It's about growth, about becoming, about standing tall in your own story while acknowledging the chapters others helped you write.

So, to the Johns, to Al, to the athletes, to my father, and to every fleeting influence that crossed my path: thank you. Thank you for showing me who I could be, who I didn't want to be, and most importantly, who I am. Your impact is in every step I take, every choice I make, every word I write.

You are the echoes that shape my voice, the shadows that sharpen my light, the roots that keep me steady as I continue to grow. And for that, I will always carry you with me—not as burdens, but as blessings.

CHAPTER THREE

BREAKING FREE: LETTING GO OF JUDGMENTS AND INSECURITIES

THE WHISPER THAT WOUNDS: GOSSIP AS THE QUIET ASSASSIN

Out of all the chapters in this book, this one has been the most challenging to write—not because the words don't come easily, but because the memories of what gossip has done to me, and the clarity it's brought me, are still sharp. Gossip is not just idle chatter. It's a force—subtle, pervasive, and destructive.

It can alter your perception of yourself, dismantle relationships, and shake your confidence. It can be a slow erosion of your character or a tidal wave of sudden upheaval.

Gossip, at its core, is an agitator. It thrives in the shadows, feeding on insecurities and creating conflict. It doesn't simply happen in isolation—it's a process, often rooted in the gossiper's own unmet desires or insecurities. And that's what makes it so dangerous. It's not just about what people say; it's about what those words are designed to do—how they aim to devalue, isolate, or control their target.

This chapter, like this book, is about clarity. It's about discovering how the experiences in your life—both good and bad—shape you. Gossip is one of those experiences, and understanding it requires more than just examining its effects; it requires understanding its origins, its mechanisms, and its motivations. Gossip is rarely about truth. Instead, it's about perception, manipulation, and often, a reflection of the gossiper's internal struggles.

I remember a moment that brought the insidiousness of gossip into sharp focus. It was during a conference at MegaFest, hosted by The Potter's House. I'd been invited to speak and found myself in a green room, engaged in conversation with Sherita Jakes, the wife of Bishop T.D. Jakes. I admired her deeply—not just for her association with The Potter's House, but for the work she has done in her role as First Lady to ground people in faith while giving them practical tools to navigate life's challenges; especially women.

As we talked, I felt a connection, an authenticity in our exchange. Then, suddenly, a young woman approached. Without hesitation, she moved directly between us, inserting herself into the space with such deliberateness that it startled me. It wasn't that she didn't see me—she saw me very clearly. But her actions were intentional, dismissive.

I stepped back, unsure of how to proceed. This wasn't my arena, and I wasn't about to cause a scene. But as I began to move away, Mrs. Jakes reached out and grabbed my hand. Her grip was firm, grounding me in the moment. She didn't let go, even as the young woman spoke—about what, I don't even remember. What I do remember is the way Mrs. Jakes handled the situation. She listened politely, her graciousness unwavering, until the woman finished and walked away without ever acknowledging me.

"Thank you," Mrs. Jakes said as she turned back to me.

"You're welcome," I replied, though I didn't fully understand what she was thanking me for.

Then she said something that has stayed with me ever since. "You need to be mindful of two kinds of people. The first are those who want to be like you."

She explained that these are the people who admire what you have—the nice car, the good job, the fulfilling relationships—and want those things for themselves. In a healthy dynamic, this admiration can be inspiring. But when it's rooted in envy, it becomes dangerous.

"The second kind," she continued, "are those who want to be you."

Her words hit me like a freight train. These aren't people who want their own version of success—they want yours. They don't just admire your job; they want your position. They don't just envy your relationships; they want to replace you in them. And that, she said, is where you need to be most vigilant. Because these are the people who will use whatever means necessary—subtle sabotage, manipulation, and yes, gossip—to achieve their goal.

That moment was a revelation. Gossip, I realized, is not just idle talk. It's a weapon, wielded by those who feel powerless in their own lives. And it's devastatingly effective, because it attacks the most vulnerable parts of us—our self-esteem, our relationships, our sense of belonging.

This is why discernment is critical. Gossip thrives in the absence of discernment—when we fail to recognize the motivations behind the words, when we allow the emotional weight of the message to overshadow the intent of the messenger. Discernment isn't just about identifying truth from lies; it's about understanding the emotional state and intentions of the person speaking.

Gossip disrupts the very foundation of transformational change by bypassing a concept that I created at Fathers Incorporated. It's called the Progressive Change Model. In the model we hypothesize that people act based on how they think, and they think based on how they feel.

We believe that to truly affect change, you must address how someone feels because feelings influence thoughts, and thoughts drive actions. Gossip, however, short-circuits this process. It doesn't engage with how someone feels—it targets their thoughts directly, sowing confusion, doubt, and insecurity. This deliberate attack on someone's thinking can derail their actions and diminish their confidence in a way that feels personal, even if the intent is entirely rooted in the insecurities of the gossiper.

Without clarity on who is speaking into your life and why, gossip becomes not just a whisper in the wind but a gale force, uprooting your sense of self and disrupting your ability to evolve into the person you are meant to be.

Through the years, I've come to identify four core aspects of gossip. These are the mechanisms by which it operates and the damage it inflicts:

1. The Reporter of Tragedy:

Some people gossip simply because they want to be the expert, the bearer of information. They thrive on being the first to share a story, often focusing on the negative because it gives their words more weight. These are often the people closest to you—the ones who know your struggles and use that knowledge as currency to elevate their own status. They frame your setbacks as breaking news, delivering it with a smugness that betrays their true intent.

2. The Bond of the Clique:

Gossip can create social bonds, forming cliques united by shared disdain for someone else. This isn't about truth or resolution; it's about power in numbers. These groups feed off each other's negativity, creating an echo chamber where the target of their gossip becomes dehumanized—a subject of scorn rather than a person with feelings and a story of their own.

3. The Moral Enforcer:

Some gossipers see themselves as arbiters of morality, using gossip to shame or embarrass their target into changing their behavior. This can be especially destructive in the age of social media, where a single rumor can spiral into a public shaming campaign. For young people, this kind of gossip can be suffocating, even life-threatening, as we've seen in the tragic rise of suicides linked to online bullying.

4. The Status Seeker:

The most dangerous gossipers are those who use it as a tool to gain power and status. They don't just share stories; they craft narratives designed to undermine and control. These are the master manipulators, the ones who understand that perception is reality and use that knowledge to bend situations—and people—to their will.

As I've aged, my perspective on gossip has shifted. When I was younger, it felt like a destroyer—something that could dismantle everything I'd worked so hard to build. But now, with the clarity that comes from experience, I see it differently. Gossip can be an evolver. It forces you to examine yourself, to confront your own actions and intentions. It challenges you to rise above the noise, to let your work and your character speak louder than the whispers.

That's not to say it doesn't hurt. Gossip still stings, especially when it's based on truth. But even then, it offers an opportunity for growth. It pushes you to reevaluate, to make amends where needed, and to strengthen your resolve.

At its worst, gossip is a thief. It steals joy, trust, and peace. But at its best, it's a teacher, revealing the areas where you need to grow and the people you need to distance yourself from. And in that way, it becomes not just something to endure, but something to learn from. Something that, with time and perspective, can help you become the person you were always meant to be.

Just two days after writing this section on gossip, I received a message that stopped me in my tracks. It wasn't the words of criticism or hearsay that I'd become so accustomed to navigating; it was a reflection of the truth I had hoped to stand on all along.

A long time friend, in an emai, shared with me this message, "I am beyond impressed (with you)! If you heard how folks advocated for your work and reputation aside from myself, your head would spin, given none of them know you personally. I was deeply moved by how others knew of your work and want to meet you! Truly speaks to your impact!"

In that moment, while I read, my heart smiling, I was reminded of a truth that can be so easy to lose sight of when you're mired in the destructive echoes of gossip: authenticity will always shine through. No matter how deeply gossip seeks to wound, no matter how persistently it tries to obscure your light, the integrity of your work and the essence of your character have a way of rising above.

It was proof that no matter how hard others tried to define me, to craft a narrative around my name or work, my authenticity had quietly but powerfully carved its own space. This message wasn't just a kind word from a friend; it was a testament to a principle I have come to live by. When you remain steadfast in your truth—when your actions consistently align with your values—there is a resonance that no amount of idle chatter can mute.

It's a strange dichotomy to exist in a world where whispers of doubt or deceit can echo louder than shouts of praise. Gossip thrives on misperception and thrives even more on the inability of the accused to defend themselves in every room. And yet, the reality is that you don't have to. Your actions, your work, and your authenticity will speak for you, often in places you never set foot in. That message wasn't just affirming—it was liberating. It reminded me that while gossip may wound in the moment, the truth is patient, steady, and enduring. The truth doesn't just heal; it restores.

WHO TOLD YOU THAT YOU WERE NAKED? UNMASKING SHAME, GUILT, AND EMBARRASSMENT

Somewhere around 30, life starts speaking to you in a language you weren't fluent in at 20. It's subtle at first, like whispers you overhear but don't quite understand. Then, it gets louder, insistent, demanding your attention. You start asking yourself questions you've never asked before, questions you didn't know you'd one day care about.

You begin to measure yourself—not against the world, but against the expectations you've silently carried, the ones you thought were background noise but now echo louder than ever.

At 30, you realize something profound: you're not 20 anymore, and 40 is closer than it feels. For the first time, perhaps, you start really analyzing where you are, what you've done, and—more importantly—what you haven't. It's like standing in front of a mirror, but instead of your reflection, you see a montage of your triumphs and failures, your unmet goals, your relationships, your career, your finances, and even your dreams. And you're left to sift through it all, wondering:

What does this all mean?

It's not just about what you've achieved. It's about what you thought you'd achieve by now. Maybe you thought you'd be financially stable, married, or living in a dream career. Maybe you imagined you'd have the perfect family or be living the kind of life that makes other people say, Wow, they've got it all together. And when reality doesn't align with the vision, that's where guilt, shame, and embarrassment creep in like uninvited guests who don't know when to leave.

> **Guilt whispers, *You should have done more*. Shame hisses, *You're not enough*. Embarrassment laughs, *What will people think?***

These emotions, tangled and heavy, can begin to consume you. But the truth is, they're not inherent. You weren't born feeling guilty, shameful, or embarrassed. Those emotions were learned, placed upon you by the people, experiences, and societal paradigms that shaped you.

And much like Adam and Eve in the garden, the pivotal question becomes: Who told you that you were naked?

In Genesis, Adam and Eve lived in a state of unselfconscious innocence. They were naked and felt no shame. But then came the serpent, planting seeds of doubt and curiosity. And when they ate the forbidden fruit, their eyes were opened, and with that newfound knowledge came something they'd never experienced before—shame. They covered themselves, hiding not just their bodies but their vulnerability.

When God walked in the garden and asked, Where are you? Adam's response was laden with fear: I was afraid because I was naked, so I hid. And God's reply cuts straight to the core: Who told you that you were naked?

That question isn't just for Adam. It's for all of us. Who told you that you should feel ashamed? Who planted the seed of guilt that now grows like a weed, choking your joy? Who made you feel embarrassed about who you are, what you've done, or where you're going?

For me, that question came to life during a simple yet pivotal moment in my childhood. I've told the story before about how my mother sent me to the store with food stamps, and I refused to go. It wasn't the task itself that bothered me—it was the fear of what my friends might think. At that moment, I wasn't just a kid sent on an errand; I was a kid terrified of being seen as poor. And the question that lingers is, Who told me that being poor was something to be ashamed of?

The answer, I've realized, isn't singular. It's not just one person or one experience. It's a collective of societal expectations, cultural paradigms, and personal insecurities that shape how we see ourselves. And as we navigate life, those layers build up, creating a distorted image that we carry with us into adulthood.

At 30, those layers start to suffocate. You begin to unpack the expectations—both yours and others'. You confront the voices that told you what you should be by now, what success looks like, and what failure means. You wrestle with the realization that some of those voices belong to people you love, people who meant well but inadvertently placed a weight on your shoulders that was never yours to carry.

And it's not just the expectations of others; it's the expectations you've internalized. You start to wonder why you feel embarrassed about things you had no control over, why you carry guilt for dreams unfulfilled, or why shame has become a constant companion. It's a heavy burden, one that threatens to crush your self-esteem and your ability to move forward.

But breaking free starts with understanding where these emotions come from. For me, it was a long journey of peeling back the layers, much like the progressive change model we use at Fathers Incorporated. The model is simple yet profound: People act based on how they think. People think based on how they feel. And if you want to change what someone does, you must first address how they feel.

Applying this model to my own life meant looking at the feelings driving my guilt, shame, and embarrassment. It meant asking hard questions: Why do I feel this way? Where did this come from? Is this belief serving me, or is it holding me back? It's a process of reprogramming your mind to understand that these emotions aren't innate—they're learned. And if they can be learned, they can also be unlearned.

One of the most profound lessons I've learned in this journey is that shame, guilt, and embarrassment are often rooted in unmet expectations. But those expectations aren't always fair, realistic, or even yours. They're a product of the environments we grew up in, the people who influenced us, and the societal norms we've absorbed. And when you begin to deconstruct those expectations, you start to see the truth: You are not defined by what you've done or what you haven't achieved. You are defined by who you are and who you're becoming.

Breaking free from these emotions isn't easy. It requires confronting the very things you've spent years avoiding. It requires vulnerability, honesty, and a willingness to rewrite the narrative you've been living by. But on the other side of that struggle is liberation—a freedom that allows you to live authentically, unapologetically, and without the weight of shame, guilt, or embarrassment.

As I reflect on this journey, I think about the many conversations I've had with men who've struggled with these emotions, particularly in the context of fatherhood. One story that stands out is from a dear friend, Joseph, who once shared his experience of being estranged from his children. He spoke about the guilt and shame he carried, not just for being absent but for feeling like he couldn't come back. His words were raw and haunting: It was hard not being in their lives, but it was even harder to come back.

That statement hit me deeply because it captures the essence of these emotions. Guilt and shame don't just make you feel bad— they create barriers, walls that seem insurmountable. They make you believe that redemption is out of reach, that the pain of facing your mistakes is greater than the pain of staying stuck. But the truth is, the only way to move forward is to confront those barriers head-on. You can't skip over the hard parts; you have to walk through them.

And that's what this chapter is about: breaking free. It's about recognizing the weight you've been carrying, understanding where it comes from, and deciding that it no longer serves you. It's about shedding the layers of guilt, shame, and embarrassment that have held you back and stepping into a life of authenticity, purpose, and freedom.

> ***So, as you read this, I encourage you to ask yourself: Who told you that you were naked? Who told you that you should feel guilty, ashamed, or embarrassed? And more importantly, who gets to decide that those emotions no longer define you? The answer, my friend, is you.***

THE SEED THAT GROWS: OVERCOMING DOUBT AND RECLAIMING CONFIDENCE

Some words carry an extraordinary weight, not because of their definition, but because of the impact they have when spoken aloud. Among those words, none perhaps are as insidious as doubt. Doubt is both a whisper and a roar, an invisible force that grows roots in the fertile soil of our minds, nourished by insecurity and watered by the careless words of others. It doesn't arrive fully formed; it sneaks in, subtle and patient, waiting for the right conditions to bloom.

For most of us, if we were to look up doubt in the dictionary, it would be easy to imagine a face beside the definition. We all have that one person—maybe it's a parent, a teacher, a mentor, or even a stranger—who planted the seed of doubt in us, intentionally or not. Doubt doesn't require an invitation. It just needs the smallest crack in your confidence to take root. And once it's there, it's relentless, wrapping itself around your self-esteem, choking the belief you have in yourself until you forget you ever had it.

Doubt, like most seeds, starts small. Sometimes it's a single comment, a seemingly harmless observation. But its impact depends on who plants it. When someone close to you—a person whose opinion carries weight—sows that seed, it doesn't just rest on the surface. It burrows deep, its roots tangling with your aspirations, your dreams, your sense of self-worth. It can come from a parent saying, Are you sure you want to try that? Or a coach muttering, Maybe you're not cut out for this. And worse, it can come from those who are supposed to nurture you, but instead use their influence to remind you of your limitations.

I've seen it happen to others. I've felt it happen to me. Doubt has a peculiar ability to linger in your mind long after the moment it was planted. It echoes, over and over, like a broken record you can't turn off. And in my case, there was one voice, one moment, that carried a sting so sharp, it still reverberates in my soul.

The fascinating thing about doubt is its dual nature. It has the power to crush a person under its weight, but it also has the power to ignite something within them—an unstoppable drive to prove it wrong. Doubt, when confronted, can transform into fuel, turning limitations into possibilities and obstacles into stepping stones. In the stories of Malcolm X, Michael Jordan, Martin Lawrence, and even my own life, I see this duality vividly. Each of us, in our unique ways, faced moments where doubt threatened to define us, and yet, we emerged not in spite of it, but because of it.

Malcolm X, before becoming the iconic civil rights leader we know, was once Malcolm Little, a young man with dreams as grand as the world around him was limiting. When Malcolm expressed his aspiration to become a lawyer, his eighth-grade teacher, Mr. Ostrovsky, didn't just plant a seed of doubt—he attempted to smother Malcolm's dreams under the weight of societal racism and lowered expectations. "That's no realistic goal for a nigger," he told Malcolm, dismissing the young boy's ambition as folly.

For a time, Malcolm internalized that doubt, believing the lies about his potential. But life has a way of flipping the narrative, and that same doubt became the fire that burned within him, pushing him to fight for justice and become one of the most eloquent voices for Black liberation.

The seed of doubt meant to diminish him instead fueled a transformation that would change history.

Then there's Michael Jordan, whose story is equally inspiring in its relatability. As a sophomore in high school, he didn't make the varsity basketball team—a blow that could have shattered his confidence. For a teenager with dreams of greatness, being told "you're not good enough" can echo loudly in the chambers of self-doubt. But Michael didn't let that voice dominate. Instead, he turned that doubt into determination, using it as the catalyst to outwork, out train, and outshine everyone. Today, Jordan isn't just a name—it's a legacy of excellence, a testament to what happens when doubt is met with resolve.

Martin Lawrence, albeit through a fictional lens, gave us a comedic yet profound look at this idea in an episode of his sitcom, *Martin*. When he returned to his high school reunion, Martin's sole purpose was to confront the seeds of doubt planted in his younger years. Facing his arch rival; Pretty Ricky, It was a moment of reclaiming power, standing before the very people who once underestimated him, and showing them not just who he had become, but who he always had the potential to be.

While the scenario was scripted for laughs, the underlying truth resonated deeply: overcoming doubt isn't just about proving others wrong; it's about proving to yourself that their words never defined you.

Years ago, I was invited to speak on a panel at the Circle of Sisters event in New York City. It was a major platform, the kind of event where you get to share your work, your passion, your vision. At the time, I was in the final stages of writing my first book, When the Tear Won't Fall. It was a deeply personal project, one that had consumed me for years. I wasn't published yet, but I was proud of the work I had done. I believed in my story.

The panel itself was inspiring. I sat alongside accomplished authors, including Reverend Run and his wife, Justine. They had just released their book, Old School Love, and the crowd was captivated by their charisma and authenticity. I spoke about my journey as an aspiring author, about the labor of writing a book that captures the rawness of life. The audience seemed engaged, nodding in agreement, clapping at the right moments. I left the stage feeling like I had made a genuine connection.

But then came the moment that changed everything.

After the panel, we were guided to an area where the authors could meet attendees, sign books, and answer questions. My wife, who was pregnant at the time, struck up a conversation with Justine. They were chatting, laughing, bonding over motherhood and life. I stood nearby, content to let them share that moment.

Reverend Run joined us, and before I knew it, we were all lining up to take a picture. My wife stood in the middle with Justine, and I stood at one end, opposite Reverend Run. It was a lighthearted moment, a snapshot of shared experiences. But then, as the camera clicked, Reverend Run turned to Justine and said something that cut through me like a blade.

"Let's Go, he doesn't even have a book," he said. His tone was dismissive, almost mocking.

Then, as if to drive the point home, he grabbed Justine's hand and led her away, leaving me standing there in stunned silence.

I wish I could say I brushed it off, that I let his words roll off my back like water. But I didn't. I couldn't. His comment wasn't just an observation—it was a judgment, a dismissal of everything I had worked for. In that moment, I wasn't an aspiring author. I wasn't a storyteller or a visionary. I was just a man without a book, reduced to a single flaw in the eyes of someone whose opinion I had given unearned power.

The sting of his words lingered. They replayed in my mind like a loop I couldn't escape. He doesn't even have a book. It wasn't just the words—it was the way he said them, the way he dismissed me as if I didn't belong, as if my story didn't matter. And the worst part was, for a moment, I believed him. I let that seed of doubt take root.

Doubt has a way of magnifying your insecurities. It doesn't just question your abilities—it questions your worth. And when that seed is planted by someone you admire, someone whose words carry weight, it becomes even harder to shake. But here's the thing about seeds: they only grow if you nourish them. Doubt only flourishes if you allow it.

In the days that followed, I made a decision. I wouldn't let his words define me. I wouldn't let that moment become a barrier to my dreams. Instead, I used it as fuel. I poured myself into finishing my book, not just to prove him wrong, but to prove to myself that I was more than his judgment.

When, "When the Tear Won't Fall" was finally published, it was more than just a book launch. It was a reclamation of my power, a declaration that I was not defined by the doubts of others.

And as I've gone on to write more books, each one feels like a triumph, a reminder that the only voice that truly matters is the one inside me.

Doubt, I've learned, is a tool. It can be used to break you, or it can be used to build you. The choice is yours. When someone plants a seed of doubt in your mind, you have the power to decide whether it will grow or wither. And as I've navigated my own journey, I've come to understand the importance of guarding my mind against those who would use doubt as a weapon.

For me, that experience with Reverend Run taught me a valuable lesson—not just about doubt, but about resilience. It reminded me that words have power, but so do I. It reminded me that I am the author of my story, and no one else gets to write my narrative. And most importantly, it reminded me that doubt, when confronted, can become the very thing that propels you to greatness.

Today, I make it a point to protect my children from the seeds of doubt. I speak life into them, affirming their dreams and their potential. I remind them that they are capable, that they are worthy, and that they are enough. Because I know how easy it is for doubt to take root, and I refuse to let it have that power over them.

Doubt, like any seed, needs care to grow. But it also needs care to be uprooted. And when you choose to confront it, to challenge it, to reclaim your confidence, you discover something powerful: you were always enough. You always had what it takes. You just needed to believe it.

WHEN THE WORLD POINTS FINGERS: BREAKING FREE FROM JUDGMENT AND INSECURITY

It was the morning after the 2025 presidential election, and while the pundits dissected the results and social media swirled with endless hot takes, I found myself in a space I'd become far too familiar with: reflection. This wasn't about party loyalty or even the outcome itself. It was about the weeks leading up to it—the rhetoric, the accusations, and the weight placed on Black men like me to carry the political hopes and dreams of a nation on our shoulders.

I was driving my son to school, a routine that had been ours for years. The same roads, the same forty-minute commute through North Atlanta, past neighborhoods lined with lawn signs, some promising hope, others, in my opinion, threatening something far from it. As I looked out the window, I realized something remarkable: today looked no different than yesterday. The streets were quiet. There were no flags waving from pickup trucks, no bands, no protests. Life just went on.

But inside me, a storm churned. For months, I'd watched as Black men were reduced to statistics, their value to the political machine measured solely by turnout percentages and voting patterns. We were labeled as the decisive factor, the demographic that could make or break an election. And when the results didn't go the way some expected, we were the scapegoats. They pointed fingers, accused us of apathy, ignorance, or worse, betrayal. It was as if our individual lives, struggles, and decisions didn't matter—only our utility as a monolithic bloc.

Let me be clear: this wasn't new. Black men have always been easy targets when things go wrong. In politics, in society, even in our own communities, we are often painted as either the saviors or the villains.

Rarely are we allowed to be human. Rarely are we seen as individuals navigating a world that, quite frankly, wasn't built with us in mind.

As I drove, my son sat quietly in the passenger seat, scrolling through his phone. He's fifteen—full of opinions, but also at that age where you're still trying to figure out who you are and how you fit into the world. I thought about the lessons I've tried to pass on to him, the balance between teaching him pride in who he is and preparing him for a world that won't always see his humanity. It's a delicate dance—wanting him to feel empowered while also being acutely aware of the landmines that come with being a young Black man in America.

That morning, I felt a familiar weight—a combination of exhaustion, frustration, and resolve. The kind of weight you carry when you've been asked to explain yourself one too many times. Why do you think this way? Why did you make that choice? Why didn't you do what we expected of you? It's a weight that many Black men know intimately, the burden of constantly having to justify your existence, your decisions, your very being.

But here's the thing: I'm done carrying that weight.

The journey to letting go of external validation is not an easy one, and I won't pretend it is. It requires unlearning years, sometimes decades, of conditioning. It requires stepping back and asking yourself the hard questions: Why do I care so much about what they think? Who am I living for? What would it mean to live authentically, to make decisions based on my values, my needs, my dreams?

For me, the answer has been a slow unfolding. It started with recognizing the difference between accountability and blame. Accountability is about ownership—acknowledging your role in a situation and doing your part to make things better. Blame, on the other hand, is a weapon. It's used to deflect, to diminish, to control. And for too long, we've allowed ourselves to be blamed for things that are far beyond our control.

This election cycle was a perfect example. Black men showed up. We voted. Some of us voted for one candidate, others for another. But instead of celebrating the fact that we are engaged, that we are thinking critically about our futures and the futures of our families, we were shamed for not voting the "right" way. As if our votes are not our own. As if we don't have the right to weigh our options, consider our priorities, and make the choice that feels right for us.

This isn't just about politics. It's about how we see ourselves and how we allow others to see us. It's about refusing to let anyone, no matter how well-meaning, define our worth. It's about stepping into our power—not as a monolith, but as individuals with diverse experiences, perspectives, and aspirations.

That morning, as I dropped my son off at school, I looked at him and saw a reflection of myself at his age—full of questions, full of potential. I thought about the world he's growing up in and the lessons I want him to carry with him. Chief among them is this: You don't owe anyone an explanation for who you are or the choices you make. Live with integrity. Live with intention. And don't let the noise of the world drown out the sound of your own voice.

As I drove back home, the streets still eerily quiet, I felt a sense of clarity. The world may not always understand us. It may not always value us. But we have the power to define ourselves. To break free from the judgments and insecurities that have held us back. To let go of the need for external validation and find peace in knowing that we are enough, just as we are.

This chapter, this moment, is about freedom. Not the kind of freedom that comes with applause or approval, but the kind that comes from within. The kind that says, "I see you. I value you. And I don't need anyone else to tell me that I matter."

THE WEIGHT OF SHADOWS: CONFRONTING SUICIDAL IDEATION AND REDISCOVERING YOUR VALUE

At the time of writing this, I was sitting in the car at my son's school, waiting for him to finish up his community service hours. I had two hours to myself. Two hours to think, to sit in my thoughts, and to finally write this section that I had been avoiding. It's December. The Georgia sky is clear, that kind of clarity you only get in winter when the sun is sharp but doesn't burn. The air is crisp, around 50 degrees, just enough to see your breath if you exhale slow.

There's a little foliage left on the trees. Most of the leaves are gone, but a few green ones still hang on stubbornly. The wind kicks up, and the remaining leaves do a slow tumble across the parking lot. Kids laugh and chase each other in the distance, their voices carried just far enough to remind me that the world goes on, even when we feel like we can't.

I've been putting this off for days. I sit down to write, and I freeze. I pace. I write a few notes. I come back, but nothing sticks. I don't know if it's because the topic is heavy, or because it's personal. Maybe both. But as I sit here now, it feels like the right time. No distractions. No excuses. Just me, my thoughts, and this subject that deserves all the honesty and weight I can give it. Because this is about suicidal ideation—the place where you don't just feel low, but where you begin to consider what it would be like if you weren't here anymore. And when you're there, it's not just a thought. It's a conversation.

A quiet, dangerous conversation you have with yourself when the world feels like it has turned its back on you. When your mind becomes a jury, your heart a witness, and you are both judge and executioner.

I know that place. I've been there. And when I was there, it was the loneliest place I've ever known. I didn't talk about it. I didn't ask for help. I just sat in it—the heaviness, the stillness, the quiet. It was years ago, but the details remain sharp. My business had fallen apart. A relationship that I thought would last had crumbled, and the shame of that failure felt like it was choking me. I was losing access to my youngest child, which cut deeper than anything else. There was gossip, too, and gossip has a way of amplifying your pain. People you thought were friends scattered, as though failure was contagious.

I remember sitting in my living room. The TV wasn't on. The radio was off. I sat there in the silence, staring at nothing, hearing nothing but the sound of my own breathing and the cruel thoughts running through my mind. When you're in that place, silence isn't peace—it's suffocation. I would tell myself the same things over and over: You're done. Nobody needs you. Nobody cares. And I believed it.

I believed it so much that it felt like my reality. Like there was nothing to look forward to, nothing to hope for, nothing worth holding onto. Hopelessness is a monster that doesn't just knock at your door—it lets itself in, sits on your chest, and whispers lies into your ear until you start to believe them. And once you stop hoping, once you start believing that your life holds no value, that's when you start thinking about ending it.

But here's the thing about that place—it sneaks up on you. It doesn't announce itself. One day, you're fine, or at least pretending to be. The next day, you're not. And by the time you realize where you are, you're already sinking. It doesn't happen fast. It's a slow slide into invisibility. You stop showing up to things. You stop returning calls. You stop reaching out. And eventually, people stop checking on you. Not because they don't care, but because they don't know. You tell them you're fine. You smile through it. And the more you isolate yourself, the deeper you go. And the deeper you go, the more you convince yourself that nobody would notice if you were gone.

That's the trick of suicidal ideation. It lies to you. It tells you that you don't matter, that nobody loves you, that the world would be better without you.

And the scariest part? You believe it. You believe it because, at your lowest point, your mind is fertile soil for those lies.

I remember sitting on that couch, thinking about what it would be like if I just didn't wake up the next morning. I wasn't afraid of dying. I wasn't even thinking about death itself—not the act, not the finality of it. I was just thinking about the relief. I just wanted the weight to go away. The shame, the failure, the gossip, the loneliness—I wanted it all to stop. And in that moment, I told God, If you don't give me a reason to get off this couch, this is where they're going to find me. It wasn't a prayer as much as it was a surrender. I didn't expect an answer. I didn't even expect Him to hear me. But He did. And in the stillness, in that suffocating quiet, I heard a voice: Go speak to the hearts of men.

That's all it took. It was short, simple, and clear. And it saved me. It didn't change my circumstances immediately, but it gave me a reason to keep going. It gave me a purpose. It reminded me that my life had value, even if I couldn't see it in that moment. I got off that couch, and I never looked back.

When I think about those dark days now, I'm reminded of how fragile life is, and how easy it is to slide into that invisible space. And that's why I believe that hope is everything. Without hope, we lose our reason to fight. Without hope, we give up on ourselves. But when you hold onto hope—even just a thread of it—it can pull you through the darkest nights.

I think about the people who didn't make it out of that place. The ones who cried out but nobody heard them. The ones who couldn't find hope, or couldn't hold onto it. It breaks my heart, because I know how close I came to being one of them. And I know how easily it could have gone the other way. That's why I tell my story. Because if sharing my lowest moment helps just one person, then it's worth it. If it reminds someone that they're not alone, that their life matters, that there's always hope—then it's worth it.

Here's what I've learned: life will knock you down. It will strip you of everything you thought you had. It will test your faith, your strength, and your will to keep going. And in those moments, you will feel like giving up. You will feel like you have nothing left. But you do. You always do. Because as long as you have breath in your body, you have value. And as long as you have value, you have purpose. And as long as you have purpose, you have a reason to fight.

If you're in that place right now—that dark, hopeless place where the silence feels like it's swallowing you whole—I need you to know something: you are not alone. Your life matters. You matter. And no matter how heavy the weight feels right now, you are strong enough to carry it. You are strong enough to get through this. And when you come out on the other side—because you will come out on the other side—you will see that the very thing that tried to break you became the thing that built you. It's not easy. It's not quick. But it's possible. And you are worth the fight.

I remember sitting in my living room during that season of my life. The house was quiet. No TV, no music—just silence. I wasn't writing, I wasn't working, I wasn't living. I was existing in my thoughts, replaying every mistake, every failure, every harsh word that had been spoken about me. I was building a case against myself, convincing myself that the world would be better off without me.

That's the danger of hopelessness. It's not just a feeling; it's a belief. Hopelessness convinces you that things will never get better, that you will always be stuck, that your pain will never go away. It strips you of your ability to see tomorrow. And when you can't see tomorrow, you don't fight for it.

THE THREE LIFELINES

You need to know that even in the darkness, there are lifelines. There are things—small but powerful—that can keep you anchored when the weight feels too heavy. For me, those lifelines are three commitments that I hold onto even now:

1. Commit to Hope.

Hope is not a feeling; it's a choice. It's the decision to believe that tomorrow can be better, even when you can't see how. Hope says, "This is not the end. This is just a moment." When I was at my lowest, hope felt like a distant concept, but I held onto it anyway. I reminded myself that seasons change, that storms don't last forever, and that even in my pain, there was purpose waiting to be discovered.

2. Commit to the Dash.

I've always talked about the "dash" on a tombstone—the line between your birth and your death. That dash represents your life.

It's the story you leave behind, the legacy you build, the impact you make. When I think about my dash, I think about my children, my family, my community. I think about the work I've been called to do and the people I've been called to serve. And I remind myself that my story is not finished yet.

3. Commit to Presence.

Presence is about showing up—not just for others, but for yourself. It's about being there, fully and completely, even when it's hard. When you commit to presence, you recognize that your life matters. Your voice matters. Your story matters. And you fight to show up, even when it feels easier to disappear.

So hold on to hope. Commit to your purpose. Commit to the dash—the life you live between your first breath and your last. And commit to your presence, because the world needs you. Someone needs you. Someone is waiting for you to show up, to be the light in their darkness, to be the hope that pulls them through. And if you ever find yourself on that couch, staring at the walls, wondering if you're worth it, I want you to remember this: you are. You always have been, and you always will be.

CHAPTER FOUR

FINDING PEACE:
NAVIGATING LIFE WITH INNER CALM

THE ROCK OF JOY: ANCHORED IN PURPOSE

There comes a point in life where the chaos that once consumed you begins to settle, and the noise that filled your mind softens to a murmur. It's not that the world has stopped moving—far from it. Bills still come, relationships still require tending, and uncertainty still lingers. But something inside shifts.

A quiet confidence emerges, filling the cracks where doubt once seeped in. It's the kind of calm that can't be shaken, the kind of assurance that whispers: "You are standing on something solid now."

This transformation doesn't happen overnight. Peace and joy don't simply waltz into your life uninvited. They are forged in fire, tempered in struggle, and born from the questions that won't let you rest—questions of why. Why am I here? Why does my existence matter? Why me? These are not simple curiosities; they are the towering, relentless mysteries that shape every decision, every hesitation, and every ambition.

And yet, within them lies the most sacred discovery of all: purpose.

Purpose isn't just about what you do—it's about who you are. It is the gravitational force that pulls you toward meaning, the quiet but insistent voice that nudges you forward even when you can't explain why. It is what makes you wake up with fire in your belly some mornings and what keeps you moving when that fire feels extinguished. Purpose is what stitches together the disjointed pieces of your life, revealing a design you couldn't see when you were in the middle of it. But here's the thing about purpose—it doesn't stand alone. It is surrounded by two equally powerful forces: passion and position.

When I look back on my journey, I see passion scattered like breadcrumbs leading me to this moment. As a young man, I chased what set my soul on fire—music, writing, storytelling, connection. At the time, I didn't realize these things were more than interests. They were teachers, shaping me long before I had the language to name them as part of my purpose.

I remember a conversation I had with God at one of my lowest points. It wasn't the kind of prayer you rehearse; it was raw, urgent, the kind that rises up when you have nothing left to lose. What is my purpose? I asked, never expecting an answer. But one came, as clear as if someone had whispered it in my ear: Speak to the hearts of men.

At first, I didn't understand. Speak to the hearts of men? How? Through what? But as I leaned into it, I began to see that every passion I had ever pursued—writing, radio, community work—had been a stepping stone toward that very calling. My time in radio taught me the power of words. Running a newspaper sharpened my storytelling. Years of community organizing built my empathy. All of it—the successes, the failures, the moments of doubt—had been shaping me for this.

And when I finally stepped fully into that purpose, something remarkable happened. My position became clear.

Position is not a job or a title. A job can be taken away. A title can be stripped. But position is sacred. It is the space you are meant to occupy, the role only you can fulfill. It is why, even when I have walked into rooms where others have more degrees, more accolades, or more experience, I have never felt out of place. Because my position isn't based on credentials—it's based on who I am.

I have doubted that position at times. I have sat at tables with experts, feeling like an imposter because I didn't have the same formal education. But then I speak, and something shifts. I realize that my life experience, my passion, and my purpose have equipped me in ways no degree ever could. I belong in those rooms because of my journey, not despite it.

And when you find your position—when you fully step into your purpose—you discover something even greater: joy.

Not happiness. Not the fleeting, conditional kind of joy that depends on circumstances. No, this is the kind of joy that anchors you. It is the unshakable kind that holds steady even in the midst of life's storms. It is the peace that remains when the world is falling apart around you. The joy that says, I am exactly where I am supposed to be, doing exactly what I was created to do.

I saw this kind of joy in my daughter not long ago. She was wrestling with the same questions I had once wrestled with: Why am I here? What is my purpose? One day, she called me, teary-eyed, saying she wanted to leave college. "Everyone around me seems to have it figured out, and I don't," she confessed.

As a father, it was hard to hear. I had my own dreams for her—dreams of a degree, of a career in sports medicine. But then she told me about her passion for becoming an esthetician. How her own struggles with skincare had led her to want to help other young women feel beautiful and confident in their skin.

And suddenly, I saw it. She wasn't just talking about a career shift. She was discovering her why. And in that moment, the uncertainty that had weighed her down was gone. In its place was peace—because she had found her purpose.

Watching her step into that purpose reminded me of a fundamental truth: when you follow the breadcrumbs of passion, they will lead you to your purpose. And when you embrace your purpose, you will find your position. And in that position, you will find joy. Not because life gets easier, but because you get stronger. Not because the chaos disappears, but because it can no longer move you.

This is what purpose does. It anchors you. It steadies you. It gives you the kind of clarity that allows you to move through life with confidence. And when you truly embrace it, joy becomes your foundation—not something you chase, but something you are.

But let's be real—this kind of joy doesn't mean life stops being hard. It doesn't mean you won't face setbacks or challenges. It doesn't mean the storms won't come. What it means is that the storms lose their power over you. You become unshakable. Because once you know who you are, once you know why you are here, nothing—not failure, not fear, not doubt—can move you from your position.

I think about my daughter again. How she stepped into her calling, found her rhythm, and never looked back. At first, I didn't fully understand it. But now, I see it for what it is—joy. The kind that comes from living in alignment with who you were created to be. The kind that is not dependent on titles, degrees, or money. The kind that lasts.

> *And that is the beauty of purpose—it doesn't have to make sense to anyone else. It doesn't have to be validated or approved by the world. It just has to resonate with you. It just has to set your soul on fire.*

Because when you live in your purpose, you become unstoppable. Your purpose becomes your anchor, your joy becomes your strength, and your position becomes your refuge. And in that space, you will find a peace that surpasses understanding. So, let the storms come. Let the critics talk. Let the world shift around you. When you are standing in your purpose, nothing can move you. The world may change, but you will remain steadfast, unshaken, anchored in joy.

Because when you live in alignment with your purpose, you don't just change your own life. You change the lives of everyone you touch. And that, my friend, is the greatest gift of all.

THE PAUSE THAT PREPARES: EMBRACING PATIENCE AS A TOOL FOR PURPOSE

Somewhere between the rush of ambition and the weight of expectation lies a space many of us try to avoid: waiting. It is uncomfortable, uncertain, and often feels like a waste of time. But patience is where clarity happens. Patience is where purpose breathes. And as much as we might want to rush through life to the destinations we dream of, I've come to understand that patience is not just a pause—it is the process that makes us ready for what's next.

I didn't always understand this. In my younger years, patience felt like the enemy. Waiting meant weakness. If you weren't actively moving, chasing, grinding, then you were falling behind. That was the mentality. There was no room for stillness because stillness felt like failure. And yet, every major moment in my life—the kind that shapes who you are—has required a level of patience that I wasn't naturally inclined to give.

Muhammad Ali once said, "I am the greatest." He said it so often and with such conviction that the world eventually believed him. But what people often forget is the patience behind his greatness. He trained tirelessly, fought strategically, and waited for the right moments to prove himself. His was not a haphazard journey; it was a deliberate one. And while the world marveled at his victories, few saw the discipline it took to prepare for them.

That's the thing about patience—it is rarely visible, but it is always working. It's the unseen effort, the moments in the dark where no one is watching, that lay the groundwork for brilliance. And yet, patience is one of the hardest things to cultivate. It demands that we trust in something bigger than ourselves, something we can't always see or control.

I've had to learn this the hard way. As a father, as a leader, as a man navigating life's complexities, patience has been both my greatest challenge and my greatest teacher. When I think about my children, for instance, I see their potential so clearly. It shines in their creativity, their curiosity, their resilience. But potential is not enough. It has to be nurtured, guided, and sometimes even restrained. That's where patience comes in.

There have been moments when I wanted to push them harder, to demand more, because I could see what they were capable of. But I've learned that growth cannot be forced. It happens in its own time, in its own way. My role is not to rush the process but to create an environment where they feel safe to grow, to fail, and to try again. And that takes patience—not just with them, but with myself.

I'll be honest: patience doesn't come naturally to me. I am a man of action. I like to see progress, to know that the steps I'm taking are leading somewhere. So, when things don't happen as quickly as I'd like, frustration creeps in. It's in those moments that I have to remind myself of something I once read: God answers prayers in three ways—yes, not now, and I have something better for you.

That last one, "I have something better for you," is the hardest to accept. It requires a level of trust and humility that doesn't always feel comfortable. But over time, I've come to see the truth in it.

There are things I've prayed for, fought for, and even begged for, only to realize later that what I thought I wanted wasn't what I needed. And in those moments, I've been grateful for the patience that protected me from myself.

Life has a way of teaching you patience, whether you want to learn it or not. Sometimes it's through the long, winding detours that keep you from rushing headfirst into danger. Other times, it's through the slow, steady climb that builds your strength for the challenges ahead. Either way, patience is not just about waiting— it's about preparing. It's about becoming.

I think about this often when I'm driving. There's nothing more frustrating than being stuck behind a slow car in the fast lane. You feel like the world is conspiring to slow you down, to keep you from reaching your destination. But what if that slow car is saving you from an accident up ahead? What if the delay is a blessing in disguise, giving you the time you need to reflect, to regroup, to recalibrate?

Patience teaches us to trust the process. It reminds us that life is not a sprint but a marathon, and that every step—no matter how small—moves us closer to our goals. It's not about being passive or complacent; it's about being deliberate. It's about knowing when to push and when to pause, when to fight and when to rest.

As I reflect on my journey, I see how patience has shaped me. It's in the moments of waiting that I've learned the most about myself—my strengths, my weaknesses, my purpose. And while it hasn't always been easy, it has always been worth it.

So, as we continue this exploration of what it means to live a life of purpose, I invite you to embrace the power of patience. It is not a weakness; it is a strength. It is the quiet confidence that what is meant for you will not pass you by, and that every moment—no matter how long it takes—has its purpose.

THE UNYIELDING DANCE BETWEEN PEACE AND CHAOS

Life often feels like an unrelenting tug-of-war between two opposing forces: peace and chaos. They are like fire and water, each seeking dominance in our lives. These two forces cannot coexist—where one resides, the other cannot. As I reflect on this fundamental truth, I've come to understand the gravity of this polarity. If peace feels elusive, it's likely because chaos has taken up residence in your heart, mind, or spirit. Chaos, by its nature, disrupts, distorts, and dismantles clarity and calm.

What's most striking is that peace and chaos are not just opposites—they're magnets. They repel one another fiercely, almost violently. You cannot hold them in the same space. If you search for peace while clinging to chaos, you will fail. And if chaos becomes your dominant reality, it will suffocate even the faintest whisper of peace. This reality has shaped much of how I live and navigate the world.

I've learned that you must choose which one you are pursuing. Peace does not arrive by accident. It must be sought, nurtured, and fiercely protected. Chaos, however, has a way of slipping in, uninvited, through small cracks in your defenses. It starts as a whisper and grows into a deafening roar before you even recognize its presence.

CHAOS LURKS IN QUESTIONS

The mind is a powerful thing, but it is also fertile ground for chaos. Some of the most significant disruption I've experienced has come not from external forces, but from the questions my mind asks in moments of vulnerability. These questions are insidious. They seem innocent, but they plant seeds of doubt, insecurity, and disruption.

1. Why wasn't I invited?

Few things sting more than realizing you've been left out. Whether it's a party, a meeting, or even a casual group chat, exclusion feels personal. You see others enjoying what you believe you had every right to participate in, and you begin to question your worth. The truth, however, is often less dramatic. Perhaps the host had limited capacity, or maybe it simply didn't cross their mind. But the question itself invites chaos into your mind and heart, creating narratives that often aren't true.

2. Why wasn't I included?

This question speaks directly to your sense of value. To be excluded from a project, decision, or opportunity feels like a direct statement about your capabilities. But again, the story your mind creates can be far from reality. Often, people don't include us not because we lack value, but because their perspective didn't align with our expectations.

3. Why wasn't I asked?

This one cuts deeper. When someone doesn't seek your advice, your help, or even your permission, it can feel like a slight. It stirs up questions about your relevance and your relationships. But much like the others, this question often says more about the asker than the situation itself. It creates chaos because it challenges your sense of importance in the eyes of others.

4. Why wasn't I mentioned?

This question feels like the sharpest cut. Recognition matters to us all, and when someone fails to acknowledge your contribution, it can feel like a betrayal. You sit in a room where accolades are being given, expecting your name to be called, and it isn't.

The chaos begins as your mind spirals through all the reasons why. Were you not good enough? Did they not notice your work? Or worse, did they deliberately leave you out? Often, the omission is unintentional, but the chaos it creates is all too real.

These questions, if allowed to fester, can consume you. They take root in your mind, weaving stories that breed chaos and steal peace. The danger lies in the fact that they don't even require external validation to do their damage—your mind does all the work.

A CONVERSATION OF CLARITY

I remember a conversation I had with my wife one evening as we sat at the dining table. We were talking about fidelity, trust, and relationships—those heavy topics that either deepen your connection or reveal cracks you didn't know existed.

She asked me, "Why do you think some people, after years and years of marriage, still step out on their spouse? Why would someone just mess up and destroy someone's life, because of their selfishness?"

I paused for a moment before replying, "You know, I can't speak for everyone. But I can tell you why I wouldn't do it."

Her eyes narrowed slightly, not in suspicion but in curiosity and anticipation of what I was about to say. "Um hum?"

"First," I began, "I love you too much. You're everything I could ever want, and there's nothing out there that compares to what we have here. Second, I have no desire. You're my peace, my center." BAM...I know, you're reading this with a side eye, but you still impressed.

She smiled, a small, knowing smile, but I wasn't finished. "And third," I added with a chuckle, "I'm too old to remember my lies."

She burst out laughing, and I joined her. "No, for real," I said, laughing harder now. "I've got no interest in keeping up with the chaos that comes with lying. Gotta tell one lie, then another. Next thing you know, I don't even remember the truth. I'm shook now just thinking about it!"

Her laughter turned into a warm, affectionate look. "That's a good reason," she said, going back to whatever she was doing that initiated the conversation..

That moment wasn't just about us. It was a crystallization of a broader truth: chaos is exhausting. Lies, drama, and disruption are all forms of chaos, and they sap your energy, your clarity, and your joy. Standing on truth, no matter how difficult, is one of the simplest ways to protect your peace.

THE PATH TO PEACE

Peace, I've come to learn, is not a destination but a discipline. It is something you cultivate daily, through intentional action and unwavering focus. Over the years, I've found three guiding principles that have helped me navigate the chaos and find my way to peace.

1. Avoid Drama

Drama is chaos's best friend. It thrives on miscommunication, misunderstandings, and emotional manipulation. Family drama, workplace drama, or social media drama—it doesn't matter where it originates. It disrupts your focus and erodes your peace.

The key is to recognize drama before it takes hold and remove yourself from its grasp. This isn't about avoiding people; it's about setting boundaries. Drama cannot survive in an environment where it is not fed.

2. Stand on Truth

Truth is the antidote to chaos. It is steady, unchanging, and liberating. Lies and half-truths, on the other hand, are the foundation of chaos.

They demand energy to maintain and create a web of complexity that traps everyone involved. Standing on truth means living with integrity and authenticity. It means being honest with yourself and others, even when the truth is uncomfortable. When you root yourself in truth, you create a firm foundation that chaos cannot shake.

3. Don't Contribute to Chaos

Perhaps the hardest principle to follow is ensuring that you are not the source of chaos. It's easy to point fingers at others, but we must also look inward. Are we engaging in gossip?

Are we stirring the pot in subtle ways? Are we allowing our unresolved issues to spill over into the lives of others? To find peace, you must first ensure that you are not sowing seeds of chaos in your own life or the lives of those around you.

PEACE AS A CHOICE

At its core, peace is a choice. It's the decision to prioritize simplicity over complexity, clarity over confusion, and calm over chaos. It's a commitment to protect your heart, mind, and spirit from the forces that seek to disrupt them. But this choice must be made daily, sometimes hourly.Peace doesn't mean a life free from challenges—it means a life where challenges don't define you. It means creating an environment where your heart can rest, your mind can think clearly, and your spirit can thrive. In this space, joy becomes not just possible, but inevitable. And joy, unlike happiness, is unshakable. It is a state of being that chaos cannot touch.

CHAPTER FIVE

THE POWER OF PERSPECTIVE: SEEING THE WORLD THROUGH SEASONED EYES

WHEN LESSONS DON'T LINE UP

There's a peculiar clarity that only time can offer. The years don't just pass—they soften sharp edges, expose what's been hiding in plain sight, and push you to revisit truths you thought were settled. I used to think that understanding was linear—that you gathered insight like bricks, stacking them one by one into a tall, sturdy tower of wisdom.

Each experience would sit neatly atop the last, building upward toward certainty. And maybe in your younger years, that illusion works. There's a kind of satisfaction in believing that if you just keep doing the work—learning, achieving, surviving—you'll reach some higher floor where it all makes sense.

But life doesn't just move up. It moves around you, beneath you, within you. At some point, you realize those bricks weren't just stacked—they were layered. Pressed by weight, cracked by weather, shifted by time. Some sink. Some resurface.

> *The lesson you learned at 20 might come back to you at 40, not because it's new, but because you're new. You've changed. You're carrying more. You see differently now—not because the world has shifted, but because your eyes have adjusted to what's always been there.*

That's the irony of wisdom. It doesn't build neatly like a tower. It settles like sediment. Some of it light and fleeting. Some of it heavy and enduring. You don't outgrow the past; you grow into it. You return to old truths with new understanding. And sometimes, what looked like a failure back then? Turns out, it was a foundation.

This shift from stacking to layering is subtle, but profound. Because it's not just about knowledge—it's about perspective. It's not about how much you've learned, but how deeply you've come to know. A younger version of me thought success was climbing. Older me has learned it's about grounding. Not just reaching for heights—but learning how to stand, how to hold your peace, how to carry your weight without collapsing under it.

That's why I no longer rush to judgment—not of others, and not of myself. What looks like a misstep today might be the very thing you'll stand on tomorrow. What feels like confusion in one season may reveal itself as clarity in another.

Because nothing is wasted. Not the wins. Not the wounds. Not the waiting. Every layer matters.

And when you start to see your life that way—as layered rather than linear—something remarkable happens. You stop chasing arrival. You stop measuring yourself by the tower you were supposed to build. And you start honoring the ground you've covered. You realize that wisdom doesn't make you taller. It makes you deeper.

That's the thing about perspective—it doesn't arrive all at once. It builds quietly, almost imperceptibly, over time. In our younger years, we imagine it works like progress: linear, predictable, goal-oriented. I used to think that if I kept moving forward, kept collecting lessons and achievements, I'd eventually build some unshakable understanding of the world. I thought wisdom was something you stacked, like bricks—each experience a block laid neatly on top of the one before it, forming a solid tower of knowledge.

But life doesn't build that way.

Understanding doesn't always stack—it settles. It seeps in like rain over soil. Some lessons land immediately. Others take decades to sink deep enough to take root. What you thought you understood at 25 might reappear at 55 with an entirely different shape, not because the lesson changed, but because you did. The context of who you've become reframes everything you thought you once knew.

That's when you realize that wisdom is not height—it's depth. It's not about building a tower that others admire. It's about allowing life to shape layers within you that make you unshakable when the ground around you shifts.

And those layers? They hold stories. Stories of wins, yes—but also stories of restraint, regret, redemption. They're made of second chances, held breaths, and the weight of lessons that had to be lived before they could be learned. And the older you get, the more you start to appreciate those layers. Not just for what they taught you, but for how they slowed you down enough to listen.

When you begin to see your life that way—not as a linear path to somewhere else, but as a layered unfolding of who you already are—your relationship with success, failure, even time itself begins to shift. You stop chasing clarity as a destination and start recognizing it as a companion. One that walks with you, changes with you, and only shows you what you're ready to see, when you're ready to see it.

THE WEIGHT OF THE SKIN I'M IN

The first time I knew my skin had weight, I was in the eighth grade in Upstate New York. My mother had sent me to live with my stepfather in a town where you could count the Black people on one hand, which accounts to why there were only three of us at the school.

Me, another girl and the janitor. On my first day there as I was walking into the middle school—sharp, cutting, unmistakable words rang out behind me, "Who's the nigger?" The words landed like a slap to the back of my head, except no one had touched me. I kept walking, staring straight ahead, but my ears burned, my stomach clenched, and my heart pounded against my ribcage. I didn't turn around. I didn't have to. I already knew. I knew that moment meant something.

That moment was the first time I truly understood that the skin I was in came with expectations, with consequences, with a weight I would carry for the rest of my life.

If you think I could tell you what shaped my life without addressing the fact that I'm Black, it would be an impossibility. Race has shaped my experiences, my lens, and how the world sees me. It is a reality that cannot be erased. A perspective that is uniquely mines. They tell me that my life expectancy as a Black man is 72 years. At 63, what does that mean for me? I hope to live to be 163, but the reality is, Black men are at the lower rung of every socioeconomic measure of quality of life. We have higher rates of heart disease and face the weight of statistics that define our mortality before we ever get a chance to thrive.

Many young Black men don't even expect to reach 18.

That kind of reality shapes the way you see the world and the way the world sees you. Being Black is not something I can hide. My skin, on sight, speaks before I do. It carries history, assumptions, and expectations, regardless of who I actually am.

Race isn't just a subject for me—it is woven into every aspect of my existence. My culture, my experiences, my perspectives are inseparable from my Blackness. Like anyone else, I take pride in who I am, just as I assume others take pride in their heritage. But for me, that pride is wrapped in both beauty and burden.

The seasoning of my years has been marinated in Blackness. My reality is important. My lens is relevant. My perspective matters. I don't have the luxury of disregarding my race, so why should I be expected to minimize it for the comfort of others?

I wasn't even thinking about race when I first outlined this book. It wasn't because it wasn't important, but because it is so interwoven into my experiences that I don't have to separate it. My wife challenged me on this, questioning how race would be relevant to those who are not Black. My response: If I can read books by people who don't look like me and still find value in them, why shouldn't others be able to do the same with mine?

And that brings me to why it is so important for me to talk about race.

First, my reality is important. I refuse to water it down for someone else's comfort. My reality is not an option; it is not up for negotiation. The weight of my skin, the experiences I have lived, and the truth of my existence all demand to be acknowledged. I will not erase the experiences that have shaped me, nor will I minimize them to fit someone else's perspective.

Second, my lens is relevant. The way I see myself is shaped by the world I have navigated. And just as my lens is shaped by my experiences, your lens is shaped by yours. But here's the thing—we learn when we engage with perspectives outside of our own. If you are willing to sit with my experiences, my lens, my truth, then maybe—just maybe—you will begin to see the world differently. Maybe you will gain an understanding that you didn't have before.

Third, my perspective matters. The stories we tell define how we understand the world. My story, my truth, my journey—these things are not footnotes. They are not addendums. They are the story. I write because my voice is necessary. Because the way I have navigated this world has value. Because the experiences of Black men in this country need to be heard, acknowledged, and understood—not just by those who look like us, but by those who don't.

History has shaped the way Black people are seen in this country. We were brought here in chains against our will. We have been systematically oppressed. These are facts. The weight of these truths sits heavy on every Black person who moves through this world.

Two things can be true at the same time. I live my reality, and you live yours. But understanding requires empathy. It requires seeing the seasoning of my life not as an isolated experience, but as part of the larger tapestry of humanity.

I have been Black all my life. I have been a man all my life. Those are two indisputable facts. My lens is shaped by that reality, just as yours is shaped by your own. But the beauty of being seasoned is realizing that difference doesn't have to divide us—it can enrich us.

This book is my truth, my perspective, my reality. And if you allow yourself to sit with it, absorb it, and understand it, you might just find something that resonates with your own journey.

THE UNSEEN GRAVITY OF IDENTITY: THE POWER OF KNOWING WHO YOU ARE

Childhood does not shield you from truth; it only delays its arrival. And when that truth comes, it does not knock—it crashes through, changing the way you see everything, including yourself.

Fast forward many decades later, and I found myself standing on the shores of Ghana, my feet sinking slightly into the warm sand, my eyes fixed on the endless stretch of water before me. The same ocean that carried my ancestors away, against their will, to a land they did not choose. The waves whispered a history that was always mine, yet I had never heard it spoken this clearly. I had come to Africa expecting to witness history. I did not expect history to be staring back at me in a way that felt so personal, so inescapable.

The irony was, Africa had never been on my list. Not because I didn't respect it, but because I didn't think I needed it. My identity as a Black man in America was forged in Brooklyn, in the heat of summer asphalt, in the rhythms of city life, in the lessons passed down from men who had survived in a country that never intended for them to thrive. I thought I knew myself. But Africa has a way of holding up a mirror that doesn't just reflect you—it reveals you. And there, standing at the Door of No Return in Elmina Castle, I felt the weight of my existence in a way I never had before.

They call it the Door of No Return because once enslaved Africans walked through it, they would never see their homeland again. The name itself is a brutal punctuation mark in history, a sentence written in blood and sorrow. Standing there, I imagined their hands touching the same stone walls, their bare feet scraping against the same floor. And then, I imagined myself in their place. What did it feel like to take that last step onto a ship bound for the unknown? What did it mean to have your identity rewritten, your past erased, your very name replaced with something foreign?

As the guide spoke, the weight in my chest grew heavier. And yet, amid the pain of that place, something else stirred in me. A quiet realization. A truth that had been buried under years of American conditioning. I was not just the descendant of the enslaved; I was the continuation of a lineage that predated slavery itself. My story did not begin in chains. It began in kingship, in artistry, in community, in resistance. This revelation did not erase the trauma, but it reframed it. It reminded me that my existence was not just survival—it was resilience.

But the most unexpected lesson came not from history, but from the present. While in Ghana, I met teachers, farmers, business-men, and students. I spoke with elders whose wisdom carried the weight of generations. And one conversation shifted something in me permanently. It was during a discussion with a local educator when he said something so simple, yet so profound: "We were never taught what happened to you after you left."

For a moment, I was stunned. Here I was, a Black man from America, carrying the weight of history on my back, assuming that those who remained in Africa carried the same knowledge. But they didn't.

The narratives that were passed down to them were different from ours. They knew of the taking, the capture, the disappearance.

But they did not know of the generations that followed—the struggle, the resilience, the fight for dignity in a land that was never meant to be ours. And just like that, I saw the missing piece. We had been disconnected, not just by distance, but by knowledge, by fractured stories that were never stitched back together.

So, where does that leave me? Where does that leave any of us who have walked through life thinking we fully understood our own existence? It leaves us with the responsibility of reclaiming, of reconnecting, of rewriting the narrative in a way that restores what was lost. It means embracing the fullness of who we are—not just the pain, but the power. It means walking into rooms with the understanding that we are not just descendants of the oppressed, but heirs to a strength that predates oppression itself.

Returning from Africa did not make me whole overnight. Identity is not something you find once and hold onto effortlessly—it is something you continuously discover, challenge, and refine. But what Ghana gave me was something invaluable: permission to embrace the full spectrum of my Blackness, to see my skin not as a burden, but as a testament to endurance and excellence.

This is why identity matters. This is why knowing who you are—fully, deeply—is the most powerful thing you can do. Because the world will try to tell you who you are. History will try to define you by the worst of what has been done to your people. But when you know your own story, when you have touched the soil of where it all began, when you have walked through the corridors of your past and emerged on the other side—you become untouchable.

And so, I move forward, carrying the echoes of my ancestors, the lessons of my travels, and the unshakable truth that I am more than what history tried to make of me. I am whole. I am here. I am enough.

THE CIRCLE OF LIFE: PERSPECTIVE CHANGES EVERYTHING

Perspective matters. Few things alter the trajectory of how you view life more than becoming a parent. It's like waking up one day and realizing that every decision, every action, every thought is no longer solely about you. It's about them—the small, fragile beings entrusted to you.

Becoming a parent changes how you see the world, how you see yourself, and what you prioritize in ways you never imagined. When I say everything changes, I mean everything. It doesn't matter your socioeconomic status, your age, or where you live. The moment your child enters this world, your life is no longer yours alone.

The transformation is profound. Priorities shift. Selfishness takes a backseat—or at least it should. Relationships change. Goals are recalibrated. The lens through which you see the world is permanently adjusted. Suddenly, the things you thought mattered fade into the background, eclipsed by the enormity of the responsibility resting on your shoulders. For better or worse, life becomes about that child.

Yet, parenting doesn't come with a manual. No one hands you a step-by-step guide to navigate the labyrinth of emotions, challenges, and decisions. What you do have, however, is the blueprint of your own upbringing. Whether you realize it or not, much of how you parent is deeply influenced by how you were parented.

For many, this is a double-edged sword. If you grew up in a nurturing, supportive environment, you're more likely to replicate that in your own parenting. But if your childhood was marked by dysfunction, chaos, or neglect, those scars don't just disappear. They shape your perception of parenting and influence your actions, often in ways you don't even recognize.

As children, we are like sponges, absorbing not just what is said to us but how it is said, not just what is done to us but how it is done. We internalize the dynamics of our households—the way conflicts are resolved, the way love is expressed, the way discipline is enforced. These lessons become the foundation of our understanding of relationships, communication, and authority.

When I reflect on my own childhood, it's clear how deeply those early experiences shaped my view of parenting and relationships. My stepfather was a dominant figure in my life, but his presence was often one of fear rather than comfort. I witnessed things no child should ever see. I watched him hit my mother, his fists landing with a force that seemed to shatter not just her physical being but the very fabric of our home. I remember standing on the other side of the door, listening to her screams, powerless to do anything but absorb the chaos.

Those moments left an indelible mark, shaping how I viewed authority, conflict, and love.

There was one instance that still plays in my mind like a film reel. I was older then, maybe in my teens, sent to live with him temporarily. We got into a heated argument in the kitchen, and things escalated quickly. Before I knew it, he had me in a headlock, his arm crushing against my neck.

Behind us was a window, and all I could think was that I wanted to throw him through it. I planted my feet, lunged back with all my might, but my footing slipped. We both fell to the floor beneath the window. As I lay there, breathless, I shouted, "You will never beat me like you beat my mother."

Even now, I don't know where those words came from.

But I know they were born from years of silent pain and suppressed rage. It was a declaration—not just to him, but to myself—that I would not be a victim of his violence. The consequence of that moment was immediate. I was sent back home, my relationship with him forever fractured.

But the scars weren't just physical; they were emotional, psychological, and generational. When I got married for the first time, I carried that baggage with me. My wife and I didn't argue—we fought. It wasn't the kind of abuse I had seen growing up, but it was physical nonetheless. And it wasn't until much later that I realized I was mimicking the only resolution I had ever witnessed: physical confrontation. I didn't know how to resolve conflict with words because I had never seen it done.

This is the reality of learned behavior. We parent as we were parented because it's what we know. Even when we vow to do things differently, the patterns of our upbringing have a way of resurfacing in moments of stress, frustration, or uncertainty. It's not enough to simply decide to break the cycle; you have to actively unlearn the lessons that no longer serve you.

For me, that unlearning process was a journey.

It required acknowledging the pain of my past, understanding how it influenced my present, and consciously choosing a different path for my future. It meant learning to communicate without anger, to discipline without fear, and to love without conditions.

It wasn't easy, but worth every releasing of that learned disfunctional behavior. It's a journey worth taking because the stakes are too high to leave to chance.

Years later, I found myself halfway across the world, standing on the vast plains of the Masai Mara in Kenya. The contrast between the chaos of my childhood and the serene, yet raw, beauty of the Serengeti was staggering. As the small plane descended, I looked out the window and saw elephants, lions, zebras, and giraffes roaming freely. There were no fences, no barriers, no signs of human control—just nature in its purest form.

When we landed, I noticed something that unsettled me: the jeeps we were riding in were open. No doors, no windows, nothing separating us from the wild animals. I turned to one of the guides and asked, "What happens if something attacks us?" He smiled and replied, "They won't. We respect them, and they respect us."

For the next few days, we drove through the Serengeti, often coming within ten feet of prides of lions. I remember one particular moment when a pride of about thirty lions walked right past our jeep. A few of them looked up, their eyes meeting mine, but they kept walking, uninterested in us. The guide explained that the animals don't see us as a threat because we don't disrupt their environment.

That trip taught me something profound about the circle of life— not just in nature but in humanity. Life is about balance, respect, and coexistence. The same principles that allowed us to coexist with lions in the wild apply to how we navigate relationships, parenting, and the world at large.

Parenting is the ultimate expression of the circle of life. It's about creating, nurturing, and eventually releasing. It's about teaching your children to navigate the world while knowing that one day, they will have to do the same for their children—and perhaps for you.

One of the most profound lessons I've learned through my work with fathers is this: the diapers you change today may one day be your own. It's a humorous yet sobering reminder that the care you give as a parent often comes full circle. When you're old and vulnerable, the love and care you poured into your children may be the very thing that sustains you.

Parenting isn't about perfection—it's about presence. It's about being there, showing up, and doing the best you can with what you have. It's about creating a circle of life that is rooted in love, respect, and balance. And when we get it right, the rewards are immeasurable.

Our children are our greatest blessings and, at times, our greatest challenges. They force us to confront ourselves, to grow, and to be better. They remind us of the beauty and fragility of life.

And they teach us, above all else, that the circle of life is a gift—one that we must cherish, nurture, and pass on.

A MEETING BORN FROM CHANCE AND PURPOSE

When I first came to Atlanta, the air smelled different—not because of the Southern humidity or the faint aroma of sweet tea and barbecue that seemed to linger everywhere, but because it carried the promise of new beginnings.

I arrived with a vision, one forged by years of hard work, frustration, and relentless ambition that had hit a glass ceiling in

New York. Atlanta wasn't just a new city; it was a blank canvas, free from the weight of old expectations and the limitations of being seen as "just Kenny from Brooklyn."

The city offered me a chance to redefine not just my work but myself. I was stepping into a space where the crabs in the barrel couldn't reach me, a place where I could climb without the pull of familiarity dragging me back down.

One of the first initiatives I launched in Atlanta was Real Dads Read, a program that fused literacy with community engagement in a way that felt deeply aligned with our mission at Fathers Incorporated. The idea was simple yet transformative: stock barbershops in metro Atlanta with children's books and encourage barbers to inspire kids to read while they waited for haircuts.

Barbershops are sacred spaces in the Black community—places where conversations flow freely, connections are made, and culture thrives. What better environment to instill the love of reading in our children?

The program quickly gained traction. Local educators, community leaders, and even national literacy advocates began to take notice.

It wasn't just the novelty of the idea that caught their attention; it was the impact. Parents shared stories of their kids picking up books for the first time, and barbers told us how their shops had become more than just spaces for grooming—they were now hubs for growth and inspiration.

The numbers told a compelling story too. Research shows that third-grade literacy proficiency is one of the strongest predictors of future success, and we knew that fathers, when actively engaged in their children's education, could tip the scales in a child's favor.

One of the most significant moments for Real Dads Read came when the executive director of Little Free Library—a global nonprofit that builds book-sharing boxes—visited Atlanta. After learning about our work, they donated 15 libraries to us, which we installed in Title I schools across the city.

These small wooden boxes became lifelines for children in underserved neighborhoods, offering them access to books even when the school doors were closed. Each library felt like a beacon of hope, a reminder that education was within reach.

Through this work, I found myself in rooms I never imagined entering. One such opportunity came when I was invited to present Real Dads Read to a group of educational leaders and policymakers at the state level led by my good friend, Mindy Benderman, CEO of GEEARS: Georgia Early Education Alliance for Ready Students.

The event was filled with decision-makers—people whose influence could shape the future of education in Georgia. I remember standing in front of the room, speaking about the intersection of literacy and fatherhood with the kind of passion that comes from knowing your work matters. I talked about the fathers I had met, the children who had been impacted, and the broader vision for what Real Dads Read could become.

After the presentation, as the room began to clear out, a woman approached me. She had a warm, confident presence and introduced herself as Stephanie Blank, the chair of the Boys & Girls Clubs of Metro Atlanta. She spoke with enthusiasm about my work and said, "I think my husband would be really interested in what you're doing. I'd love to connect you with him."

I've had similar conversations before, where someone offers to connect me with someone else who might share an interest in our work. Often, those offers fade into the background noise of unful-filled good intentions. But there was something different about Stephanie's tone—an urgency, a sincerity that suggested this wasn't just polite small talk. I thanked her and agreed, still not fully grasping who she was or what doors she might open.

It wasn't until later, after doing some quick research, that I understood the gravity of that conversation. Stephanie wasn't just anyone; she was the ex-wife of Arthur Blank, the billionaire co-founder of Home Depot and owner of the Atlanta Falcons. She wasn't simply making a casual suggestion—she was offering to connect me with one of the most influential figures in the city, someone whose resources and reach could amplify the work we were doing in ways I hadn't even dared to imagine.

Before I could even process the magnitude of this opportunity, our office phone rang and my wife called me to tell me the news. It was Arthur Blank's office, calling to schedule a meeting. The speed of it all left me almost breathless. Within hours of my conversation with Stephanie, a date and time were set. It felt surreal, like the universe had decided to align in my favor at that very moment.

As I hung up the phone, I drove the rest of the way home in silence, letting it sink in. This wasn't just a meeting; it was a chance to showcase everything we had been building. It was an opportunity to share our vision with someone who could help us take it to heights we hadn't yet reached. But more than that, it felt like validation—not just of the work we were doing, but of the decision to leave New York, to step out of my comfort zone, and to embrace the unknown in Atlanta.

I knew the meeting itself would be important, but I also knew that the path leading to it was just as significant. It was a reminder that every presentation, every conversation, every sleepless night spent crafting a vision wasn't just for nothing.

It was all part of a larger journey, one that had brought me to this moment. And as I prepared to walk into that meeting, I carried with me not just the hopes of Fathers Incorporated, but the dreams of every father and child whose lives we were working to change.

IS THE JUICE WORTH THE SQUEEZE?

When I think back to the meeting with Mr. Arthur Blank, it wasn't just an encounter; it was a collision—a defining moment. But before we get to the crescendo, let me take you back to the emotions that stirred within me as I prepared for that meeting.

In those days, I was chasing more than just opportunities; I was chasing validation. Not in the small sense of wanting to impress someone, but in the larger, weightier way of proving that my work, my purpose, and my very being deserved a seat at tables I'd never imagined sitting at.

The lead-up to that day was electric in my household. The idea of sitting face-to-face with someone whose wealth and influence could change the trajectory of not only Fathers Incorporated but my life entirely—well, it made every moment leading up to it feel monumental. My wife was buzzing with excitement, and I was too, though my excitement was laced with a simmering anxiety. It wasn't the anxiety of fear, but the heavy pressure of wanting to make every second count. I couldn't afford to fumble this opportunity.

The night before, I hardly slept. My mind replayed potential scenarios like a movie reel. What if I stumbled over my words? What if he asked me something I wasn't prepared to answer?

What if he saw me as just another guy with a nonprofit and no real vision? That last one stuck with me the most.

The nonprofit space is filled with dreamers, but dreams don't always translate to action, and I wanted him to see that I wasn't just another idealist. I wanted him to see my fire, my conviction, my belief that the work I was doing mattered—really mattered.

Morning came, and it was game time. I dressed with care, making sure every detail of my appearance reflected the seriousness of my intent. My suit was pressed, my tie was straight, and my shoes shone like a mirror.

As I stood in front of the bathroom sink tying my tie, I looked at myself in the mirror and whispered, "You got this." But deep down, I knew that it wasn't about having it; it was about being it—being the man who could step into a billionaire's office and articulate a vision so compelling that he'd see the value in walking alongside me.

When we arrived at his office, the grandeur of it all hit me. This wasn't just an office; it was a monument to achievement. The walls were adorned with memorabilia that spoke of victories—both personal and professional. Every detail of the space screamed success, but not in a gaudy way. It was refined, intentional, and intimidating. I felt small, not because I lacked confidence, but because the sheer magnitude of his world dwarfed mine.

He greeted us warmly, extending his hand with a smile that seemed both genuine and discerning. As we sat down, I could feel the weight of his presence. This wasn't just a man; this was a legacy in motion. He didn't need to impress anyone, and yet, his very existence was impressive.

As we exchanged pleasantries, I could see that he already knew about me. He had done his homework. He wasn't just meeting me out of courtesy; he was meeting me with purpose.

And then came the moment—the question that would define our meeting. "So, what can I do for you?" he asked, leaning back in his chair, his hands folded casually in his lap. It was an invitation, but it was also a test.

I took a deep breath, steadied myself, and laid out my grand idea. I spoke with passion, describing my vision of filling Mercedes-Benz Stadium with 10,000 fathers and their children, all reading Green Eggs and Ham together. I painted the picture vividly, emphasizing the Guinness World Record we'd set and the ripple effect it would have on literacy, fatherhood, and community. As I spoke, I could feel the excitement building in my chest. This was it—this was my shot.

When I finished, there was a pause. It wasn't an uncomfortable pause, but it was long enough for me to start second-guessing myself. Then, he leaned back a little further, looked me in the eye, and said, "Do you know how much it costs to turn the lights on at the stadium?"

"No, sir," I replied, my voice steady but my confidence beginning to waver.

He smiled slightly and delivered the line that would stay with me forever: "Anytime I get involved with something, I always ask myself one question: Is the juice worth the squeeze?"

It took me a moment to process what he meant. My idea, as grand as it felt to me, was small in comparison to the scale at which he operated. To him, it wasn't about hosting an event or setting a record; it was about creating lasting impact—transformational impact. My dream was too small for the room I was sitting in, and in that moment, I felt the sting of inadequacy. But it wasn't a crushing blow; it was a revelation.

He went on to say that his foundation would consider supporting smaller initiatives and connected me to another team member for follow-up.

The meeting ended cordially, but as I walked out of that office, I felt a mix of emotions—disappointment, humility, and an undeniable spark of inspiration.

For days, I replayed his words in my mind. "Is the juice worth the squeeze?" It wasn't just a question; it was a challenge—a challenge to think bigger, to dream bigger, to be bigger. Over time, I began to see the wisdom in what he had said.

My idea, while well-intentioned, was a single drop in the ocean of possibilities. If I wanted to truly make an impact, I needed to think on a scale that matched the magnitude of the work I claimed to care about.

Years after our encounter, I was driving down Interstate 85 and drove past the Arthur Blank Children's Hospital, a stunning testament to his vision and commitment. It opened October 2024. As I looked at that building, I thought about all the lives it would touch—lives he would never meet but would impact forever. And in that moment, I understood what it meant to create a legacy. It wasn't about the immediate reward; it was about the enduring impact.

Looking back, that meeting wasn't a missed opportunity; it was a masterclass. Arthur Blank didn't give me money, but he gave me something far more valuable—perspective.

He challenged me to rise above the limitations of my own thinking and to see the world not as it is, but as it could be. And for that, I will always be grateful.

THE WEIGHT OF CAPACITY: LEARNING TO SUSTAIN, SERVE, AND RISE

Capacity matters. Why would one say that? Why would anyone stop and take the time to frame their life around such a statement? I want to give you the answer to that question upfront, then walk you through why it holds so much weight. Capacity matters because it informs others—and more importantly, it informs you—about your ability to sustain.

It tells you about your ability to endure, to weather the storms, to hold steady under pressure. But it also reveals your ability to help, to serve, to be present for others when they need you the most. In essence, capacity is not just about you; it's about who you can become to the people who rely on you, whether they know it or not. It is about whether you can show up, fully and consistently, when the time comes. That's why it matters.

Here's what I've learned: capacity doesn't happen overnight, and it doesn't come by accident. It requires three things—you must learn, you must earn, and you must be concerned. Those three elements are the pillars of capacity. Learning expands the mind, earning secures the means, and concern stretches the heart. If you leave any one of these untouched, your capacity to serve will be limited, your impact diminished.

During the COVID-19 pandemic, I saw the true meaning of capacity play out in real time. While the world was shutting down, while businesses were closing their doors and families were struggling to stay afloat, Fathers Incorporated doubled in size. We grew our staff, expanded our reach, and deepened our work—not because we had magic or luck on our side, but because we had spent years building capacity. For me, that growth was personal.

It was validation of a belief I've held since the day I started this work: people don't need you when things are easy. They need you when everything around them is falling apart. They need you when life is heaviest, when the weight feels impossible to carry alone. In those moments, your capacity matters most.

Capacity is what separates those who merely talk about serving from those who are able to do it. And it's not just about organizations or businesses—it's about all of us. As a parent, you need capacity to love, to nurture, to guide, even when you're tired, frustrated, or unsure. As a spouse, you need capacity to hold your partner's hand through sickness and health, through abundance and lack. As a friend, as a mentor, as a community leader, your capacity to stand strong, to lift others, to remain reliable—even in your own storms—becomes the quiet currency of your life.
It is what people will remember.

The first tenant of capacity is learning. I've said this before, but it bears repeating: you cannot serve others well if you are not always learning. Life is a classroom, and every experience—good or bad—is a lesson waiting to be studied. You have to be a student of your craft. Don't just show up—master your space.

Become the kind of person who knows what they're doing, who understands the nuance of their work, who doesn't cut corners or make excuses. If you're in the human service business, as we are at Fathers Incorporated, then you better know people. You better understand their struggles, their habits, their fears. You better be willing to sit in their shoes, to feel what they feel. Learning doesn't just build knowledge; it builds empathy. And without empathy, your capacity to serve will always fall short.

The second tenant is earning. Earning is about resources. It's about putting in the work to build the means to sustain your calling. It's about recognizing that free isn't free—not really. The kind of help people need, the kind of help that matters, requires resources. It requires financial capital, yes, but also emotional capital, spiritual capital, and human capital. You have to earn those things. You have to earn trust, earn respect, earn credibility.

That doesn't happen just because you say you want to help. It happens because you show up and put in the work, day after day, when no one is watching. It happens because you prove yourself— not through words, but through action.

And then there's concern—the third and, I believe, the most critical tenant of capacity. Concern is about heart. It's about care. It's about having the kind of soul that doesn't just see people but feels for them. The work I do is not hard work; it's heart work. And if your heart isn't in it, you're not ready to serve. You can't fake concern—not in this space.

People know when you're just going through the motions. They know when your care is transactional and when it's real. Concern means showing up not because you're obligated, but because you're invested—fully, completely, without reservation. Concern is what gives you the stamina to sit with people in their pain. It is what compels you to put yourself second so that someone else can breathe easier. It is the thing that makes serving a calling, not a chore.

Capacity takes time. It takes patience. It takes resilience. You don't wake up one morning with a full tank ready to serve the world. You build it, day by day, through learning, earning, and concern. And while capacity is built slowly, it can be tested in an instant.

> *Life will show up and ask you to prove what you're made of—and you won't get to pick the time or the circumstances.*

There's a story I often think about when it comes to capacity. It's the story of a grandmother who always cut the tail off her chicken before cooking it. Her family watched her do it for years, assuming it was some special secret to making the chicken taste better. One day, they decided to ask her why she did it. Her answer was simple: "Because the chicken wouldn't fit in the pot." That's how we are sometimes. We limit ourselves without realizing it. We shrink our capacity because we've never stopped to question why. We've never expanded our vision or grown our understanding.

We've been cutting the tail off the chicken because that's how it's always been done. Capacity matters because it stretches you. It demands growth. It pushes you to challenge yourself, to ask bigger questions, to expand beyond what you thought was possible. It requires vision—the kind of vision that sees not just where you are, but where you're going. It requires empathy—the kind of empathy that lets you feel someone else's pain so deeply that you can't rest until you've done something about it.

In Matthew 25:14-30, Jesus tells the parable of the talents. A master gives three servants varying amounts of gold, asking them to use it wisely. Two of the servants double their talents, earning praise for their faithfulness. The third buries his talent out of fear, returning it unused. The master calls him "wicked and lazy," taking his talent away. The lesson is clear: capacity is a responsibility. Whatever gifts, resources, or opportunities you've been given are not for you to bury.

They are for you to use, to multiply, to grow.

At the end of the day, capacity matters because it defines your ability to fulfill your purpose. It shapes who you can be to others and what you can leave behind. It tells the world what you're made of. So I ask you: Are you learning? Are you earning? Are you concerned? Are you building the capacity to serve not just when it's easy, but when it's hard? Because when the moment comes, and people are looking for help, your capacity will be what makes the difference. And that, above all else, is why capacity matters.

THE BATTLE FOR VALUE: FINDING WORTH WITHIN YOURSELF

One of the most critical questions you can ask yourself, no matter your age or stage in life, is this: Can I find value in my life despite what others think of me? But more importantly, can I find value in myself? This isn't just a rhetorical question; it's the cornerstone of self-worth, the very thing that insecurity attacks with surgical precision.

And the truth is, value isn't just determined by you. Sometimes, it's dictated by others, like a market assessing supply and demand. How much of you does the world need, and what is your worth in that equation?

But here's the deeper question: When the world stops affirming you, when the applause fades and the recognition dwindles, can you still find value in yourself? Can you hold onto your sense of worth when all the external markers are stripped away? That's the real challenge, and it's one I've grappled with personally, professionally, and spiritually.

For me, value has often been tied to what I've accomplished.

What have I contributed to the world? What have I achieved? What have I done that matters? These are the questions I've asked myself in quiet moments of doubt, and sometimes the answers felt insufficient. Even when I've had the accolades, the platforms, the opportunities that others might envy, there were still moments when I doubted my value. And if I'm being honest, some of those moments were the darkest of my life.

There's a dream I had once that I've never forgotten. In the dream, I was standing in front of a burning house. Fire engines surrounded the scene, lights flashing, chaos everywhere. There were firefighters and bystanders, news crews capturing the drama, the kind of scene that draws a crowd for all the wrong reasons. Then, a voice spoke to me, clear and calm amidst the chaos. "What do you see?" it asked.

"I see a burning house," I replied. "And people running out." "Those people," the voice said, "are the ones who understand the urgency of their situation. They have the ability to save themselves, and they're doing so. They have a voice that calls out to others, a voice that warns, a voice that guides. They are capable."

The scene shifted, and I saw people being carried out of the house.

"What do you see now?" the voice asked.

"I see people who can't move on their own," I said. "People who need help."

"Yes," the voice replied. "These are the ones who have a voice but lack the strength to escape alone. They need others to carry them, to guide them to safety. Their lives are no less valuable than those who ran out themselves."

Finally, the scene shifted again. The house was still burning, but now it was silent. "What do you hear?" the voice asked.
I strained to listen. "I don't hear anything," I said.

"Listen closely," the voice urged. "What do you hear?"
"Nothing," I repeated.

"Those are the ones still inside," the voice said. "The ones who don't have a voice. They can't call out for help. They're trapped, silent, but their need is just as urgent. These are the people you must learn to hear. They are the ones who need you the most."

That dream has stayed with me, etched into my memory as a metaphor for life. It taught me that everyone has value, whether they're running, being carried, or too silent to cry out. But it also taught me that the ability to see and affirm that value—in others and in ourselves—is not always easy. It requires intentionality, empathy, and sometimes, the courage to confront our own insecurities.

Insecurities have a way of creeping in, don't they? They whisper lies into our minds, planting seeds of doubt that grow into thickets of fear and self-loathing. For me, those whispers have been the toughest battle I've ever fought. They tell you that you're not enough, that you're irrelevant, that the world doesn't need what you have to offer. And the irony is, those whispers often come from the little boy inside me, the younger version of myself who didn't yet have the tools to fight back.

We all have that younger self within us. For some, it's a little boy; for others, a little girl. That inner child carries the weight of our early experiences, our first encounters with rejection, failure, and doubt. And while that child is a part of us, it doesn't define us. Yet, too often, we let it. We let that voice dictate how we see ourselves, how we measure our value.

That's why affirmations are so important. They are the antidote to those whispers, the counter-narrative to the stories of insecurity we tell ourselves. Affirmations are not just words; they are declarations of truth. They remind us of who we are and who we can become. And they have the power to transform our self-perception, to shift the narrative from doubt to confidence, from fear to courage.

Think about superheroes for a moment. Why do you think Spider-Man is called "The Amazing Spider-Man"? Doesn't the world already know he's amazing? Of course it does. But sometimes, even Spider-Man needs to be reminded. Sometimes, Peter Parker wakes up feeling like just Peter Parker, burdened by the weight of his responsibilities, doubting his ability to rise to the occasion.

In those moments, the title "The Amazing Spider-Man" is not just a label; it's an affirmation. It's a reminder to himself and to the world that he is capable, that he is enough, that he is, in fact, amazing.

The same goes for the Hulk. Why is he called "The Incredible Hulk"? Because some days, he's just Bruce Banner, a man grappling with his own inner turmoil. But when the moment calls for it, he transforms, and in that transformation, he becomes incredible. The title is both a declaration and a reminder of his potential, of the power within him.

We all need those reminders. We all need to wake up in the morning and tell ourselves that we are amazing, incredible, and super. Because the truth is, we are. We are all the superheroes of our own lives, capable of overcoming obstacles, defying odds, and making a difference in the world. But we have to believe it. We have to speak it into existence.

I've met some incredible people in my life. I've stood on stages, spoken to thousands, traveled the world, met legends like Oprah Winfrey and Coretta Scott King, and worked with some of the most impactful organizations in the country. And yet, there have been moments when I doubted my value.

Moments when the whispers of insecurity drowned out the applause. Moments when I couldn't see the worth in my own accomplishments.

One such moment was tied to my experience with Coretta Scott King. Years ago, while serving on the board of the Capital Region YMCA, I was tasked with helping to bring the Black and Latino Achievers Program to Albany, New York.

It was an ambitious project, one that required community support, funding, and a powerful voice to inspire others to get involved. During one of our planning meetings, someone asked who we could invite as a keynote speaker for our fundraising dinner. Without hesitation, I suggested Coretta Scott King, though I doubted we could afford her honorarium.

To my surprise, a generous supporter of the YMCA didn't hesitate. He wrote the check on the spot, and just like that, we had Coretta Scott King confirmed as our speaker. That day, I had the privilege of spending hours with her, sitting in her hotel suite, listening to her stories about the Civil Rights Movement and her late husband, Dr. Martin Luther King Jr. She spoke with such grace and wisdom, sharing insights that left me in awe.

At one point, she signed books for a few guests and expressed frustration about inaccuracies in some of the writings about Dr. King. "Kenny," she said, "look at this. They got the date of the March on Washington wrong.

This is why it's so important to protect his legacy."

That experience should have been a defining moment for me, a memory to treasure without reservation. And while it is a cherished memory, it's also one that stirs a lingering sense of insecurity.

You see, even after 15 years of success with that program, I've never been adequately recognized as one of its co-founders. Despite the impact it's had on countless young lives, my role in its creation has been minimized, almost erased. It's a painful reminder that sometimes, no matter how much you contribute, others can diminish your value, intentionally or not.

While I've long since stopped agonizing over the lack of recognition, it doesn't erase the sting of being overlooked. It doesn't eliminate the questions that creep in late at night: Was my contribution not enough? Did I not fight hard enough to protect my own legacy? These are the echoes of insecurity, the whispers that try to undermine the value I know I've brought to the world.

And yet, I choose not to let those whispers win. I choose to focus on the lives that were changed, the young people who found inspiration and opportunity through that program. Because at the end of the day, my value isn't determined by accolades or acknowledgments. It's determined by the impact I've had and the legacy I continue to build.

It's a lesson I'm still learning, one affirmation at a time. I am amazing. I am incredible. I am worthy. And so are you.

WHEN DOES LIFE STOP BEING ABOUT YOU?

Life is a paradox, isn't it? On one hand, we're told to take care of ourselves, to focus on our own goals, our happiness, and our well-being. On the other, we live in a world that constantly reminds us of our responsibilities to others. Somewhere between those two truths lies the question: is life ever really about you? And if it isn't, when does it stop being about you?

I've asked myself this question many times, not as a philosophical exercise but as a way of reconciling the push and pull of life's demands. At times, the answer has felt clear; other times, it has been as murky as a foggy morning. But what I've come to realize is that life is rarely, if ever, just about you. It can feel like it is in certain moments—in the quiet spaces where you reflect, or in the decisions you make that seem to serve only yourself—but even those moments are connected to the lives of others.

Take the example of being on a plane. When the flight attendant gives the safety briefing, they always emphasize that you should put on your oxygen mask first before helping someone else. At first glance, this seems selfish—a declaration that your life matters more. But think about it: the only reason you're instructed to do that is because, without oxygen, you won't be able to help anyone else. So even in the act of saving yourself, the larger purpose is to save others. The two are interconnected.

The word that often comes to mind when I think about this dynamic is selfishness. A good friend of mine, Janks, once told me during an interview that selfishness is at the root of so many of life's problems. He said, "People get divorced because they're selfish.

They don't take care of their children because they're selfish. They quit their jobs because they're angry at the other parent because they're selfish." His words stuck with me because they spoke to the heart of a truth many of us avoid: selfishness isolates us. It makes life small, narrow, and ultimately unfulfilling.

But here's the thing: humans aren't born selfless. We come into this world as infants, entirely dependent on others for survival. We cry when we're hungry, scream when we're uncomfortable, and demand attention without a thought for what it costs those around us. It takes time, guidance, and experience to grow out of that state. Some people never do.

For others, the realization that life isn't about them comes in stages—small awakenings that reshape their understanding of the world.

I often wonder when most people start to think about their legacy, about what they'll leave behind when they're gone. I submit that for young people, this thought rarely crosses their minds. When you're young, you believe you'll live forever. Death is an abstraction, something that happens to other people. It's not until you've lived a little, until you've lost someone or faced your own mortality, that you begin to grasp the impermanence of life.

And yet, even in youth, we leave impressions. Our absence, whether through death, distance, or abandonment, creates a void in the lives of others. People notice the holes we leave behind. They feel the weight of our absence. But it's hard to see that when you're young, because the world revolves around you—or at least, that's what it feels like.

There are some, however, who grow up in environments that force them to confront the fragility of life much earlier than others. In communities where violence is rampant, where death is a constant presence, young people often resign themselves to the belief that they won't live to see adulthood. I've heard the number "18" repeated countless times. "I never thought I'd make it past 18," they say. "I never thought I'd see 30."

When you believe your time is short, it's easy to live selfishly, to focus on the here and now because the future feels out of reach.

For those of us who are seasoned, the perspective is different. With age comes the realization that our lives are deeply interconnected with the lives of others. We begin to see the ripple effects of our actions, the way our choices impact those around us. We recognize that our absence—whether temporary or permanent—leaves a mark.

I think back to a trip I took with my daughters to Atlanta years ago. They were young, and we were excited to explore the city, to visit landmarks and create memories together. As we were getting ready to go out one morning, I noticed how they were dressed. It wasn't overly provocative, but it was more revealing than I thought appropriate for the day's activities. I voiced my concern, and I could see the resistance in their eyes. They didn't understand why it mattered.

So I explained. I told them that when they're out with friends, they can dress however they like because they're in their own circle, surrounded by people their age who understand their context. But when they're out with me, their father, things are different.

I told them there are men who won't respect the fact that they're with their father, men who might behave inappropriately. I explained that if something happened, I would have to protect them, and that protection could escalate into something serious— something that could separate me from them.

It was a heavy burden to place on their young shoulders, but I needed them to understand that their choices didn't exist in a vacuum. Their actions had the potential to impact me, just as my actions impacted them. That moment was a lesson for all of us about the interconnectedness of life.

As a parent, I've learned that life stops being about you the moment you realize your actions have consequences beyond your-self. Whether it's the way you raise your children, the way you treat your partner, or the way you engage with the world, your life is always part of a larger story.

The same is true when you embrace a life of service. When you commit to serving others—whether as a parent, a professional, or a member of your community—you begin to see the profound truth that life is not about you. It's about what you can give, what you can contribute, and how you can leave the world better than you found it.

Faith also plays a role in this understanding. For those of us who believe in a higher power, there's a sense that our lives are part of a divine plan. When you give your life to that purpose, when you trust that your steps are ordered, you relinquish the illusion of control. You come to see your life not as your own, but as a vessel for something greater.

There's a freedom in that realization. When you stop trying to make life about you, you open yourself up to the beauty of connection, the joy of service, and the fulfillment that comes from living with purpose. You begin to see that every decision, every action, every moment is an opportunity to contribute to something larger than yourself.

So, is life ever just about you? I don't think it is. And the sooner we realize that, the sooner we can start living in a way that truly matters. Because life, at its core, is about what we can do for others—and in doing so, what we can become for ourselves.

CHAPTER SIX

LIVING WITH PURPOSE: DEFINING AND PURSUING WHAT TRULY MATTERS

THE BUCKETS OF A PURPOSEFUL LIFE

At some point in our journey, we're confronted with a question that refuses to be ignored: What truly matters? It's not the kind of question that whispers politely in the background.

It's a question that stands boldly in front of you, arms crossed, daring you to answer with more than a shrug. It's a question that demands clarity, one that insists you examine your life—not just the surface, but the depths, the corners you've ignored, and the places you've tucked away for another day.

I've spent a lot of time thinking about this question, both for myself and for the people I've met along the way. Writing this book has been an exercise in confronting that question again and again, peeling back the layers of my own life to uncover the moments, the choices, and the experiences that have shaped who I am. It's not an easy process.

In fact, it's downright uncomfortable at times. But it's necessary, because if we don't know what matters, how can we know how to live?

When I think about the framework of this book and the journey we've taken so far, I see it as a mirror. A reflection of the stories, lessons, and experiences that have framed my life, shaping how I think and how I move through the world. We've explored the influences of relationships, the echoes of our past, and the ways we navigate the opinions of others. All of it matters, but now it's time to shift the focus inward, to pause and assess where we are.

This chapter is about that assessment. It's about slowing down and asking yourself the hard questions: What truly matters in my life? What am I pursuing, and why? What drives me to keep going, to strive, to dream, to push forward even when the odds feel insurmountable? These aren't questions with easy answers, but they're questions worth asking, because the answers define the trajectory of our lives.

When I reflect on my own journey, I find that most of what matters in life can be placed into four buckets: family, legacy, health, and faith. These buckets aren't exhaustive, but they hold the weight of the things that give life meaning.

They are the pillars that ground us, the anchors that keep us steady, and the compass that guides us forward.

Family is everything. It's where we begin, and for many of us, it's where we find our greatest joys and deepest pains. Family teaches us who we are, often before we've had a chance to decide for ourselves. Whether functional or dysfunctional, supportive or absent, family leaves a mark that shapes how we see the world and our place in it.

I've often said that family is the incubator of life. It's where we learn our first lessons about love, trust, and conflict. It's where we're nurtured—or not—and where the seeds of our identity are planted. But family is not static. It changes as we grow, as we create families of our own, and as we redefine what family means to us.

Legacy is the thread that connects the past, present, and future. It's what we leave behind, not just in terms of wealth or accomplishments, but in the values we instill, the relationships we nurture, and the impact we make on the lives of others. Legacy asks us to think beyond ourselves, to consider how our lives will resonate in the hearts and minds of those who come after us.

I've often thought about the concept of the dash—the small line that separates the date of our birth from the date of our death on a tombstone. That dash, though small, holds the entirety of our lives. It represents every choice we've made, every relationship we've built, and every moment we've lived.

> *The question is, what are we doing with our dash? What are we creating, contributing, and leaving behind that will endure?*

Health is the foundation upon which everything else rests. Without it, nothing else matters. Yet, it's often the thing we take for granted until it's gone.

When you're young, you feel invincible, as though your body will carry you forever without complaint. But age has a way of humbling you, of reminding you that health is not a given—it's a gift.

I've heard the saying, "Youth is wasted on the young." I'm not sure I entirely agree, but I understand the sentiment. When you're young, you don't think about your health. You don't think about the toll that poor choices will take on your body over time. But as you grow older, as the aches and pains begin to creep in, you start to realize that health is not just a physical state—it's a form of wealth.

Faith is the thread that weaves it all together. It's what gives us hope in the face of uncertainty, strength in the midst of struggle, and purpose in the midst of chaos. For me, faith has been a guiding force, a source of comfort and clarity. It's what I turn to when the path ahead feels unclear, when the weight of life feels too heavy to bear.

Faith is not the same as religion, though the two are often intertwined. Faith is belief in something greater than yourself, in the unseen and the unknown. It's the assurance that there is meaning in the mess, purpose in the pain, and beauty in the brokenness.

I often think about the small acts of faith we engage in every day without realizing it. When we cross a bridge, we have faith that it will hold us. When we sit in a chair, we have faith that it will support us. These small acts remind us that faith is not about certainty—it's about trust.

As I write this, I am reminded of the many lessons life has taught me about these four buckets. They are not separate—they are interconnected, each one influencing and shaping the others. Family teaches us about love and legacy.

Legacy challenges us to prioritize our health and faith. Health reminds us to cherish the time we have with our family. And faith gives us the strength to pursue our legacy, even when the road is difficult.

My hope is that as we delve into these buckets together, you will find pieces of your own story reflected in mine. I hope you will take the time to examine your own life, to consider what truly matters to you, and to begin living in alignment with those values.

Because at the end of the day, what truly matters is not what we achieve, but who we become. It's not about the milestones we reach, but the moments we share. It's not about the legacy we leave behind, but the love we give along the way.

This is the journey we're on together—to define and pursue what truly matters, to live with purpose, and to create a life that reflects the best of who we are. Let's take the next step.

THE CORNERSTONE OF LIFE: FAMILY

There are few things in life as foundational, as grounding, as the presence of family. It's where most of us begin, and it often shapes who we are long before we even understand ourselves. Family is not just a collection of people connected by blood; it is a tapestry of relationships, responsibilities, and shared experiences that create the fabric of our existence.

It defines us in ways we don't always see and influences us in ways we can never fully measure.

Family is often where our first lessons are learned. As children, we look to our parents, siblings, and extended family members to understand the world. These are the people who teach us about love, conflict, forgiveness, and resilience. They model behaviors, instill values, and set expectations—both spoken and unspoken. Whether functional or dysfunctional, family leaves an indelible mark on our development, shaping how we see ourselves and how we engage with others.

When I think about family, I think about the profound responsibility it carries. For parents, it's about more than just providing food, shelter, and clothing. It's about creating an environment where children feel safe, loved, and encouraged to reach their potential. It's about giving them the tools to navigate the world with confidence and integrity.

For children, it's about learning the value of respect, the importance of contribution, and the role they play within the family unit.

But family isn't just about immediate relationships—it extends to the connections we form with those who enter our lives by choice or circumstance. Aunts, uncles, cousins, grandparents, and even close family friends become part of the intricate web of relationships that define our sense of belonging. Each of these relationships carries its own weight, its own lessons, and its own challenges.

One of the complexities of family becomes even more evident when we enter into marriage. Marriage doesn't just join two people—it interlocks two families. When you marry someone, you don't just become a partner to your spouse; you become part of their family dynamic, and they become part of yours.

This blending of families can be a beautiful and enriching experience, but it also comes with its own set of challenges.

I often reflect on the biblical directive that a man shall leave his father and mother and cleave to his wife.

I've come to understand that while this scripture speaks to prioritizing your spouse, it also raises questions about navigating the boundaries between your new family unit and the family you were born into. Does leaving your parents mean leaving your family entirely? Not in a literal sense, but it does mean that your spouse must come first.

In my own marriage, my wife's family taught me lessons I hadn't anticipated—lessons about loyalty, forgiveness, and the sanctity of protecting what we've built together. My wife is one of the most forgiving people I've ever known. Her heart is open, her nature facilitative, and her willingness to see the redemptive qualities in others is nothing short of remarkable.

But that same openness has, at times, required me to put up boundaries on her behalf. While I admire her ability to extend grace, my protective nature often steps in to safeguard her emotional well-being. I've seen the dynamics of family impact her in ways that ignited my instinct to shield her from harm. How her family presented themselves then and now, is still extremely painful for me to absourb and tolerate for anyone, but certainly to allow my wife to endure.

As a result I had to create firewalls—spaces where I could protect our family unit from external dysfunctions that threatened to infiltrate our home.

This balancing act is not easy. It's difficult to reconcile the importance of family with the need to set boundaries. Family is sacred, yes, but it can also be one of the most destructive forces in our lives if we're not careful. The key is in recognizing when to hold on and when to let go, when to embrace and when to step back.

For me, growing up in a single-parent household taught me early on the value of resilience and sacrifice. My mother was a pillar of strength, often carrying the weight of the world on her shoulders while ensuring that my siblings and I had what we needed. Her dedication taught me the importance of showing up, even when it's hard, and the power of love that transcends circumstances.

But I also learned that family is not immune to pain or conflict. It is within family that we often experience our greatest joys and our deepest wounds. There ain't a perfect family ever created; starting with the first family born out of Adam and Eve. Disagreements, misunderstandings, and unmet expectations can create rifts that feel impossible to bridge. Yet, it is also within family that we learn the true meaning of forgiveness and the strength that comes from reconciliation.

As I've grown older, my perspective on family has evolved. I've come to see it not just as something I was born into, but as something I have the power to build and nurture. I've seen how family shapes the trajectory of our lives and how the choices we make within our families can ripple outward, impacting generations to come.

One of the most powerful aspects of family is its ability to ground us. In a world that often feels chaotic and uncertain, family can serve as an anchor—a place where we are known, accepted, and loved. It reminds us of who we are and where we come from, providing a sense of continuity that is both comforting and empowering.

But family is not static; it is ever-changing. Relationships evolve, roles shift, and dynamics are constantly in flux. This fluidity can be both a challenge and an opportunity. It requires us to adapt, to grow, and to continuously invest in the relationships that matter most.

Family is also a reflection of our values. The way we show up for our loved ones says a lot about who we are and what we prioritize. Do we make time for the people who matter? Do we listen, support, and encourage? Do we offer grace when mistakes are made? These are the questions that guide us as we navigate the complexities of family life.

In my work with fathers, I've seen firsthand the transformative power of family. I've witnessed the impact of fathers who step up and embrace their roles with intention and love. I've seen how a strong family foundation can change the trajectory of a child's life, giving them the confidence and stability they need to thrive.

At its core, family is about connection. It's about the bonds that tie us together, the moments that shape our memories, and the love that sustains us through life's challenges. It is both a gift and a responsibility—a privilege that requires effort, patience, and a willingness to grow.

As we explore the things that truly matter in life, family stands out as a cornerstone. It is where we learn to give and receive love, where we find our first sense of belonging, and where we discover the beauty of living in relationship with others. Family is not perfect, and it is not always easy, but it is undeniably one of life's greatest treasures.

In the end, it is family that reminds us of what is truly important. It grounds us in our humanity, connects us to our purpose, and teaches us the value of living a life that is bigger than ourselves. It is a cornerstone worth building upon, a legacy worth leaving, and a blessing worth cherishing.

THE SACRED WEIGHT OF COMMITMENT

There's something about the word "marriage" that holds an almost sacred weight in society. It's more than a legal contract, more than a declaration of love. Marriage, at its core, represents something deeply symbolic—a merging of lives, dreams, and futures.

For some, it's a spiritual bond, a covenant that holds divine significance. For others, it's a practical institution, a structure that offers stability and legitimacy. But regardless of how you define it, marriage is one of those elements of life that carries a profound influence on how we see ourselves and how the world sees us.

In my life, marriage has been both a teacher and a mirror. It has taught me about commitment, sacrifice, and the intricate dance of balancing individuality with partnership. It has forced me to confront my flaws, adjust my expectations, and redefine what love looks like. And perhaps most importantly, it has been a journey of discovering what truly matters—not just in the context of a relationship, but in life as a whole.

I've learned that marriage has a way of framing everything—how you view the world, how you engage with others, and how you perceive yourself. It becomes a lens through which you navigate life, a foundation upon which so many other aspects of your existence are built.

> ***But marriage is not just about love. It's about purpose. It's about intention. It's about building something greater than yourself.***

When I reflect on my first marriage, I see a young man who was still trying to figure out who he was. I was 18, freshly enlisted in the military, and newly married to my high school sweetheart.

We had a child, and like so many others of our generation, we followed the tradition that said marriage was the next logical step. It was what you did to legitimize your family, to show the world that you were committed and responsible.

But the truth is, I didn't fully understand what I was committing to. I had grown up in a single-parent household and had never seen a healthy marriage up close. My understanding of relationships was shaped by what I saw on TV or heard in conversations—a patchwork of ideals and expectations that didn't quite fit together. So, when I said, "I do; I didn't." We got married more out of obligation than understanding.

Our wedding was a modest affair—a courthouse ceremony with a few close friends as witnesses, followed by a reception in a two-bedroom apartment. It was intimate and unassuming, but beneath the surface, there was a lack of clarity about what we were truly stepping into.

We loved each other, yes, but love alone wasn't enough.

Looking back, I realize that our marriage lacked the tools to withstand the storms that inevitably come. We didn't know how to communicate effectively, how to resolve conflicts without letting them fester.

We were navigating life as individuals rather than as a team, and when the challenges piled up, we didn't have the foundation to hold us together.

When that marriage ended, it was painful in ways I couldn't have anticipated. It wasn't just the loss of a partner—it was the loss of a dream, the shattering of an ideal. And yet, it was also a turning point. It forced me to confront the gaps in my understanding, to ask myself hard questions about what I wanted and what I was willing to give.

By the time I entered my second marriage, I was a different man. I had lived enough life to know what I valued and what I needed. I had seen examples of strong, enduring marriages, and I had learned from my own mistakes. This time, I approached marriage with a sense of intentionality, understanding that it wasn't just about love—it was about partnership, growth, and purpose.

One of the most significant lessons I've learned is that marriage is a journey, not a destination. Saying "I do" is not the culmination of a love story—it's the beginning of a new chapter, one that requires constant work and commitment. It's about showing up every day, not just for your partner, but for the life you're building together.

In my second marriage, I learned an important truth about sacrifice—not just in terms of personal wants and desires, but in the complexity of managing linear relationships. When you marry someone who has children from a previous relationship, and you have children of your own, the family dynamic becomes a delicate web of interconnected relationships.

There is your relationship with your spouse, the central pillar of the marriage. But then there is your relationship with your spouse's child, your spouse's relationship with your child, and the relationship between your respective children. Add to that the adjacent relationships with the other parents of those children, and suddenly, you're managing seven distinct relationships, each of which plays a critical role in the health and harmony of the family.

Maintaining these relationships requires intentional effort and sacrifice. It means prioritizing the well-being of the entire family unit over personal preferences or individual grievances. It means navigating the challenges of blended family dynamics with patience and understanding. And it means recognizing that every relationship within the family impacts the larger whole.

This is the sacred weight of commitment—that in choosing to build a life with someone, you are also choosing to embrace the complexities that come with it. You are choosing to invest in not just your spouse, but in the relationships that make up the fabric of your shared life. And that investment, while demanding, is what creates a foundation strong enough to weather life's storms.

Marriage demands intentionality. It requires you to set goals, both individually and as a couple, and to work together to achieve them. It requires honesty, resilience, and a willingness to adapt. But above all, it requires a commitment to something greater than yourself—a commitment to the life you are building together, the family you are nurturing, and the legacy you are creating.

As I reflect on my journey, I am grateful for the lessons marriage has taught me. It has shown me the power of love, the beauty of sacrifice, and the importance of living with intention. And it has reminded me that the most meaningful pursuits in life are those that connect us to others, that call us to something greater than ourselves.

This is the sacred weight of commitment. This is the beauty of living with purpose.

WHEN LOVE BECOMES THE COMPASS

At some point in life, there comes a moment when you start to sift through all the noise, all the distractions, and all the fleeting pursuits, and ask yourself: What really matters? It's a question that feels simple on the surface but carries a depth that can take a lifetime to explore. The answer isn't always clear, and it certainly isn't always easy, but I've come to believe that finding what matters is what gives our lives true meaning.

For me, the journey toward understanding what matters started with a shift—a shift in how I saw the world, in how I saw myself, and in how I saw love. I didn't always have the clarity I do now. In my younger years, I was driven by ambition, by the need to prove something to myself and to others.

I thought success, recognition, and material accomplishments were the markers of a meaningful life. And for a while, they were. They served their purpose, filling the voids left by insecurity and doubt.

But life has a way of humbling you, of teaching you that what you thought mattered isn't what truly matters at all. For me, that realization began to crystallize when I got married.

Marriage has a way of shifting your perspective. It grounds you, centers you, and forces you to confront the parts of yourself that you might otherwise avoid. It's not just about love—it's about commitment, purpose, and building a life together.

I'll never forget the early days of my relationship with my wife. She tells the story of how, before she even moved to Albany, that she had a dream about her husband being in Albany. She told me that God told her in a dream; "you're going to find your husband there." She never misses an opportunity to tell anyone who listens that narrative. Oh, the tale gets better.

Years later when I met her while doing some community work that, God doubled down and told her that, I in fact, was the man she was going to marry. I always chuckle when she tells that story. My response has always jokingly been, "Well, that's cool that He told you, but until he told me, it really didn't matter!"

That level of faith and patience she has, still astounds me to this day. After we were married I asked her, how did she know I was ready? She explained to me that God told her, "When you can follow Me through him, he'll be ready." It wasn't until years later, looking back, that I understood what she meant.

When I began to align my life with purpose, to walk a path of commitment and clarity, something shifted within me. It became clear who she was to me, and who I wanted to be for her.

Marriage, in many ways, became the space where I began to understand what truly mattered. It wasn't just about love—it was about intentionality. It was about creating a life that reflected our values, our goals, and our shared vision for the future.

One of the first lessons marriage taught me was the importance of communication. In my first marriage, communication was often fraught with misunderstanding and unresolved conflict. I carried the learned behavior of my upbringing into that relationship, where disagreements were met with silence or physicality, not dialogue. By the time I met my wife, I knew I wanted something different.

I wanted to build a relationship where we could talk—really talk— and work through challenges without tearing each other down.

But even with the best intentions, communication wasn't always easy. My wife and I were both yellers. It wasn't the kind of yelling born out of anger or disrespect—it was just how we expressed ourselves in moments of frustration. One day, during one of our heated exchanges, I told her, "Stop yelling." She fired back, "I'm not yelling!" And there we were, stuck in a loop of disagreement over the very act of yelling.

It wasn't until we had a deeper conversation about our upbringings that the root of the issue became clear. She grew up in a large, boisterous household where raising your voice was the norm. In her family, yelling wasn't a sign of conflict—it was just how you made yourself heard. I, on the other hand, grew up in a quiet home where even a slightly elevated voice carried weight. What she considered normal, I perceived as shouting.

Once we understood this about each other, we made a conscious decision to define our own way of communicating. We agreed on what yelling meant to us as a couple, and from that moment, the dynamic shifted. We rarely, if ever, raise our voices now. Instead, we've learned to navigate disagreements with patience and understanding.

That lesson—one of many—showed me that when something truly matters, you find a way to make it work. You don't let pride or stubbornness get in the way. You adapt, you compromise, and you grow.

Marriage also taught me the importance of boundaries and roles. In any relationship, but especially in marriage, it's essential to understand your responsibilities and respect the boundaries that keep the relationship healthy. This doesn't mean rigidly adhering to traditional gender roles—it means finding a balance that works for both partners. It means knowing when to step up, when to step back, and when to stand side by side.

But perhaps the most profound lesson marriage has taught me is the power of sacrifice. When I married my wife, I didn't just commit to her—I committed to her daughter, just as she committed to mine. We became a blended family, with all the complexities and challenges that come with it.

I quickly realized that our marriage wasn't just about the two of us. It was about the seven distinct relationships within our family: my relationship with my wife, her relationship with me, my relationship with her daughter, her relationship with my daughter, the relationship between our daughters, and our relationships with the other parents of our children. Each of these relationships required care, attention, and intentionality.

Maintaining those relationships wasn't always easy, but it was necessary. It required sacrifice—sacrificing time, ego, and even certain dreams to ensure that our family could thrive. But what I learned through that process is that sacrifice, when born out of love, doesn't feel like a burden. It feels like purpose.

That's the thing about marriage—it has a way of clarifying what matters. It strips away the superficial and brings you face-to-face with the things that truly hold value: love, commitment, trust, and the bonds we create with one another.

I often think about the words of Proverbs 18:22: "He who finds a wife finds what is good and receives favor from the Lord." Those words resonate with me because they speak to the transformative power of marriage. It's not just about finding a partner—it's about finding purpose. It's about building a life that reflects the best of who you are and who you aspire to be.

Marriage is not for everyone, and it's not a prerequisite for a meaningful life. But for those who choose it, it can be one of the most profound expressions of love and purpose. It can be a journey of growth, discovery, and transformation—a journey that reminds us of what truly matters.

Love matters. Commitment matters. Purpose matters. And when you find someone who shares those values, someone who is willing to walk that journey with you, it becomes clear: this is what life is about. This is what truly matters.

THE LOVE THAT MATTERS

There's something about being a father to daughters that changes a man. It's a sacred kind of responsibility, one that feels both heavy and light, profound and personal. Raising girls isn't just about teaching them how to navigate the world; it's about equipping them to see themselves as worthy of love, respect, and all the things the world may try to deny them.

For a father, the hope is always to set the bar so high that any man who enters their life must rise to meet it.

I've often joked that raising daughters is like sharing company secrets—giving them the inside scoop on how to recognize the good, avoid the bad, and see through the charm that too often masks intentions. It's a delicate balance, trying to prepare them for the romantic world while hoping they don't encounter the worst of it. But in the back of every father's mind, there's the unspoken truth: we're raising them to avoid versions of who we might have been at their age.

I remember a particular conversation with my middle daughter. She's the one who took my advice on dating quite literally, keeping her romantic life almost entirely under wraps. One day, I couldn't help but bring it up.

"You know," I said, "I don't see you bringing anyone around. No cookouts, no reunions, not even a Fourth of July picnic. What's going on? Are you even dating?"

She laughed, a little sheepishly, and said, "I've dated a few guys. Nothing serious. Nobody who resonates."

"Resonates?" I asked. "What does that mean?"

"Just... no one who feels right. No one who fits."

Her response intrigued me, so I pressed further. "Is it the dating scene? Or do you think the myth is true—there aren't any good men out there?"

"No," she said with confidence. "I think my standards are just high."

At first, I felt a sense of pride. Standards should be high. When you're looking for someone to spend your life with, expectations should be elevated. But what she said next floored me.
"I just haven't met anyone like you."

It stopped me in my tracks. Her words were both flattering and sobering. On one hand, there was immense pride in knowing that she saw me as a model of what a man should be. On the other hand, I felt a pang of sadness, because I understood the weight of her words.

I took a moment to absorb it before responding. "That's... a lot to carry, you know. I'm honored that you see me that way, but I also don't want that to make things harder for you."

She smiled, and we let the conversation hang for a moment. Then I said, "Let me tell you a story. It's about how your mother and I got together."

I told her about the first time I truly connected with her mother. I'd known her casually for a while, as a coworker and a friend in community spaces. But our interactions had always been surface-level, nothing that hinted at what was to come.

At the time, my life was in shambles. I'd just come out of a destructive relationship. My business had failed. My reputation in the community was bruised, and I was carrying the weight of isolation and broken trust. My circle of friends had grown smaller, and I was struggling to find my footing.

One afternoon, I ran into her mother outside a restaurant near where she worked. I don't even remember who I was with, or why I was there, but our paths crossed, and we started talking. She asked me how I was doing, and though I didn't share all the gory details, I was honest enough to let her know life wasn't great. She must have sensed the heaviness I was carrying, but instead of pity, she offered kindness. "We should get together sometime," she said casually.

I hesitated. "I'd like that, but to be honest, I'm not in a position to take you out the way you deserve. I'm in between jobs, and life's a bit chaotic right now."

Her response caught me off guard. "I'm not worried about all that," she said with a smile.

"Well," I said, half-joking, "I can offer you a peanut butter and jelly sandwich at my place. That's about all I've got."

She laughed and then said, "I like peanut butter and jelly."
That simple exchange changed everything. It wasn't just the words—it was the way she said them, with sincerity and ease, as if to say, "I see you, and that's enough."

So, she came over. We sat in my modest apartment, eating peanut butter and jelly sandwiches and drinking Kool-Aid, and we talked. We laughed. We shared pieces of ourselves.

There were no grand gestures, no extravagant plans—just two people connecting in the simplest, most genuine way.

As I told my daughter this story, I emphasized the lesson I wanted her to take away. "Sometimes," I said, "you have to be able to see the prince in the frog. Your mother saw something in me when I couldn't even see it in myself.

She looked past the warts and the failures and saw my potential. And because of that, I was able to grow into the man she believed I could be."

I told her about how her mother and I built our relationship, piece by piece, growing together through life's challenges. We didn't start with everything figured out. We had to navigate our own dysfunctions, past wounds, and uncertainties. But what made it work was our mutual commitment to see the best in each other and to bring out that best whenever possible.

Our love story wasn't about fairy tale moments or perfect circumstances. It was about two imperfect people choosing to build something meaningful together.

And as I reflected on that journey, I realized that love—real love—isn't about the initial spark or the butterflies. It's about the deep, abiding connection that grows over time.

> *When you love someone, truly love them, it transforms how you see the world. Their happiness becomes your priority. Their sadness feels like your own. Their victories are your greatest joys, and their struggles are battles you willingly fight by their side.*

I wanted my daughter to understand that love isn't always glamorous or easy. It's not about finding someone who checks every box or fits an ideal. It's about finding someone who makes you better, who challenges you, who sees the best in you even when you can't see it yourself.

"Your mother," I told her, "is the reason I am the man I am today. She saw the prince in the frog, and because of that, I was able to become who I was meant to be. That's the kind of love I want for you—not perfect, but real. A love that matters."

As I finished telling her the story, I could see the wheels turning in her mind. I don't know what her future holds or who she'll choose to share it with, but I hope that when the time comes, she'll remember this conversation. I hope she'll look for someone who sees her for who she truly is and who inspires her to be the best version of herself.

Because at the end of the day, love isn't just about romance. It's about purpose. It's about finding someone to walk the journey with, to build a life that reflects what truly matters. And that, more than anything, is the kind of love worth waiting for.

THE LEGACY IN THE BATON

One of the most profound lessons I've come to understand about life and leadership is knowing when and how to pass the baton. In the relay race of life, passing the baton is a delicate yet decisive act, one that requires full speed, trust, and seamless coordination.

It is a symbol of continuity, a shared understanding that the race is not ours alone to run. The mistake so many of us make—leaders, parents, visionaries alike—is holding on too tightly, too long, until the baton becomes more a weight than a tool of progress.

In this metaphorical race, the baton isn't just a tool; it's a symbol of legacy. It represents everything we've built, nurtured, and poured our lives into. Passing it is not just about relinquishing control but about entrusting someone else to carry forward the essence of who we are and what we've contributed to the world. It is about the continuation of vision, and more importantly, it's about legacy.

Bishop Darren Ferguson, a colleague, friend, and the Board Chair of Fathers Incorporated, shared a story that struck me deeply. Bishop Ferguson, a former mentee of the late Dr. Calvin A. Butts of the historic Abyssinian Baptist Church in Harlem, recounted a pivotal moment in leadership and legacy that I've carried with me ever since.

Dr. Butts was a giant of a man in the faith and community, a pillar whose leadership transformed Abyssinian Baptist Church into a beacon of hope and progress. He was the kind of leader you rarely come across—a visionary, a warrior for justice, and a man whose life's work touched countless people. But even giants must one day rest.

The story Bishop Ferguson told was one of reverence but also caution. Dr. Butts, despite his many accomplishments, clung to leadership well beyond his prime. His dedication was undeniable, his contributions immeasurable. Yet, as time took its inevitable toll, he could no longer run the race with the same vigor. By the time he was ready—or perhaps forced—to let go, it was too late. The baton had not been passed. Instead, it was held tightly until the very end, buried with him in the figurative sense.

The church he had so lovingly built was left in a state of uncertainty. Employees didn't know who would take over. Leadership was confused. The structure, so dependent on his presence, struggled to find its footing without him. They had to rebuild, essentially starting from scratch, because the baton had not been passed while the race was still in motion.

This story is a vivid reminder of the delicate balance between holding on and letting go. It is a cautionary tale about the dangers of waiting too long, of believing that holding onto the reins will somehow preserve our youth, our vitality, or our sense of purpose. It is a reminder that legacy is not in the act of holding but in the art of passing.

There is an almost primal fear among many of us—especially as we age—that letting go is akin to letting go of life itself. We tie our identity so deeply to what we've built, to the successes we've achieved, that the mere thought of stepping back feels like a kind of death.

And yet, what is a legacy if not something meant to outlive us, to thrive in the hands of those we have mentored, inspired, and guided?

Holding on to leadership, to influence, to control, doesn't keep us young. It doesn't even keep us relevant. What it does is stall the momentum of the race. Just because things won't be done the way we've done them doesn't mean they won't be done well—or even better. True wisdom is recognizing the potential in others, mentoring them, and equipping them to carry forward the vision in their own way.

I've seen this principle play out in my own life, both in the lessons I've learned from others and in the choices I've made myself. In the context of Fathers Incorporated, I've had to think deeply about what it means to build something that will last beyond me. The work we do is too important, too impactful, to hinge on one person. It must be bigger than me, sustained by the collective vision and the strength of those who will one day take up the baton.

This is not a lesson easily learned. The baton, after all, is deeply personal. It carries the weight of late nights, hard decisions, and sacrifices made along the way. It is a symbol of our blood, sweat, and tears, the culmination of years of dedication. But as much as it represents us, it is not ours to keep.

I think about my children when I consider legacy. My role as a father is not to hold on to them, to make them extensions of myself. It is to guide them, to prepare them, to pass the baton of life's lessons so they can run their own race. The same is true of leadership. The same is true of life.

I've often said that one of the most profound responsibilities we have as we grow older is to transition from being warriors to being wise generals. Warriors are in the trenches, fighting the battles, pushing forward. But wise generals step back. They strategize. They mentor. They guide the next generation of warriors, ensuring they are equipped to fight the battles of their time.

This transition is not about relinquishing relevance or resigning oneself to obscurity. It is about understanding that our impact is amplified through others. It is about recognizing that the seeds we plant in the lives of others will grow into legacies far greater than anything we could achieve alone.

As I reflect on my own journey, I recognize the critical importance of this transition. Over the next decade or so, I know I will encounter individuals—perhaps they are already in my life—who are ready to take the baton. My responsibility is to mentor them, to pour into them the knowledge and wisdom I have gained, to ensure they are equipped to carry the vision forward.

The beauty of legacy is that it is not diminished by being shared. In fact, it grows. By passing the baton while we are still running, we ensure that the race continues with momentum, with energy, with purpose. We ensure that what we have built does not crumble but thrives, adapting to the needs and challenges of a new generation.

Bishop Ferguson's story of Dr. Butts serves as both a warning and a call to action. It challenges us to reflect on our own lives and ask, "Am I holding on too tightly? Am I preparing the next generation to carry the vision forward?" It reminds us that legacy is not about us—it is about those who come after us.

In the relay race of life, passing the baton is not an act of surrender. It is an act of faith, an acknowledgment that the race is bigger than any one runner. It is an act of love, ensuring that those who come after us are equipped to succeed.

And so, as I think about my own baton—the work I've done, the lessons I've learned, the lives I've touched—I am reminded that my greatest legacy will not be in how tightly I held on, but in how gracefully I let go.

HEALTH AS LEGACY: THE WEIGHT OF WHAT WE CARRY

Health is one of those things that often feels invisible until it isn't. For so many of us, it exists in the background, unnoticed and unappreciated, until the moment it demands our attention.

But when we talk about living with purpose and pursuing what truly matters, health cannot be overlooked. It's more than a personal concern—it's a legacy, a thread woven through generations, carrying both the gifts and burdens of those who came before us.

I've come to see health as more than just the state of one's body. It's a connection, a lineage, a responsibility that extends beyond our individual lives. It's the genetic markers we pass on to our children, the habits and behaviors they witness, the lessons they absorb without ever realizing it. Health is, quite literally, life's foundation, and it's a foundation that can either strengthen or weaken the generations to come.

When I think back to my childhood in Crown Heights, Brooklyn, I see the early markers of health—both the blessings and the challenges. I had asthma, as did my brother and sister. It was something passed down, I believe, from my grandfather's side of the family. Our lives were punctuated by moments of breathlessness, inhalers, and trips to the emergency room. Kings County Hospital became a familiar place for me, particularly on the weekends when asthma episodes seemed to strike the hardest.

If you've never been to Kings County Hospital, let me paint you a picture. On a Saturday night, the emergency room felt like the set of a chaotic movie—people with gunshot wounds, stab wounds, parents cradling feverish children, doctors and nurses moving in controlled chaos. For a kid like me, sitting there in the midst of it all, it was overwhelming. But asthma had a way of jumping the line, especially for children.

I remember the relief of being rushed to the front, a mask placed over my face, the cool rush of oxygen easing my lungs. As much as those memories stay with me, they also remind me of how little I understood health as a legacy back then.

Asthma wasn't just my condition—it was part of my family's story, a thread that connected us across generations. Today, my son also has asthma. Thanks to advancements in medicine, it hasn't defined his life the way it sometimes defined mine, but it's a reminder that our health isn't just ours. It's a gift we pass on, for better or worse.

Health isn't only about genetics. It's also about behaviors, habits, and the culture we create within our families. Growing up in the 70s, physical activity wasn't something we scheduled or signed up for—it was simply how we lived.

There were no PlayStations or Xboxes keeping us inside. We had the schoolyard, and it was the epicenter of our social lives and our exercise routines.

I can still see it clearly—kids running everywhere, the air filled with the sound of laughter and shouts, sneakers pounding against asphalt. In the mornings, before school started, we'd gather in the schoolyard after breakfast.

For 30 to 40 minutes, we'd run, play tag, jump rope, and just let our energy spill out in every direction. After lunch, it was the same thing. More running, more playing, more movement.

It was a different time. Our parents didn't have to drag us outside—we couldn't wait to get out of the house. Saturdays and Sundays were spent playing stickball, freeze tag, handball, or just running around for the sheer joy of it. Our mothers would call us back inside only for dinner or when the streetlights came on. Those moments of play weren't just about fun—they were shaping our bodies, our stamina, and our understanding of what it meant to move and be alive.

But here's the thing: even in those simpler times, health wasn't something we actively thought about. We ate what was in front of us, whether it was nutritious or not. We didn't talk about choles-terol or blood pressure or the long-term impact of what we put in our bodies. Our youth felt invincible, and we lived like nothing could touch us.

That invincibility fades as you get older. By the time I hit my middle years, health became less of an abstract concept and more of a necessity. I needed my body to work. I needed it to provide for my family, to show up for my children, to be the anchor I wanted to be. But even then, it was easy to fall into patterns that weren't sustainable. Eating on the go, skipping exercise, ignoring the signs that my body was asking for more care.

Men and health have always had a complicated relationship. For many men, the very idea of focusing on health is often viewed as a concession, a sign of weakness, or even an inconvenience. It's the kind of thing that gets brushed off with phrases like, "I'm fine," or "It's nothing to worry about." There's a cultural narrative—one that's deeply ingrained—that to be a man is to be invincible, unshakeable, and unbreakable.

> *You're supposed to push through the pain, shake off the discomfort, and keep moving forward. And yet, that very narrative has cost so many men their lives.*

The truth is, men often wait until it's too late to address health concerns. I've seen it time and time again—friends, colleagues, even myself, brushing off warning signs until the issue becomes unavoidable.

There's an unspoken rule among men that if it's not visibly broken, bleeding, or falling off, then it doesn't need attention. And when we do finally seek help, it's often because someone else—our wife, our partner, our child—has pushed us to go to the doctor. Men tend to rely on external reminders, as though caring for our own health isn't something we're naturally entitled to do.

This mentality is especially dangerous in the Black community, where access to healthcare can already be limited by systemic barriers. For Black men, health often becomes an afterthought, overshadowed by the daily grind of providing, surviving, and navigating a world that doesn't always value our presence.

The stigma around vulnerability compounds the problem. To admit you're unwell, to show up in a doctor's office, is to admit you're not invincible. And for many men, that's a reality they'd rather avoid.

What's missing from the conversation is the understanding that strength isn't about ignoring your health—it's about taking charge of it. True strength lies in recognizing that your body, your mind, and your spirit are the vessels through which you live your purpose. It's not weakness to get your blood pressure checked, to schedule a prostate exam, to talk to someone about the weight you've been carrying in your heart.

It's courage. It's wisdom. It's love—not just for yourself, but for the people who depend on you.

As men, we owe it to ourselves to rewrite the script. Health is not the enemy; it's the ally. It's what allows us to be present for our families, to lead, to protect, to provide, and to live fully. It's time we stop seeing health as something that diminishes us and start seeing it as the foundation of everything we are and everything we hope to be.

Now, at 63, health feels like both a gift and a burden. I take my medications each night, those little pills that remind me of choices I made—or didn't make—decades ago. High blood pressure, prediabetes, cholesterol management—these are the realities of a body that has lived a full life but didn't always get the care it deserved.

And yet, I'm here. I'm here, and I'm learning. I'm learning to listen to my body in ways I never did before. I'm learning to see health not just as a personal concern but as a legacy I owe to my children and grandchildren.

When I think about my grandchildren, I think about the responsibility I have to them—not just to be around, but to be present, to be engaged, to be healthy enough to leave them with stories, wisdom, and love.

> ***Proverbs 13:22 says, "A good man leaves an inheritance to his children's children." That inheritance isn't just about money or possessions. It's about health, knowledge, and the example we set.***

Health isn't just about what we do for ourselves. It's about what we pass on. It's about teaching our children to prioritize their well-being, to move their bodies, to eat with intention, to rest when they need it. It's about breaking cycles of neglect, ignorance, and avoidance.

And it's not just physical health—it's mental health, too. In communities like mine, mental health has long been stigmatized. Words like "crazy" were thrown around carelessly, and seeking help was often seen as a sign of weakness. But mental health is just as critical as physical health. Stress, anxiety, depression—these are burdens that can weigh us down, affect our families, and ripple through generations if left unaddressed.

As I look back on my life and think about the lessons I want to leave behind, health stands out as one of the most important. It's not something to take for granted, not something to put off until tomorrow. It's a daily commitment, a legacy we build with every choice we make.

For the young people reading this, I hope you'll take this to heart. Pay attention to your health now, not later. Exercise, eat well, rest, and take care of your mind as well as your body. For those of us who are more seasoned, it's never too late to make changes. Every small step matters.

Health is a cornerstone of life. It's the foundation upon which we build our families, pursue our dreams, and create our legacies. It's what allows us to live with purpose, to show up for the people we love, and to leave the world better than we found it. It matters. It has always mattered. And it will always matter.

WHEN PASSION AND FAITH LEADS YOUR LIFE

What do you do when one morning God wakes you up and starts your day by saying, "They will hear my voice in your silence and see my power in your actions"? Those words, simple yet profound, left me sitting at the edge of my bed, the morning light not yet cutting through the curtains. It was the kind of moment where clarity hits, but not with the thunderclap of certainty—more like a whisper that resonates in the corners of your soul.

The world moves so fast. Today, we're saturated with feelings about all kinds of things, each emotion pulling us toward decisions that either solidify our purpose or stray us further away from it. But even amidst the noise, we feel that stirring—that undeniable urge to pause and check in with the source of those feelings. "God, is that you?" we ask, almost breathless. The battle between divine conviction and personal justification is relentless. Some call it conscience, others an inner voice.

For me, it's the Holy Spirit—that quiet, persistent guide we often mistake for our own musings.

Growing up, this battle was a familiar one. Saturday mornings often found me glued to the cartoon antics of Looney Tunes. Remember the scenes where a character had a devil on one shoulder and an angel on the other? They argued incessantly, each trying to sway the character one way or another.

Life felt like that. Small decisions, big decisions—each moment came with the pull of influences that demanded attention and action.

Those voices drive more than just decisions; they stir passions. Whether it's how we dress, who we love, or the work we do, there's a voice shaping the intention behind every action. It whispers about the stranger in line at the supermarket, the colleague who slighted you years ago, or even the person sitting next to you on the plane. But amidst the chaos of these competing voices lies the quiet directive of purpose.

Years ago, I worked in an office where conversations spilled over cubicle walls. They were like tiny windows into people's lives. In that sea of voices, there was one man I'll never forget. He often muttered to himself, not loudly, just low enough to be noticed.

At first, I thought he was on the phone or maybe rehearsing an important presentation. But one day, I walked by his desk and realized he wasn't speaking to anyone but himself. He wasn't crazy; he was contemplative.

"It's okay to talk to yourself," they say, "as long as you don't answer back."

But maybe he wasn't talking to himself. Maybe he was talking to God—a conversation so personal, so sacred, that it didn't require an audience. Watching him, I began to understand that passion isn't always loud or demonstrative. Sometimes, it's quiet—a fire that smolders in the silence, waiting for the right breath of wind to ignite it.

Passion isn't born fully formed. It's a process, a cycle that reveals itself over time. Awareness, when you begin to feel the nudge, the tug of something greater calling you. Grinding, when you pour yourself into it, struggling, learning, and refining your purpose. Shedding, when you let go of distractions and doubts, peeling away what doesn't serve the mission.

Awakening, when clarity emerges and you step fully into the understanding of your calling. Resonating, when your passion begins to ripple outward, touching others and amplifying its reach.

The greatest motivators of legacy and impact are tied to the realization that life isn't about fleeting recognition but meaningful contribution. You've heard it said, "How can you find comfort in living if you don't have something worthwhile to die for?"

That question has anchored me on many sleepless nights. Legacy isn't built on applause; it's built on action.

I think of a quote by Roald Dahl: "If you are interested in something, no matter what it is, go at it full speed ahead. Embrace it with both arms, hug it, love it, and above all become passionate about it." Dahl's words resonate deeply because passion isn't lukewarm. It's not content with half-measures. It's white-hot, unapologetically fervent.

Purpose builds legacy, and legacy shapes the future. But purpose often begins in small, personal moments of surrender. For me, it began the day I stopped wrestling with God's whispers and started letting them guide my actions.

There's a difference between striving and aligning—one exhausts you; the other sustains you. When you align your life with divine purpose, you're not just working; you're building.

Years ago, Pastor Tre, my previous pastor in New York, said, "I served my way into position." Those words struck me because they encapsulated the quiet truth of greatness. True leadership, true impact, begins with service. It's not about climbing ladders or demanding recognition. It's about showing up, time and time again, to do the work God has placed before you.

This truth has been a cornerstone of my journey. I've learned that the loudest expressions of purpose aren't in speeches or accolades. They're in the silent actions that ripple through generations.

They're in the way you show up for your family, your community, and the strangers who cross your path. Purpose isn't about being seen; it's about being felt.

The morning God woke me with those words—"They will hear my voice in your silence and see my power in your actions"—was the morning I stopped questioning His call. That's the thing about purpose: it doesn't require fanfare. It requires faith.

When you lean into it, you become a vessel through which something far greater than yourself can flow. So, what do you do when God whispers purpose into your ear? You answer. Not with words, but with action. You let His voice guide your silence, and you let His power speak through your life. In doing so, you create a legacy that changes the world—not with noise, but with resonance.

WHEN ECHOES FADE: THE QUIET PAIN OF WHAT CANNOT RETURN

There's a strange silence that comes with age. It's not the silence of an empty room or a paused conversation—it's deeper than that.

171

It's the silence of things lost, of moments that will never return, of echoes that once resonated loudly but now fade into the background like whispers in the wind. It's a silence that speaks not of absence, but of transformation, of the inevitable changes that time insists upon.

I used to think of death as a singular event. A moment when the heart stops, when breath ceases, when life gives way to stillness. But as I've grown older, I've come to understand that death is rarely so definitive. Death is a process. It is the slow unraveling of what once was, the gradual departure of the things that tether us to our youth, to our strength, to the world as we knew it.

It starts small. A forgotten name, a misplaced item, a moment of confusion that you laugh off at first. "Getting old," you joke, as though humor can soften the sharp edge of reality. But the moments accumulate. You begin to notice the way your knees creak when you stand, the way your muscles resist the movements that once felt effortless. You notice the way recovery takes longer, the way sleep feels less restorative, the way your body becomes a map of aches and limitations.

And then there are the other losses. The ones that aren't so easily laughed away. The friends who no longer call because they're no longer here. The places that once held memories but now stand empty, their walls echoing with the ghosts of laughter and love. The traditions that fade because the people who carried them forward are gone, leaving you to wonder if you should pick up the mantle or let it rest.

I remember the first time I truly felt the weight of this kind of death. It wasn't at a funeral, though I've been to plenty. It was in the quiet of my own home, standing in front of a mirror.

I was looking at myself—really looking—and for the first time, I didn't recognize the man staring back. My hair, once jet black, had surrendered to gray. The lines on my face told stories I hadn't consented to share. My shoulders, once broad and proud, slumped under the weight of years. It wasn't vanity that struck me in that moment; it was the realization that the version of myself I'd always known was slipping away. That was a kind of death I hadn't prepared for.

But physical changes are only part of the story. The deeper pain comes from the death of things that can't be touched but are felt in every fiber of your being. The death of dreams you've outgrown or abandoned. The death of relationships that once defined you but now exist only in memory. The death of opportunities you let pass, either because you didn't recognize them for what they were or because you were too afraid to seize them.

And then there's memory itself. Oh, how cruelly it can betray you. I've spent hours searching for a word, a name, a detail that once came easily to mind. The frustration is maddening. It's not just the inconvenience of forgetfulness—it's the fear of losing pieces of yourself, of losing the ability to frame your life in the context of your experiences. Without memory, who are we? What becomes of the stories we've carried, the lessons we've learned, the love we've shared?

I think often about my mother, who is now 85 years old. She is still sharp in many ways, though time has slowed her just a bit. Her wit remains intact, even as moments of forgetfulness creep in.

Recently, she came to visit, and I had the chance to witness her joy in a way I hadn't seen in years. My mother is a die-hard New York Mets fan, and it just so happened that both the Mets and the Atlanta Braves were battling for first place in their division during her visit. I decided to take her to a game—a small gesture, but one that revealed so much about life and time.

As we arrived at the stadium, I noticed the long walk from the car to the entrance. Though my mother is still mobile, I found myself worrying about whether the distance would be too much for her. Once inside, I fretted over the steepness of the steps leading to our seats. But as we settled in and the game began, all those worries faded. My mother's face lit up when I handed her a bag of popcorn, her smile stretching wide as she watched the players on the field. It struck me then that this might have been her first live Mets game.

Growing up in Brooklyn, she'd spent countless hours watching games on television, but this was different. I saw in her eyes the joy of reliving a piece of her youth, of connecting with a simpler time when baseball was the heartbeat of her community.

On the drive home, she began telling me a story. I can't recall all the details now, but what stood out was how she repeated it. She started and ended in the same place each time, as though the story was a circle she couldn't quite break out of. It was a bittersweet moment. I was reminded of her age, of the inevitability of time, but I was also grateful.

Here she was, at 82, still able to walk to a stadium, to savor popcorn, to share stories—even if they looped in repetition. I found myself thinking that if I could carry even half of her resilience and joy into my later years, I would be blessed.

There is a Star Trek: Enterprise episode that often comes to mind when I reflect on the nature of memory, time, and the things we lose along the way. In the episode, the crew encounters a derelict ship, its inhabitants suspended in cryonic stasis. These people had frozen themselves in hopes that future medical advancements could cure their ailments. The premise is both fascinating and sobering. Three individuals are revived, their illnesses cured, but they awaken to a world that is completely unrecognizable. Their families are gone, their culture has evolved beyond what they knew, and the memories they cherished have become relics of a forgotten past.

The revived individuals grapple with a haunting truth: while their bodies have been preserved, their lives as they knew them have ended. The people and places that gave them a sense of belonging have vanished. The episode underscores a profound reality about life and aging: even if we could pause the physical decline, we cannot stop the world from moving forward without us. We cannot hold onto the echoes of our past forever.

This story feels relevant not because it mirrors my mother's experience, but because it highlights the delicate balance between preserving the past and embracing the present. Watching my mother at the game, I saw someone deeply rooted in her history yet fully alive in the moment. It reminded me that while time may take away certain things—youth, strength, even clarity—it cannot rob us of the joy we choose to experience here and now.

And maybe that's the lesson we're meant to learn as we age: how to let go. How to mourn the things we've lost without letting that mourning consume us. How to honor what's gone while still embracing what remains. How to find beauty in the echoes, even as they fade.

The truth is, we are always dying. From the moment we take our first breath, we are moving toward an end we cannot escape. But we are also always living. Every moment, every choice, every connection is an affirmation of life, a declaration that we are here, that we matter, that we are part of something greater than ourselves.

I don't fear death, not in the way I once did. What I fear is not having lived fully enough, not having loved deeply enough, not having left behind a legacy that speaks to the truth of who I was. And so, I choose to live—not in denial of death, but in defiance of it. I choose to see the beauty in the wrinkles, the wisdom in the gray, the strength in the scars. I choose to cherish the moments I have, knowing that they are fleeting but precious.

Because even as echoes fade, they leave behind a resonance. A vibration that lingers, that shapes the world in ways we may never fully understand. And perhaps that is the greatest gift of all: to know that even when we are gone, a part of us remains. In the memories we've created, the love we've shared, the lives we've touched.

So here's my advice, for what it's worth: Live your life unapologetically. Embrace the mess, the beauty, the heartbreak, the joy. Leave nothing unsaid, nothing undone. And when the time comes to let go, do so with grace, knowing that you have lived well, that your echoes will linger, that your life mattered. Because it does. It always has. And it always will.

THE INVISIBLE BRIDGE: FAITH AS THE PATH TO BELIEF

There is a certain stillness that overtakes a room when someone asks, "What do you believe in?" It's not the stillness of quiet reflection but the loaded pause of vulnerability. Because to answer that question honestly is to reveal the core of yourself—your fears, your hopes, your very essence. And if you're not careful, the weight of that question can pin you to the floor.

I've found myself in countless conversations about faith, where the word itself seems to rise like an insurmountable mountain between two people. For some, faith is an anchor—firm, unyielding. For others, it's a whisper of doubt, a fog that never quite lifts.

176

But regardless of where you stand, faith demands something from you: belief in the intangible.

To believe in faith, you have to confront the unseen. You have to trust the bridge that you can't touch, the path that you can't see. And yet, the paradox of faith is this: even as it asks you to trust in the unseen, it insists that your actions, your works, give substance to what is intangible.

Faith is not a quiet thing; it's a verb. It moves. It builds. It becomes.

The words of James 2:14-26 echo in my mind whenever I think about faith: "Faith without works is dead." This isn't just scripture; it's the heartbeat of what it means to live fully, to give life to the things you believe in. Because faith, without action, is like a bridge you never step on. And what good is a bridge if it doesn't take you somewhere?

I'll never forget the day my family and I decided to take a leap of faith that would redefine everything we knew about ourselves. We were living in Albany, New York, a place that had become both a comfort and a cage. The ceilings in my life felt too low, the opportunities too scarce. I looked at my children, growing up in an environment that no longer felt expansive enough for their potential, and I knew we needed a change.

The kind of change that rattles your foundation.

Atlanta became the dream. A city where ceilings seemed to stretch skyward, where opportunities felt abundant, and where we could start fresh. But dreams don't come without cost. At the time, Fathers Incorporated was tethered to a federal contract that provided our primary income. The contract was up for renewal, and the rebid process was fraught with uncertainty.

The first time we bid for the contract, it felt like a battle on all fronts. Personal attacks, professional challenges, and betrayal from people I thought were allies turned what should have been a moment of triumph into a test of resilience.

And yet, there we were, contemplating a move to Atlanta without knowing if the contract would be renewed. Without knowing if the income that sustained our family, our organization, our dreams would continue. It was the kind of uncertainty that could paralyze a person. But we moved anyway. We packed our lives into boxes, gathered our courage, and stepped onto the bridge of faith, trusting it would hold us.

The first weeks in Atlanta were surreal. The city felt alive in a way Albany never had. But beneath the surface of that excitement was a quiet, persistent fear. What if the contract didn't come through? What if we had uprooted our lives for nothing? Each morning, I'd wake up and look out at the Atlanta skyline, searching for reassurance in its silhouette. And every morning, I'd remind myself: "Faith without works is dead. Keep working."

The contract was renewed. When the call came through, it felt like a floodgate of relief opening all at once. But the true gift wasn't just the contract itself. It was the realization that we had chosen faith over fear and found our way to the other side.

Faith, I've learned, is not a one-time decision. It's a daily practice, a commitment to believe in something bigger than your circumstances. And perhaps most importantly, it's a muscle that grows with use. The more you step out on the invisible bridge, the more you trust that it will hold you.

I think about this often when I'm working with fathers who have been incarcerated. These men—some of whom have spent decades defined by their worst mistakes—are asked to step out onto a bridge of faith every single day. Society doesn't make it easy. We label them with words that imprison them long after the bars have disappeared: convict, criminal, ex-con. But when you strip away those labels and replace them with words like returning citizen, you begin to see the person beneath the stigma. You begin to see the faith it takes to rebuild a life from the ground up.

Freedom, in its truest sense, is as much a state of mind as it is a physical condition. And faith is the engine of that freedom. It's the belief that your current circumstances are not your permanent reality. It's the hope that even in the silence of your most desperate moments, there is a voice calling you forward. My mother, God bless her soul, taught me more about faith than any scripture ever could. She was a woman of unshakable belief, the kind of belief that comes from necessity. We were in church almost every day of the week, and while I resented it as a child, I see now how deeply those roots of faith were planted. My mother's faith wasn't just about religion; it was about resilience. It was about believing that there was a way, even when every door seemed closed.

She believed in the power of hope, a power that resonates deeply in my own life. Hope, after all, is faith's twin. When Barack Obama launched his first presidential campaign, the word "hope" became a rallying cry for a nation. But as he often reminded us, hope is not passive. It's not wishful thinking. Hope requires action. It demands that you plant seeds, even when you can't see the harvest.

As I sit here, reflecting on the many leaps of faith that have defined my life, I am struck by one undeniable truth: faith is not about certainty. It's about trust. It's about believing that the things you cannot see, the things you cannot touch, are just as real as the ground beneath your feet. And it's about understanding that the bridge you step onto is built not just by your belief, but by your willingness to work.

So I ask you: What bridges are you standing before today? What leap of faith are you hesitating to take? Whatever it is, know this: the bridge will hold you. But you have to take the first step. And as you do, let your faith guide your works, and let your works give life to your faith.

Because in the end, it's not about what you believe. It's about how you live it.

CHAPTER SEVEN

EMBRACING THE TRANSITION: FROM RELEVANT WARRIOR TO WISE GENERAL

THE TRANSITION: FROM RELEVANT WARRIOR TO WISE GENERAL

There comes a time in every seasoned person's life when the echo of the past calls louder than the noise of the present. It's not an intrusion—it's an invitation, one that whispers, "Reflect on who you've been to understand who you are." Lately, I've been sitting with this idea, contemplating the journey from being a Relevant Warrior to stepping into the role of a Wise General.

My life has been marked by battles, some fierce and external, others silent and internal. The warrior in me fought for relevance—for a voice in rooms that would have otherwise ignored me, for validation in spaces that didn't see my worth. The warrior is instinctual, reactive, charging forward with passion and energy. But the general? The general is calculated, intentional, reflective. And here's the hard truth: the world rarely tells you when it's time to transition. It simply waits to see if you'll recognize the call.

This journey has been marked by names—nicknames, to be exact. Each one, like a breadcrumb, tells a story about a moment in my life, about who I was and how the world saw me at that time. People close to me call me "KB," a straightforward shorthand for my name. It's simple, almost unassuming, but it's also intimate. When someone calls me KB, I know they're part of my circle— they've earned the right to that familiarity.

But then there's "DJ Quiet Storm." That name is a time capsule, a remnant of my younger years when I was a professional DJ. I started spinning records in high school, the music flowing through me like a second language. The name was given to me by a friend who said, "Man, you're like a quiet storm.

You're a force—strong, deliberate—but at the same time, there's a calmness about you. People don't see you coming until you're already there." The name stuck, and I carried it through my years as a DJ. It was more than a name; it was an identity. It captured a duality in me—a powerful presence wrapped in quiet restraint.

Then there's "Braz." It's funny how people just seem to gravitate toward shortening "Braswell," cutting it down to "Braz" or even "Brazie." It's a name that comes with a laugh, a nod, a sense of camaraderie.

Even people who don't know me well seem to land on it naturally, as if the name itself carries an unspoken invitation to familiarity. It's light, playful, but it also holds weight. It's a reminder that sometimes, the simplest names carry the most history.

But of all the names I've been called, none has intrigued me as much as "General." It was Shawn Dove who first spoke it into existence. "What's up, General?" he said, like it was already written. At first, I didn't know how to live up to it.

A general is a leader, a strategist, someone who carries the weight of others on their shoulders. I wasn't sure I was ready for that. I wasn't sure I deserved it. But Shawn saw something in me I hadn't yet seen in myself. He saw the battles I had fought, the wisdom I had gained, and the way others began to look to me for guidance. He saw the general long before I did.

The nickname took on a life of its own. Soon, others in my circle were calling me General too. And with every mention, I felt the weight of it, the responsibility it carried. It wasn't just a name—it was a reflection of who I was becoming. The warrior in me bristled at the idea of stepping back, of trading instinct for strategy, of slowing down to see the bigger picture. But the general in me knew it was time.

A warrior fights battles, but a general fights wars. And wars are not won by brute strength alone—they are won by strategy, by patience, by understanding the bigger picture. Battles are about survival, but wars are about purpose. A warrior focuses on the immediate threat; a general focuses on the ultimate goal.

This transition is not just about age or experience—it's about perspective. It's about realizing that the lessons of the battles you've fought were not for the fight itself but for the wisdom they imparted. It's about understanding that every scar is a map, every loss a teacher.

A warrior charges headfirst into the fray, driven by adrenaline and instinct. The battle is in front of them, immediate and urgent, and they fight with everything they've got. But the general steps back.

The general surveys the battlefield, not just to see the fight but to understand the terrain, the resources, the timing. A warrior is focused on the opponent before them; a general is thinking three steps ahead, considering not just this battle but the next one, and the one after that.

A warrior thrives on action, on momentum, on the thrill of combat. They are the heartbeat of the fight, the energy that drives it forward. But a general? A general is the mind behind the movement. They plan, they strategize, they anticipate. The warrior asks, "What can I do right now to win?" The general asks, "What must be done to win it all?"

The warrior relies on strength, speed, and precision. Their victories are measured in moments, in immediate outcomes. The general relies on wisdom, patience, and vision. Their victories are measured in legacies, in the lasting impact of their decisions. A warrior's focus is narrow, but intense—a laser beam slicing through the chaos.

A general's focus is broad, encompassing not just the fight but the people fighting, the resources they need, and the purpose they serve.

And perhaps the most profound difference is this: a warrior fights for themselves. Even when their cause is noble, their fight is personal—proving their worth, their strength, their capability. A general fights for others. Their focus is on the soldiers, the civilians, the people who will benefit from their leadership. A general understands that their role is not to be the strongest, but to bring out the strength in others.

As I navigate this transition, I carry with me the wisdom of the battles I've fought, the names I've been given, and the lessons I've learned. Because this is what it means to become a Wise General:

184

to see the war as more than just a series of battles, to understand the purpose behind the fight, and to lead with grace, wisdom, and a steady hand.

The warrior in me will always be there—a fire that cannot be extinguished. But the general in me knows that fire must be tempered, guided, and used with purpose. And in this season of my life, I choose to lead with clarity, to strategize with intention, and to carry the weight of the general with honor. Because in the end, it's not about the battles I've won—it's about the lives I've touched, the wisdom I've shared, and the legacy I leave behind.

GUARDING THE LEGACY: A GENERAL'S STRATEGY FOR SUSTAINING WHAT MATTERS

The evolution from warrior to general is marked by a deliberate shift in perspective. It's a transition that requires more than just time—it demands reflection, discipline, and a recalibration of priorities. As a warrior, the focus is on the fight—on the immediate, the urgent, the battle at hand. But as a general, the vision broadens.

The battlefield is no longer the defining space; it's the strategy room, the map table, the long view that takes precedence. And with this shift comes the recognition of what must be guarded above all else.

In this season of my life, I've learned that leadership—true leadership—is not just about winning battles. It's about safeguarding what matters most. It's about protecting the things that sustain us, define us, and empower us to keep going.

This is where my focus now lies: not on the fleeting victories of the moment, but on the enduring legacies we build over time.

And that begins with a principle I hold close: protect the business, protect the brand.

As I've gotten older, one of the most valuable lessons I've learned is the importance of protecting the business and the brand. Now, I'm not just talking about business in the narrow sense of the word—like a company or an organization—I'm talking about anything in your life that you hold dear. For some people, business is their literal business; for others, it's their job, their passion, their family, or even their health. For me, I've come to use the term "business" as a way to describe everything that requires protection, nurturing, and vigilance in my life.

This idea didn't come to me overnight. It's something I've learned over time, from both successes and failures, as I've built my career and my life. When I was younger, I thought protecting the business was just about setting boundaries—knowing who could come into my space, how far they could go, and how long they could stay. But as I've matured, I've realized that protecting the business is about so much more than that. It's about making sure that no one can infiltrate or disrupt the things I've worked so hard to build.

The business might be your career, your family, or your personal passion. It might be your physical health, like it is for an athlete, or your voice, like it is for a singer. Whatever it is, we all have something that needs to be protected because it sustains us. It's the thing that provides for us, the thing that represents who we are, and the thing that helps us navigate through life. And it's our responsibility to protect it.

I often tell my employees, "Protect the business." I stress this not just as a professional standard but as a life philosophy. Don't leave blind spots. Don't let anyone or anything come in and take from you, break you down, or disrupt what you've built.

Whether it's your finances, your career, your family, or your peace of mind, everything requires stewardship.

There's a scripture that speaks about being a good steward over what you have before God determines you can handle more. I think about that often. To be a good steward, you have to maintain control over your business, no matter what form it takes. People may not see things the way you do, or they may not care for your business the way you care for it, but that doesn't change your responsibility to protect it.

It's like a singer who has to protect their voice. They can't be around smokers, or in places where they have to yell, or eat foods that damage their vocal cords. An athlete's body is their business; they can't afford to take risks that might injure them because their body is what sustains their career. It's the same for any of us.

We have to protect what we rely on—whether it's our mind, our health, or our passion—because without it, we're vulnerable.

I've seen what happens when people fail to protect their business. I've watched leaders hold on to power for too long, thinking they were invincible, only to leave their legacy in ruins. They didn't protect what mattered, and in the end, it cost them. And then there are those who come into your business thinking they are more valuable than you are. They'll tell you, "If it wasn't for me, this wouldn't have happened."

But the truth is, no one builds anything alone. You provided the opportunity, you built the environment, and you deserve all the credit for that.

You have to protect your business from people who will try to claim credit for your success, and from those who don't have the same investment in it as you do. Not everyone who works for you cares about your business the way you do. Some are just there for a paycheck, some because they have nowhere else to go. That's why setting boundaries and standards is essential. Protect your finances, your time, and your energy. Don't let anyone come in and diminish your efforts.

But protecting the business isn't just about the day-to-day operations. It's about protecting your mental health, your sanity. The hardest part of running any business, or even just managing life, is dealing with people. People can be the most destructive force in your environment, whether through competition, jealousy, or simply not understanding your vision. They'll test you, push you, and sometimes, they'll even attack what you've built.

Then there's the brand. To me, the brand is the essence of who you are. It's how people think of you, how they talk about you when you're not in the room. Your brand is a reflection of your values, your work ethic, your passion.

It's the lasting impression you leave on the world.

I've always told myself, and those around me, to protect the brand. Don't allow anything or anyone to damage the integrity of who you are or what you represent. Your brand is what people associate with your name, with your business, with your legacy. And sometimes, protecting the brand means saying no to opportunities that don't align with your values, or letting go of people who don't respect the standards you've set.

Take Michael Jordan, for example. His brand is excellence—never giving up, holding people accountable, striving for greatness. That's the brand he's built, and it's how people think of him. Magic Johnson has a different kind of brand—one of pulling people together, compassion, and leadership. Both men built brands that reflect who they are at their core, and their brands speak for them long before they even walk into a room.

As I've gotten older, protecting my business and my brand has become more than just a professional necessity. It's become a personal standard. It's how I've learned to protect my peace of mind, my integrity, and my legacy. Running a business is an isolated experience. People who aren't entrepreneurs don't understand the sacrifices you make to protect something that seems intangible to them. They don't see the hours you work, the holidays you miss, or the stress you carry.

But as an entrepreneur, your business and your brand become extensions of who you are. They are the foundation of everything you've built.

In the end, the wisdom I've gained from my experiences can be summed up in one simple lesson: protect the business, protect the brand. Your business might be your literal business, your health, your family, or your passion. Whatever it is, it's yours to nurture and protect. And your brand? That's your legacy. It's how people will remember you long after you've left the room.

PROTECTING THE MISSION, DREAMING AS GENERALS

When I came back home from the military, I wasn't just lost—I was untethered. Not the kind of lost where you can't find your way home, but the kind where you don't know who you are or where you belong. The Army had given me structure, purpose, and direction—every part of my life was mapped out.

From what to wear to where to be, every decision was made for me. But stepping back into civilian life was like stepping into a battlefield with no map, no mission, and no commanding officer.

Suddenly, it was all on me: to take care of myself, my wife, my daughter. And I wasn't ready.

I remember having a conversation with my brother before he went into Desert Storm. After praying for his safety, I told him two things that had played a role in my own financial struggles after serving. The first was the way our mother handled money. She worked tirelessly to make sure we had what we needed, always finding a way to stretch every dollar.

But she never had the chance to teach me about saving, planning, or thinking beyond the next paycheck. Watching her hustle was like learning to swim by standing on the shore—I saw the effort, but I never learned the stroke.

The second was the military itself. The Army had been a safety net—housing, food, healthcare, and even extra allowances if you were married. It took care of everything, so when I came back home, I didn't know how to take care of myself.

I hadn't been taught how to build a foundation outside of the military, how to navigate the real world, or how to provide for my family without the structure of the Army. I stepped off the battle-field, but I wasn't equipped to be the general of my own life.

I had to start somewhere. I still remember sitting in a workforce skills development program, writing down my goals for the next ten years. At 20, I aimed to make $20,000 a year. By 30, $30,000. By 40, $40,000. Back then, that seemed like an audacious dream for someone with no degree and only a GED. At the time, I thought I was setting the bar high. But now, looking back, I realize I was still thinking like a soldier—focused on survival and immediate goals—not like a general, who sees the entire battlefield and plans for the future.

Back then, I didn't dream of owning a home, starting a business, or sending my kids to private school. Those ideas weren't even on my radar. Growing up in Brooklyn, we didn't talk about things like generational wealth or building empires. Our focus was getting through the day, not planning for the decades.

But a general must learn to adjust strategy, and I've come to understand the value of dreaming bigger. What if I'd been taught to think beyond the immediate? To plan for what could be instead of what was? It's not just about what I didn't know back then—it's about how I've used those lessons to shape the man I am today. Running my own business, I understand now that protecting the mission isn't just about financial stability. It's about safeguarding the things that matter most: my family, my peace, and my purpose.

Protecting the mission means thinking like a general—anticipating challenges, fortifying your resources, and making decisions with wisdom and clarity. It means showing my kids that their lives can be more than just reacting to what's in front of them. I teach them to think beyond the block they grew up on, to see the world as full of opportunities instead of obstacles.

That's why I take them traveling, expose them to different cultures, and show them possibilities I never imagined at their age. I want them to dream like generals—not just of surviving the fight, but of building something worth protecting.

People often say, "I wish I knew then, what I know now." And while there's truth in that, I don't dwell on it. Instead, I focus on what I can do with what I've learned. Every morning, I wake up and pray for purpose. I ask God to guide me because as long as I have purpose, I'm still in the fight. And as a general, the fight isn't about me—it's about those I'm leading, those who depend on me to see beyond the immediate.

I still think about those early days—the small dreams and the narrow vision. But more than that, I think about how to pave a path forward for my family, my community, and the next generation of warriors. I want them to know they don't have to wait to think bigger or dream beyond what they've been taught to expect.

They can step into their roles as generals now—commanding their lives with vision, wisdom, and purpose.

The lesson is clear: Protect the mission, dream like a general, and never stop advancing. The battlefield may change, but the strategy remains the same.

Keep moving forward, with the next generation in mind and a legacy worth defending in your heart.

THE APEX OF STRATEGIC VISION: THINKING LIKE A GENERAL

As you read this book, I want to remind you why I'm sharing these stories. They might seem like scattered memories or moments that don't fit neatly into why I've stopped caring or why I feel like I'm too seasoned to care anymore. But trust me, every story is a part of the map that led me here.

Each moment laid the foundation for who I am now, transitioning from a warrior fighting to survive to a general strategizing to thrive. These aren't just memories—they're lessons, turning points, and battle plans that shaped the way I see the world and the life I'm building.

Take this moment right here. It's about learning from the past—about protecting the mission and ensuring the legacy. For years, I struggled with finding mentorship. It was hard to find someone who could guide me through uncharted territory because I was constantly evolving.

You've probably heard the saying, "If you're the smartest person in the room, you need to find a new room." Growing up, I also heard, "Show me your five closest friends, and I'll show you your future." We become reflections of the people we surround ourselves with, and those people either sharpen us for battle or dull our edge.

For me, though, it was always difficult to find someone who felt like a true general—someone who had walked the same path, faced the same challenges, and carried the same weight. Maybe that's why, for so long, I kept thinking like a soldier.

I kept my goals small and manageable because dreaming big felt like walking into battle without armor. Small dreams make life easier. They don't demand as much risk or require as much sacrifice.

I'll never forget a conversation I had with someone I worked with years ago. He used to say, "My biggest hope is to live long enough to see my reality exceed my dreams." At the time, I couldn't wrap my head around it. How could your reality ever surpass your dreams? But looking back, I see the truth in those words. When your dreams are small, it doesn't take much for life to outpace them.

No one ever pushed me to think bigger. No one handed me the map to navigate the uncharted terrain of my potential. So, I stayed in my comfort zone, thinking small, dreaming cautiously, and keeping my head down. But generals don't win wars by playing it safe. I had to learn to take command of my own life, to step out of the narrow confines of what I thought was possible and into a larger vision for my future.

Mentorship was elusive for me because I didn't understand if mentors were found or if they found you. Over time, I've realized that mentors aren't perfect—they're not meant to be.

They're guides, not saviors. I've had people come into my life who showed me glimpses of what was possible, who shifted my thinking in ways that made me grow. They weren't traditional generals, but they had strategies I could borrow, and that made all the difference.

One of the greatest lessons I've learned is that striving for excellence moves you from thinking like a warrior to thinking like a general. Excellence isn't just about winning the battle in front of you; it's about preparing for the long campaign.

It's about holding yourself to a standard that reveals who is ready to march beside you and who isn't. When you live with excellence, you don't have to question the loyalty or competence of your troops. The ones who can't match your discipline, your vision, or your accountability will show themselves—and that's okay.

Not everyone is meant to fight at your side.

For a long time, I felt guilty about this. Guilty for wanting more, for raising the bar, for outgrowing people who weren't ready to rise to the challenge. But here's what I've come to understand: generals don't apologize for leading. They don't shrink their vision to make others comfortable. And they don't limit the size of their dreams because someone else lacks the capacity to see them.

Excellence exposes everything—weaknesses, strengths, opportunities, and risks. When you strive for it, you set a standard that ensures the people around you are either sharpening you or stepping aside. It's not selfish; it's strategic. Because protecting the mission and achieving the vision requires focus, discipline, and clarity.

The size of my dream isn't contingent upon who believes in it. The work I do to fulfill that dream is my responsibility alone.

And I've learned that the size of my dream can't be limited by the way you see me. As a general, my dreams must be vast, not for my sake alone but for the sake of those who follow. I'm not just strategizing for myself—I'm building a legacy that will outlast me.

So, if you find yourself in a place where your dreams feel small or your circle feels limiting, remember this: generals don't settle for surviving the skirmish. They plan for the victory that reshapes the entire battlefield. Dream bigger. Lead boldly. And never apologize for aiming higher than the world expects. The journey from warrior to general demands it.

REDEFINING THE LEGACY: FROM ENDANGERED SPECIES TO WISE GENERALS

"Kenny, we have an opportunity here, and I don't think we can afford to miss it," Bishop Darren Ferguson told me, his voice carrying that familiar mix of conviction and urgency. "You see, Black men like us were never bred to grow old. Historically, we've been labeled an 'endangered species,' cut down too soon, not given the tools or insights to navigate beyond the ages at which so many of our heroes expired.

Malcolm X at 40. Martin Luther King Jr. at 39. Jackie Robinson taken far too young. These icons—men who could have reshaped the world for decades longer—left us early. And for those who did live longer, they often fell into patterns that didn't serve them or us well."

He paused, leaning forward as if to emphasize the weight of his words. "Think about it: we saw legends like Willie Mays and Hank Aaron fade into the background, smiling from the sidelines.

We watched others pretend they weren't aging at all, like Jesse Jackson, or cling to power far past their prime, unable to see the harm it caused. I saw this firsthand with our brother, the Rev. Dr. Calvin Butts III. His reluctance to pass the baton left a whirlwind of confusion at my former church home and pain for his family. That kind of holding on—it's not wisdom. It's fear."

His words settled in my chest like a heavy stone, not because they were harsh, but because they were true.

"Kenny," he continued, "this isn't just a book we're talking about. It's bigger than that. It's a blueprint, a tour, a masterclass for our brothers. This is about making the shift from relevant warriors to wise generals. We need to show Black men that aging isn't the end of the story—it's a new chapter, one we get to write with power, purpose, and just the right amount of not giving a damn anymore."

He laughed lightly, but his eyes held a steady fire. "Yes, we should expect to grow old, and we should demand that our lives be full. Look at us—we still look good for our age. We're still strong. We may not throw hands for as many rounds as we used to, but we know how to fight smart. This next season isn't about brute force; it's about strategy. It's about mentoring, about passing on the wisdom we've gained to the next generation. We need to redefine what it means to age as Black men."

His voice softened, but the intensity never wavered. "Aging doesn't mean losing relevance or power, Kenny. It means gaining wisdom. It means walking into a room, commanding respect, and show-ing the younger ones that we're still here, still thriving, and still leading. But it also means letting go when the time is right—not of our values or our fight, but of the need to be the loudest voice in the room. That's how we make room for the next generation to rise, equipped with the lessons we've passed on."

He leaned back, a small smile breaking through his serious expres-sion. "We're the first generation of Black men who can truly change this paradigm, Kenny. We can model what it looks like to embrace aging without fear or shame. We don't have to clutch at relevance or cling to the past. Instead, we can walk boldly into our 60s, 70s, 80s, and beyond with dignity, with joy, and with the knowledge that we're leaving a legacy of strength, wisdom, and resilience."

He let his words hang in the air for a moment, giving them time to sink in. "This is our moment, Kenny. Let's use it."

THE WEIGHT OF WISDOM: FROM YODA TO POPS

There's a strange irony in how life cycles back on itself, how the things we once mocked or misunderstood come to define us in ways we never expected. I think about that often these days, especially when I hear myself saying something that starts with, "Back in my day..." I always swore I'd never be that guy, the one clinging to old stories like a tattered coat, but here I am—leaning on the tales of my youth to give meaning to the present. And the thing is, it's not just me. It's all of us who reach a certain point, where time begins to stretch out behind us like a long shadow, and the future seems less about chasing and more about reflecting.

But let me be clear: there's danger in those words, "Back in my day." They can become a wall, a way to dismiss the present as inferior, to look at the world through the fogged-up lens of nostalgia. It's a fine line, isn't it? Between using the past to illuminate the present and using it to overshadow it entirely. And that's where the sages come in.

You see, the role of a sage isn't to cling to the past but to draw from it. The great sages—the ones we revere in fiction and in life—didn't spend their time lamenting the way things used to be.

They leaned into the present, using their accumulated wisdom to guide those still trying to find their way. Think about Yoda from

Star Wars. That little green creature didn't sit around waxing poetic about the golden age of the Jedi. He took Luke Skywalker—broken, unsure, raw—and helped him see the path ahead, not by dwelling on what was lost but by showing him what could be gained.

I've always been drawn to characters like Yoda. There's something about the quiet, unassuming power of a true sage that resonates deeply with me. It's the way they listen more than they speak, how their words carry weight not because they're loud but because they're earned. And it's not just Yoda.

There's Mr. Miyagi from The Karate Kid, whose wisdom came wrapped in chores like "wax on, wax off." At first glance, it seemed like busywork, a meaningless task. But hidden within those simple movements was a lesson—a foundation for something greater.

> ***That's the essence of a sage: they don't just give you the answer; they help you discover it for yourself.***

And then there's the raw, unpolished wisdom of Mudbone, the old storyteller character created by Richard Pryor. Mudbone was rough around the edges, full of humor and grit, but beneath the laughter was a deep well of truth. He carried the weight of history in his words, using his stories to shine a light on the pain and resilience of Black life in America.

That's what I mean when I say wisdom isn't always polished. Sometimes it's messy, delivered in a way that makes you uncomfortable because it forces you to confront things you'd rather avoid.

I think about these figures often when I'm sitting with younger men, listening to them wrestle with questions they're just beginning to articulate. And it's funny because sometimes they'll call me

"OG" or "Pops." At first, it grated on me. I'd bristle at the words, hearing in them an implication that I was somehow past my prime, relegated to the sidelines of relevance. But over time, I've come to see it differently. Those names—OG, Pops—aren't insults. They're acknowledgments.

They're a way of saying, "I see you. I respect what you've been through. Teach me."

It's a humbling thing, to realize you've become someone others look to for guidance. It's also a responsibility. Because let's be real: not every elder deserves the title of sage. There's a difference between being old and being wise, between accumulating years and accumulating understanding. Wisdom doesn't come automatically with age. It comes from reflection, from learning, from a willingness to grow even when the world tells you your growing days are over.

That's why I try to stay rooted in the present. It's easy to fall into the trap of thinking the best days are behind you, to dismiss the younger generation as lost or misguided. But that kind of thinking does no one any good. It creates a divide, a gap where there should be a bridge. And if there's one thing I've learned, it's that wisdom isn't about standing above others; it's about walking alongside them.

I remember a conversation I had with my son not long ago. We were watching basketball, debating whether today's players could hold their own against the legends of the past. He turned to me and said, "Yeah, Dad, but that was back in the 1900s."

The 1900s!

The words hit me like a punch to the gut. To him, the era I grew up in might as well have been ancient history. And for a moment, I felt defensive, ready to launch into a tirade about how much better things were "back in my day." But then I caught myself. What good would that do? Would it make him see the world differently? Or would it just reinforce the idea that I was out of touch?

So instead, I laughed. "You're right," I said. "But you know what? The lessons from the 1900s still apply today. The game might look different, but the fundamentals haven't changed."

That's the balance, isn't it? Honoring the past without being trapped by it. Drawing from its lessons without using it as a weapon to dismiss the present. It's a tricky thing to navigate, but it's essential if we're going to be the sages our communities need.

I think about Darth Vader's words to Obi-Wan Kenobi in Star Wars: "I was but the learner; now I am the master." It's a powerful line, but it's also a warning. Because mastery, if not tempered by humility, can become arrogance. And arrogance has no place in wisdom. The moment you think you've learned everything, that's the moment you stop growing. And a sage who stops growing is no sage at all.

So here I am, embracing the titles of OG and Pops, leaning into the role of sage not because I have all the answers but because I'm willing to share what I've learned. I've made peace with the fact that my stories start with "Back in my day," because I've learned how to use them as bridges, not walls. I've stopped worrying about being seen as "relevant" and started focusing on being present.

Because at the end of the day, wisdom isn't about relevance. It's about resonance. It's about planting seeds of understanding and trust, even if you never get to see them bloom.

The danger of living in the past is real, but so is the danger of dismissing it. The challenge for those of us stepping into the role of sage is to honor both—to weave the threads of yesterday into the fabric of today, creating something strong enough to carry the weight of tomorrow. And that, my friend, is what makes the journey worth it.

THE ECHO OF WISDOM: EMBRACING THE SAGE WITHIN

There comes a time when the weight of life—its victories, its losses, and all the quiet in-betweens—gathers into a single moment of clarity. It's the kind of moment that feels like stepping into a room where everyone has been waiting for you to speak, though you hadn't planned to say a word. That's what it feels like to become a sage.

But let me tell you, it doesn't happen overnight. The transition from warrior to general, from fighter to thinker, from student to teacher, is rarely marked by ceremony. It's quiet. Subtle. Like waking up one morning and realizing you've been carrying the answers to questions you'd long forgotten to ask.

I've spent years trying to understand what it means to be a sage. It's not a role you volunteer for; it's one you grow into. It's not about age, though age certainly helps. It's about perspective. It's about recognizing that your experiences—all the pain, joy, and lessons—aren't just for you. They're for the ones coming behind you.

The ones still learning, still struggling, still searching for the wisdom they don't yet know they need.
Let me set the scene for you.

It's a cool autumn evening, the kind where the air feels crisp and alive, as though it's been infused with the quiet hum of change. I'm sitting in a circle with a group of young men, each one at a different crossroads in his life. Some are fresh out of college, their dreams still shiny and untested.

Others are a few steps into fatherhood, already feeling the weight of responsibility pressing against their shoulders. And then there are the ones who've stumbled, who've seen what happens when life doesn't play fair, who've felt the sting of failure and are wondering if redemption is possible.

We're sitting around a firepit, the flames dancing and throwing shadows across their faces. They're talking, sharing stories about their families, their fears, their ambitions. There's laughter, but there's also a heaviness in the air, the kind that comes when people are trying to figure out how to carry what feels too heavy to bear. They look at me occasionally, not as an elder but as someone who's been where they are—someone who might have something useful to say.

And I'm quiet. Listening. Waiting. Not because I don't have anything to say, but because I've learned that the first rule of being a sage is to listen more than you speak.

Then, a question breaks the silence.

"How do you know when you've done enough?"

It's a young man named Jordan. He's in his late twenties, his face a mix of weariness and determination. He's talking about his father, a man who worked three jobs and still struggled to make ends meet.

Jordan's voice cracks as he speaks. "He died before he got to enjoy any of it. How do I make sure that doesn't happen to me?"

The fire crackles, filling the space where his words hang heavy.

All eyes turn to me. And this is where the sage steps in.

"You don't," I say finally, my voice steady but soft. "You don't make sure it doesn't happen. What you do is make sure the journey is worth it."

The words aren't rehearsed. They come from a place I can't quite name, but I've learned to trust it. It's the place where my mother's quiet strength lives, where my father's absence left room for resilience to grow. It's the place where decades of mistakes and triumphs have been distilled into something that feels true.

"The truth is," I continue, "your father's work wasn't just about the money. It was about you. It was about making sure you had a chance to ask the question you just asked me.

That's his legacy. And your job isn't to avoid his struggles; it's to honor them by living fully, by finding joy even in the hard places. That's how you know you've done enough—when you've lived in a way that makes the struggle meaningful."

Jordan nods, his eyes glistening, and the circle falls silent again. But it's not the heavy silence from before. It's the kind that feels like something has shifted, like the air has been cleared just enough to make space for hope.

This is what it means to be a sage. Not to have all the answers, but to offer what you have when it's needed. To hold space for others to find their own truths. To remind them that they're not alone. I think about the sages who shaped me. My mother, who taught me the power of quiet perseverance. My mentors, who showed me what it meant to stand tall even when the world tried to knock you down. The elders in my community, whose stories were like breadcrumbs leading me back to myself.

They didn't wear the title of "sage," but they wore the responsibility of it every day.

Being a sage isn't about having wisdom—it's about sharing it. It's about understanding that your experiences, your scars, your stories, aren't just yours. They're part of a collective memory, a shared inheritance meant to guide, to heal, to inspire.

And it's not always easy. Sometimes the wisdom you offer won't be heard. Sometimes it will be misunderstood. Sometimes it will be ignored altogether. But you offer it anyway. Because that's what sages do. They plant seeds, knowing they might not be around to see them grow.

As the fire dies down and the young men start to drift away, I sit for a moment longer, staring at the glowing embers. The air is cool now, the kind of cool that seeps into your bones and reminds you that time is always moving, always changing. And I'm grateful. Grateful for the questions, for the stories, for the chance to be a part of something larger than myself.

The journey from warrior to sage isn't a straight path. It's messy, unpredictable, and often uncomfortable. But it's also beautiful.

Because at the end of it, you realize that the wisdom you've gathered isn't just about what you've learned—it's about what you've shared. And that, more than anything, is what makes the journey worth it.

CHAPTER EIGHT

AUTHENTIC RELATIONSHIPS: BUILDING CONNECTIONS THAT MATTER

BAD RELATIONSHIPS: THE QUIET THIEF OF PEACE

If there's one thing I've come to know with certainty, it's this: nothing in life is more capable of destroying your peace than a relationship. Relationships—so critical to the human experience, so deeply embedded in who we are—have the unique power to build us up or tear us down.

They can inspire, comfort, and elevate, but they can also devastate, unravel, and leave scars that last a lifetime. And the thing about relationships is they are never simple. They are layered, complex, and intertwined with emotions, expectations, and unspoken rules that shift and evolve over time.

One of the most profound truths I've learned about relationships is that they demand something of you. When you engage in a relationship, you give a piece of yourself—your time, your trust, your love, your vulnerability. What you give is directly proportional to the value you place on that relationship, especially in its early stages. If you invest more than the other person, you leave yourself vulnerable. And if the other person invests more than you, they are the ones left exposed. The imbalance creates a chasm, one that widens over time if the relationship isn't clearly defined.

It's the lack of definition that often breeds chaos. When two people enter into a relationship—whether familial, romantic, professional, or spiritual—without a shared understanding of its purpose or boundaries, misalignment becomes inevitable. One person's expectations don't match the other's, and that disparity can unravel even the strongest bonds. Relationships, when left unchecked, become breeding grounds for miscommunication, resentment, and ultimately, the destruction of peace.

But here's the thing: life is relational. No man is an island. We are not built to exist in isolation. We are connected by blood, by choice, by fate, and sometimes by circumstance. Some connections are intentional—born of shared values or mutual goals—while others are random, the result of life's unpredictability. A shared tragedy, a fleeting encounter, or a collaborative project can create bonds that feel unshakable, yet are often as fragile as they are profound. These connections, while deeply meaningful in the moment, can become sources of pain when their season ends.

There's a saying I've come to appreciate: relationships can be for a reason or a season. Some relationships are meant to serve a specific purpose, to teach us something, to help us grow, or to guide us through a particular chapter in our lives. Others are seasonal, thriving for a time before fading into the background. The problem arises when we mistake a seasonal relationship for a lifelong one. We cling to something that was never meant to last, and in doing so, we create unnecessary hurt for ourselves.

This lesson becomes clearer with age. As a young man, I didn't understand the transient nature of many relationships. I agonized over friendships that ended, over people who left, over bonds that frayed without warning. It wasn't until later in life that I realized not every relationship is meant to endure. Some are simply not equipped to weather the transitions of adolescence, adulthood, and beyond. And that's okay. But it's a hard truth to accept, especially when you've invested deeply.

Take family, for example. Family relationships are some of the most powerful—and potentially painful—connections we experience. With family, you don't get to choose. You are bound by blood, by shared history, by the circumstances of your birth. And while the depth of these relationships can be a source of immense joy and comfort, they can also be a source of deep hurt. The bond between parent and child, for instance, is unparalleled. There is no relationship more formative, more impactful, or more capable of shaping a person's self-worth.

When the parent-child relationship is fractured, the effects are profound and often lifelong. A parent's absence—whether physical, emotional, or both—leaves a void that is difficult, if not impossible, to fill. Issues of fatherlessness, for example, have rippled through generations, creating cycles of pain and loss that are hard to break. And while much attention is given to absent fathers, motherlessness carries its own unique and devastating weight. The absence of a mother's love, guidance, and presence is a wound that cuts deep, often leaving scars that manifest in other relationships throughout life.

The history of slavery provides a stark illustration of the destruction wrought by severed family bonds. One of the most inhumane tools of control used during slavery was the deliberate breaking apart of families. Mothers torn from children, fathers stripped of their roles, siblings separated—these actions weren't just acts of physical displacement; they were acts of emotional and spiritual violence. The echoes of this systemic destruction are still felt today in the fractured family structures within many communities, particularly Black communities. The pain of those broken bonds lingers, a haunting reminder of how deeply relationships shape and define us.

Romantic relationships, too, hold incredible power—both to uplift and to destroy. When love is good, it feels invincible. But when it goes bad, it can leave devastation in its wake. Romantic relationships demand an emotional investment unlike any other. Love requires vulnerability, trust, and a willingness to share parts of yourself that you guard fiercely in other relationships. And when that love is betrayed or broken, the pain is not easily undone.

Trust is often the first casualty in a bad romantic relationship. Once trust is broken, it's hard to rebuild. The doubts creep in, the questions linger, and the connection begins to erode. And even when the relationship ends, the wounds remain. They shape how you approach future relationships, how willing you are to open your heart again. Sometimes, the scars are so deep that they prevent you from fully engaging in love again, even when you desperately want to.

Abusive relationships, whether physical, emotional, or psychological, take this pain to another level. Abuse creates cycles of control, fear, and dependency that are hard to break. Victims of abuse often find themselves trapped—not just by the abuser but by the emotional and logistical entanglements that come with the relationship. Leaving is not as simple as walking away. The ties that bind are complex, layered with threats, manipulation, and the lingering hope that things might change.

These relationships are among the most damaging, leaving deep emotional scars that take years, sometimes a lifetime, to heal.

Working relationships, though seemingly less personal, can also disrupt your peace. The time we spend at work, the connections we form with colleagues, and the dynamics of workplace interactions all have the potential to impact our emotional well-being. A toxic work environment, an envious coworker, or an unsupportive boss can turn a job into a daily source of stress and anxiety. When work relationships go bad, the effects ripple into other areas of life, disrupting not just your professional life but your personal peace as well.

Congregational relationships—those formed within spiritual or religious communities—carry their own unique complexities. Church hurt, as it's often called, is a deeply personal pain. These relationships are rooted not just in shared beliefs but in shared vulnerability. You bring your spiritual self to these spaces, seeking guidance, connection, and purpose. When these relationships are fractured, the hurt runs deep because it feels like a betrayal of something sacred. Leaving a congregation, or losing trust in a spiritual leader, isn't just a logistical decision—it's a spiritual wound that takes time to heal.

Bad relationships, in all their forms, leave a trail of triggers. These triggers are the emotional landmines we carry into new relationships, often without realizing it. A harsh word, a familiar behavior, or even an innocent action can set off memories of past hurts, shaping how we engage with others. This baggage complicates new connections, creating barriers to trust and intimacy. And when two people enter a relationship with their own sets of baggage, the potential for miscommunication and conflict multiplies.

There's a saying that has stood the test of time: misery loves company. This phrase has taken root in our cultural lexicon because it speaks to a universal truth. People who are unhappy often seek to spread that unhappiness, consciously or unconsciously, by pulling others into their emotional turmoil. Misery, when left unchecked, doesn't sit quietly—it reaches outward, seeking validation, connection, or even power through the disruption of others' peace. Recognizing this dynamic is critical, especially when navigating relationships.

If someone's misery is consuming your peace, it's essential to set boundaries, protect your emotional well-being, and resist the pull into their chaos. Peace, after all, is a choice—and sometimes, that choice means walking away.

As I've grown more seasoned, I've come to understand the importance of protecting my peace. I no longer have the tolerance for dramatized relationships, whether they're familial, romantic, professional, or congregational. My peace is too valuable, too central to my well-being, to be disrupted by unnecessary chaos.

And while I can't control how others show up in relationships, I can control how I engage. I can set boundaries, prioritize truth, and choose connections that nurture rather than drain me.

The reality is this: relationships will always be a part of life. They will shape us, challenge us, and sometimes hurt us. But as we grow, we gain the wisdom to discern which relationships are worth investing in and which ones we need to let go of. We learn to value our peace above all else, recognizing that a life lived in peace is a life well-lived. And in that peace, we find the strength to navigate even the most complex and challenging connections, emerging not unscathed, but stronger, wiser, and more deeply aligned with who we are meant to be.

BRIDGES OF BELONGING: THE POWER AND PERILS OF FRIENDSHIP

When I think about friendship, I realize it's as essential as breathing, yet as complex as a beating heart. Friendship is the first bridge we cross in life that isn't built by our family but by choice—by small gestures, shared secrets, and the unspoken trust that begins to tether us to others. There's a rawness in it, a fragile tenderness that makes these bonds feel sacred. For me, understanding the depth of friendship has been a journey, one that has revealed the essential role these connections play in our lives, shaping our perceptions of ourselves and the world around us.

From the earliest days, we start to learn about connection through family. That's the initial blueprint. For me, family taught me resilience, the importance of integrity, and the strength to keep pushing forward even when times were tough. But as much as family gave me, I also found limits there—limits on how big I dared to dream. Growing up in Brooklyn, surrounded by the hum and grit of the city, dreams weren't extravagant. We lived with just enough, and so our vision often stayed close to home, close to what we knew. I had to reach beyond those walls to start seeing what was possible, and friendship became the ladder that helped me climb to new perspectives.

The friendships I made were like stepping stones, each one teaching me a little more about myself. My friends in those early days were like extensions of my family, but with one critical difference: they weren't bound by blood but by choice. It's a powerful feeling, knowing that someone chooses to be in your life, to share your struggles, to celebrate your wins, to walk beside you simply because they want to. That choice is what makes friendship unique. These are the bonds that grow not from obligation but from shared experiences, from mutual respect, and sometimes, just from laughter shared over nothing in particular.

But as I've gotten older, I've seen how friendship has changed, too. When I was growing up, friendship wasn't as instant as clicking "accept" or "follow." Friendship was earned. We spent hours together—playing handball on the schoolyard, walking the streets with no particular destination, or just talking, really talking. In those moments, we opened up, trusted each other, let each other in.

Now, with social media, friendship has taken on a different texture. Friends have become lists, and connections are measured in numbers, likes, and comments. But numbers don't tell the story of friendship. A true friend doesn't need an algorithm to stay connected.

Friendships today sometimes feel thinner, stretched out over the surface of a screen. There's something missing, something that can't be captured by a profile picture or a status update. It's the depth, the weight of shared history, the unspoken language between two people who have walked through life together. We've become so accustomed to quick connections that we often forget what it means to have a friend who truly knows us, who has seen us at our worst and loved us anyway.

I was recently reminded of something that Bishop T.D. Jakes once shared. He described three kinds of people in our lives: confidants, constituents, and comrades. Confidants are the rare ones. They're the friends who will stand by you, no matter the season, who will weather storms with you. Constituents are there because you have a shared goal or purpose; they're there as long as you're walking a similar path.

Comrades are even more temporary; they're the ones who may share a fight with you, a common cause, but they aren't necessarily there for you. They're with you for the journey, but not for the destination.

These distinctions matter because so often, we label anyone we cross paths with as "friend." But friendship isn't casual. It's a commitment, a deep and profound commitment. It's about presence—about being there, not just physically, but emotionally, spiritually. It's about knowing that when the world turns dark, there's someone who will stand by you without asking questions, without expecting anything in return.

For a long time, I tried to answer a question my daughter once asked me: "Dad, who's your best friend?" It should have been an easy answer, but the truth was, I didn't have one person who filled that role entirely. Instead, I had a circle of people, each one holding a different piece of my trust, my respect, my love. I came to understand that I don't need a best friend. I need a circle of confidants, people who inspire me, who challenge me, who keep me grounded. I need people who love me enough to tell me the truth, even when it hurts, and who are there to pick me up when I stumble.

It was a revelation to realize that friendship doesn't have to be all or nothing. There's no need to put the weight of every need, every expectation, on one person. Life is too complex for that. Instead, I've learned to surround myself with different kinds of friends—friends who each bring something unique into my life. And in doing so, I've been able to give more freely, without the pressure of trying to make one person into my everything.

Losing a friend, though—that's a lesson in heartbreak. When someone you've let into your life decides to walk away, it's not just their absence that you feel. It's a loss of the history you shared, the laughter, the secrets, the times they saw you in a way no one else did. It leaves a scar. I've come to see that every friendship leaves a mark, some deeper than others. I still carry the marks of friends who've come and gone, and each one has taught me something— about trust, about resilience, about letting go.

There's a loneliness that follows that kind of loss. When a friend leaves, it's as if part of you leaves, too. But I've learned that friendships, like life itself, have seasons. Some are meant to last a lifetime; others are only with us for a moment. I used to think that every friendship needed to be forever, that any ending was a failure. But now I see that every friendship serves its purpose, whether it's to teach us, to heal us, or simply to bring us joy for a time.

I've come to think of friendships as gifts, not promises. They're God's way of placing the right people in our lives at the right time. Some friends are there to lift us up; others are there to ground us, to remind us of where we came from. And then there are the ones who challenge us, who push us to grow in ways we didn't know we needed. Each friendship is a chapter in the story of who we are, and together, they create a mosaic that is uniquely ours.

Sometimes, the hardest part of friendship is knowing when to let go. We hold on because we fear the void, but letting go is sometimes the greatest act of love. It allows space for new connections, for new growth. I've learned that as much as we may want to, we can't keep everyone in our lives forever. People change; we change. And with that change comes the painful realization that not every friendship will fit into every season of our lives.

If there's one thing I've learned, it's this: don't hold too tightly. Friendships are fluid, not fixed. They ebb and flow, they evolve, and that's okay. Some friends are here to teach us a lesson, to help us through a chapter. And if we're lucky, a few will be there for the whole journey. But time is not a measure of loyalty. Some of the deepest friendships are the ones that come into our lives suddenly, intensely, and leave an indelible mark.

Friendship, like love, is a risk. We open ourselves up to the possibility of joy and the inevitability of pain. But without it, life would be empty. Each friend I've had, whether for a season or a lifetime, has been a blessing, a reminder that we are not meant to walk this journey alone. Friendship is the bridge that connects us, that allows us to see ourselves through someone else's eyes. And when those friends are gone, the bridge may no longer be there, but the lessons, the love—they stay with us. They become a part of who we are, woven into the fabric of our lives.

So if you take anything from this, let it be this: friendships are gifts. Treasure them, but don't cling. Appreciate each one for what it is, for as long as it lasts. And remember that some friends will stay in your life, not because of how long you've known them, but because of how deeply they've touched your heart.

THE FAMILIAR MASK: NAVIGATING THE DICHOTOMY OF FRIENDS AND ENEMIES

The dichotomy of friends and enemies is one of the most perplexing aspects of human relationships. It's this strange occurrence, a contrasting duality that is sometimes nearly impossible to distinguish. I've wrestled with this concept for years, trying to unpack how the familiar and the unknown coexist in the same space, how the masks people wear obscure their true intentions, and how the lines between friend and foe often blur.

This idea of dichotomy took root in my mind while thinking about the masks we wear in life. There's a public service campaign by the Ad Council that speaks to this, showcasing how humans function much of the time by hiding behind facades. We present faces that are palatable, even familiar, while concealing the unknown parts of ourselves. It's a concept that's both profound and unsettling, because it begs the question: How well do we truly know the people in our lives?

The Bible, as it often does, offers wisdom on this topic. In Mark 6:4 and Luke 4:24, the scripture says, "A prophet is honored everywhere except in his own hometown and among his own relatives and in his own home." That line has always stuck with me.

It speaks to how familiarity can breed contempt, or at the very least, diminish respect. People who have grown up around you, who have seen your flaws, your mistakes, your masks—those people often struggle to recognize your greatness, your potential, your authenticity. Their familiarity with the surface blinds them to the depth of who you are.

Richard Pryor once joked about this very phenomenon. When he went back to Peoria, Illinois, his old friends would approach him in the bathroom and say, "Man, you ain't shit. I knew you when you mama was hoeing. Let me get a dollar," followed by some embarrassing anecdote. Pryor's story, while humorous, underscores a painful truth: The people closest to you, those who know your history, are often the ones who struggle the most to see your value. It's a bitter irony that the familiar can so easily mask the extraordinary.

This dichotomy between friends and enemies is made even more complex by the notion that the devil often wears a familiar face. Angela Bassett said it best in 9-1-1: "The devil tricks you with his lies and wears a familiar face." There's a chilling truth to that statement. It's not the obvious enemies who pose the greatest threat; it's the ones who come close, who gain your trust, who know your vulnerabilities. They don't announce their intentions. They move quietly, subtly, hiding behind the mask of friendship.

This brings me to one of the most painful experiences of my life, a time when I was not the betrayed but the betrayer. It was a circumstantial betrayal, not premeditated, but that doesn't lessen the sting or the consequences.

The friend I betrayed was someone I was once very close to, some-one whose life and trust I shattered in a way that still haunts me. The betrayal involved his wife. At the time, he and I were not seeing eye to eye. There was tension between us, a growing rift that neither of us fully acknowledged but both felt. In that space of discord, lines were crossed. I'm not proud of what happened. In fact, I've spent years trying to understand how I allowed myself to engage in such a betrayal, knowing full well the ethical boundaries I was trampling.

There are unwritten rules in life, and this was one of them: You don't covet another man's wife. You don't cross that line, no matter the circumstances. But I did. And while I've tried to reason and justify my actions to myself, the truth remains: I betrayed a friend. Whether circumstantial or premeditated, the impact was the same. Trust was broken. Relationships were destroyed. The ripple effects of that betrayal spread far and wide, touching people who had no part in the act itself but were still affected by its fallout.

In the aftermath, I lost more than just a friendship. I lost oppor-tunities, connections, and a sense of belonging. I felt isolated, vilified, and deeply ashamed. But amid the wreckage, there were lessons. I learned the importance of boundaries, of regulating my emotions and actions. I learned that no matter how deep the rift, betrayal is never the answer. And I learned that even in the dark-est moments, there is room for redemption.

The irony of that betrayal is that it ultimately led me to my calling. The pain and loss I experienced became the foundation for my servant life. It was as if God took my brokenness and used it to build something new, something meaningful. Proverbs 16:4 says, "The Lord has made everything for its purpose, even the wicked for the day of trouble." That scripture resonates deeply with me. My actions were wicked, but they served a purpose—not just for my growth, but for the work I do today.

And yet, as much as that chapter of my life was marked by pain and loss, it wasn't without its lessons and even a few blessings. Through that situation, I found myself forming deeper relationships with children I hadn't previously connected with. I became more present, more aware of what it meant to be a meaningful presence in someone's life. Those relationships remain strong to this day, and they serve as a reminder that even in the midst of failure, something good can emerge.

On a personal level, that experience changed me profoundly. It motivated me to grow, to evaluate my boundaries, and to commit to never allowing my emotions to override my principles again. It taught me the importance of aligning my actions with my values and the necessity of being intentional in how I navigate relationships.

But even as I've found purpose in the aftermath, the scars remain. I've apologized to those I hurt, but apologies can only go so far. They can't undo the damage. They can't erase the pain. And they can't change the fact that some friendships will never be mended.

This dichotomy of friends and enemies is something I've seen play out in countless ways. From the biblical story of Cain and Abel, where jealousy led one brother to kill another, to the betrayal of Michael Corleone by his own brother Fredo in The Godfather, the line between friend and enemy is often razor-thin. Even in pop culture, we see this duality. Tupac and Biggie started as friends, but lies, gossip, and ego turned them into rivals, ultimately leading to their tragic deaths.

These stories, whether biblical, fictional, or real, highlight the complexity of human relationships. They remind us that the people closest to us have the greatest capacity to hurt us, precisely because they know us so well. They know our strengths and our weaknesses, our hopes and our fears.

And when those relationships turn sour, the pain is profound.

I've often wondered how we navigate this dichotomy. How do we protect ourselves without becoming jaded? How do we cultivate meaningful connections without letting the fear of betrayal hold us back? For me, the answer lies in boundaries and authenticity. It's about being intentional with who you let into your life and ensuring that the relationships you build are based on truth, not masks.

At this stage in my life, I've become more selective with my friendships. I've learned to value quality over quantity, depth over breadth. And I've learned to recognize that even the strongest friendships can falter, that people can change, and that sometimes, the best thing you can do is let go.

But letting go doesn't mean forgetting. It doesn't mean erasing the lessons or dismissing the pain. It means holding onto the wisdom those experiences brought and using it to build a stronger, more intentional future.

So, as I reflect on the dichotomy of friends and enemies, I'm reminded of this simple truth: Life is messy. Relationships are complicated. And the line between friend and foe is often blurred. But in the midst of that messiness, there is always an opportunity to grow, to learn, and to become the best version of yourself. And that, perhaps, is the greatest lesson of all.

CAN YOU HOLD MY WEIGHT? THE SACRED CIRCLE OF TRUST

I've often been told that trust is a two-way street, but I've come to believe it's more like a suspension bridge—a structure that must hold steady under the weight of life's heaviest moments. The road beneath you is nothing without the tensile strength of what holds it together: authentic relationships. Without those, the entire bridge collapses. And when you're standing in the middle of it, burdened by something you can't carry alone, the stakes are immeasurable.

So, let me ask you—when life's weight presses down, do the people around you hold steady, or do they buckle?

I've carried my share of weight. Some of it self-inflicted, some of it dropped on me by the careless hands of others. And in those moments, I've looked around my circle and asked a question that's both sobering and liberating: Can you hold my weight? Not just any weight, but my weight. The weight of my vulnerability, my pain, my shame, and my dreams. The kind of weight that, if not supported, can break a man in half.

A long time ago, Pastor Creflo Dollar posed a thought experiment that stopped me in my tracks. It was during one of his sermons, the kind that slows your heartbeat and makes you sit still long after he's finished speaking. He asked us to imagine needing an amount of money so large it felt almost absurd. Think of a number, he said, one that's beyond your reach—a number that would make you feel small just to admit it out loud. Then, imagine the people in your circle who could provide it. But here was the catch: they had to give it to you without asking questions. Not why do you need it, not when will you pay it back.

Just give it. No conditions. No hesitation.

That exercise shook me.

I closed my eyes and pictured my circle—friends, family, colleagues. People I'd laughed with, cried with, broken bread with. And as I sifted through those faces, the number of people I could truly depend on dwindled. It wasn't that they didn't love me, or that they didn't care. It was that the weight of trust and generosity required in that scenario was something else entirely. To give without question requires not just resources but faith—faith in you. It demands a depth of relationship that transcends surface connections.

As Pastor Dollar wrapped up, he dropped one final challenge. "If you don't have at least five people in your life who can hold your weight in that way, you need to reevaluate your circle." And let me tell you—that hit like a gut punch.

But weight isn't always financial, is it? Money is just one manifestation of what it means to hold someone's burden.

Often, the heaviest loads are intangible: emotional wounds, the sting of betrayal, the ache of loss, or the quiet desperation of a man trying to hold it all together. When I think about the weight I've carried in my life, the financial burdens pale in comparison to the moments when I needed someone to see me—really see me—and say, "I've got you."

In those moments, I've learned that not everyone is built to carry your weight. Some people will fold under it. Others will disappear. And then there are those who will lift you without hesitation, without resentment, without needing to know why. Those are the people you hold close. Those are the people you pour into because they are rare, sacred, and worth every ounce of energy you've got.

And yet, asking for that support is one of the hardest things to do. There's a vulnerability in the ask that feels like stepping out onto thin ice, unsure if it will hold. To ask for help means admitting that you can't do it alone, and for many of us, that feels like failure. We're taught to be self-reliant, to soldier on, to keep our struggles hidden beneath a facade of strength. So, when the moment comes to reach out, the words often stick in our throats. What if they say no?

That's the question that haunts us, isn't it? The fear of rejection. The fear that your need, your weight, might be too much for someone else to bear. And worse, the fear that their "no" isn't just about their capacity but about you. What does it say about your worth if someone can't or won't help? That fear can be paralyzing, keeping us locked in our struggles, too ashamed or afraid to ask.

But even a "yes" carries its own complexities. When someone agrees to help, what does that yes mean? Does it come with strings attached? Expectations? A timeline? Asking for help is never just about the need itself; it's about navigating the unspoken rules and dynamics that come with someone else stepping in.

You're not just handing over your burden—you're handing over a piece of your trust, and that's no small thing.

Nowhere is this more complicated than when money and family are involved. There's a unique tension in those situations, a push and pull between love and obligation, trust and resentment. Money has a way of magnifying everything—the good, the bad, and the ugly. It's not just about the dollar amount; it's about what that money represents.

In family, money becomes entangled with identity and history. It's not just a loan; it's a reflection of decades of shared experiences, grievances, and expectations. A sibling might say yes because they feel they should, not because they want to. A parent might give but expect that gift to come with obedience or deference. And when things go wrong—when the money isn't repaid, or the gratitude isn't shown—the fallout can be devastating. Families have fractured over less.

I've seen it happen. I've lived it. I've watched as relationships unraveled not because of the money itself but because of what it symbolized: unmet expectations, unspoken resentments, and the weight of a "yes" that was given grudgingly. It's why some people refuse to mix money and family at all—not because they don't care, but because they care too much to risk it.

Let's talk about the ones who can't hold your weight. It's not always their fault. Sometimes, their inability to support you says more about their own limitations than your worth. But the pain of realizing someone you counted on can't meet you in your moment of need? That pain cuts deep. It's the friend who says, "I wish I could help," but their eyes betray their relief at not being responsible for your pain. It's the family member who ghosts you because your struggle makes them uncomfortable. And perhaps worst of all, it's the silence—the non-response that leaves you questioning whether you ever mattered to them at all.

Empty support—that's what I call it. And empty support is more damaging than no support at all. Because it creates an illusion of safety, a mirage of reliability that evaporates the moment you reach for it. It's the promise of a bridge that collapses under your first step. And when that happens, it's not just disappointing—it's devastating. It shakes your faith in people, in relationships, in trust itself.

But then there are the others—the ones who surprise you with their strength. The ones who step up in ways you didn't even know were possible. I've had moments when someone I least expected became my rock, my anchor. Like the friend who showed up on my doorstep with a hot meal and no expectations, or the mentor who sat with me in silence when words felt too heavy.

> *Those are the moments that restore your faith. Those are the moments that remind you that while not everyone can hold your weight, some people were built for it.*

As I reflect on this, I'm reminded of a conversation I had with my son about social capital. He's a private school kid, surrounded by peers whose parents are CEOs, entrepreneurs, and influencers.

I tell him often: "Your relationships matter more than you know. Build them authentically. Because one day, you'll need people who can hold your weight."

It's the same lesson I've had to learn over and over again. Your circle is not about quantity; it's about quality. It's about surrounding yourself with people who can weather the storm with you, who can see your humanity even when you're at your lowest. It's about finding those five people Pastor Dollar talked about and pouring into them as much as they pour into you.

Authentic relationships are a two-way street. You can't expect someone to hold your weight if you've never shown up for them. And showing up doesn't always mean grand gestures. Sometimes, it's as simple as listening without judgment, checking in without being asked, or offering a hand when you notice someone's struggling.

Relationships are built in the small, quiet moments that often go unnoticed. But those moments? They're everything. So here's my challenge to you: take stock of your circle.

Who can you call when the weight feels unbearable? Who would call you? And if the answers leave you feeling uneasy, maybe it's time to reevaluate.

Not just your relationships, but how you show up in them. Because the truth is, you don't just need people who can hold your weight— you need to be the kind of person who can hold theirs.

And when you find those people? Hold onto them with everything you've got. Because in this life, where the weight can feel crushing and the bridges are few, there's nothing more sacred than a circle that can hold you steady.

So, I'll ask you again: Can you hold my weight? And just as importantly, can I hold yours?

THE FAMILIARITY OF PAIN: WHY WE RUMMAGE THROUGH THE PAST

The past has a peculiar way of calling out to us. It doesn't whisper; it beckons like an old friend standing on a distant shore, waving you back toward waters you've already swam. Or maybe it's more like the pull of an undertow, subtle and strong, dragging you beneath the surface just when you thought you were wading toward new horizons. I've found myself rummaging through the remnants of yesterdays I thought I'd discarded, searching for something—redemption, understanding, closure, or maybe just a reason why.

I've come to believe that people go back to what's familiar, even if it's broken. Pain, when repeated enough, becomes an echo—a sound you recognize in the dark, a rhythm that feels like home even as it tears you apart. And yet, we return. We return to the arguments we swore we'd never have again, to the relationships we promised we'd outgrow, to the memories that feel more real than the moment we're standing in.

There was a time in my life when I couldn't stop looking back. I'd open the trash bag of discarded relationships and sift through the fragments, hoping to find something I might've missed. It's like you tell yourself, Maybe I threw this away too quickly, or Maybe it wasn't as bad as I remember.

You convince yourself that the familiar—no matter how messy, no matter how painful—is better than the uncertainty of starting over.

> ***But here's the truth I've come to understand: If you rummage long enough, you'll find the dirt you thought you buried. You'll carry it with you, thinking it's something precious when all it is, is weight.***

I remember a particular relationship that felt like this. We'd broken up for all the right reasons, but the pull to return was stronger than logic. There's something about shared history that feels magnetic, as though the good times outweigh the bad simply because they came first. I went back. I justified it with phrases like, "We were young back then" or "People change." And for a moment, it felt like I was right.

We laughed at old jokes, revisited the places where love once lived, and convinced ourselves that time had healed the wounds we'd inflicted on each other.

But the cracks resurfaced. They always do. I realized I hadn't returned to find something new; I'd returned to validate the part of me that didn't want to let go. And in doing so, I'd put myself in the same cycle of pain I thought I'd escaped. The truth is, going back didn't mend the broken pieces; it only reminded me why they broke in the first place.

People romanticize the idea of second chances. They talk about redemption and forgiveness like they're the key to unlocking a better version of something that's inherently flawed. And while I believe in the beauty of forgiveness, I've learned it's not synonymous with reconciliation. Forgiveness is about release—letting go of the anger and hurt so it no longer defines you.

But reconciliation? That's a rebuilding process, and it only works if both parties bring new materials to the table. If you're still building with the same rotted wood, the structure won't hold.

I've thought a lot about why we go back. Part of it, I think, is fear. The fear of being alone. The fear of starting over. The fear that maybe we were the ones who were wrong all along. But there's another layer, too: comfort. Even pain, when it's predictable, can feel safer than the unknown. There's a twisted logic in choosing the familiar hurt over the uncertainty of healing.

I think about my mother when I reflect on this. She was a quiet woman in many ways, not one for grand gestures or dramatic displays of emotion. But her strength was like a current—steady, powerful, and often unseen. She had this phrase she'd say when I'd come to her with my heartbreaks and my confusion over why people I cared for couldn't seem to love me the way I needed them to. "You can't make a tiger change its stripes," she'd say, her voice calm but resolute. "You just have to decide if you can live with them."

At the time, I didn't fully understand what she meant. I thought she was telling me to give up on people, to stop believing in the possibility of growth. But that wasn't it at all. She was telling me that change is rare and that the kind of change worth waiting for doesn't come because you want it to. It comes because the other person chooses it—not for you, but for themselves.

Looking back, I see how those words have shaped my approach to relationships, to friendships, and even to my own self-reflection. They've reminded me that love, real love, doesn't require you to rummage through the trash of past mistakes, hoping to find something salvageable. Real love builds anew. It starts fresh, with materials that haven't already been worn down by regret and resentment.

But it's not just about romantic relationships. We do this with friendships, with jobs, with dreams we've outgrown but can't seem to let go of. We go back to old habits, old places, old versions of ourselves, hoping that familiarity will bring peace. But it rarely does. More often than not, it's like revisiting a childhood home and realizing the rooms are smaller than you remember, the paint is chipped, and the magic you once felt there was less about the space and more about the time in your life.

If there's one thing I've learned in my seasoned years, it's this: The past is a teacher, not a home. It's a place to visit for lessons, not a place to live. There are treasures to be found in its corners—wisdom, growth, and even forgiveness—but there's also the risk of getting stuck, of letting nostalgia blind you to the present and the future. The echoes of yesterday can be comforting, but they can also drown out the new melodies waiting to be written.

So, when you feel the pull to go back—to revisit what you've left behind—ask yourself why. Are you searching for closure, or are you avoiding the discomfort of moving forward? Are you honoring the lessons of the past, or are you trying to relive them? And most importantly, are you carrying those lessons into the future, or are you letting them weigh you down?

Here's where the balance lies: there are things worth looking back for. Lessons, for instance. The past is a reservoir of lessons, and if you're willing to reflect, you can draw from it a wealth of insight. Look back to understand where things went wrong, but don't stay there. Carry those lessons forward, using them to navigate the challenges ahead with wisdom you didn't have before.

Wisdom is another treasure worth seeking in the past. It's the ability to see patterns, to recognize the cycles that keep you stuck, and to decide differently next time. The past, if you let it, can whisper truths that help you grow—truths about who you were and who you're capable of becoming.

Answers, too, can sometimes be found in the rearview mirror. There are questions that only the passage of time can clarify. Why did that relationship fail? Why did that opportunity slip through my fingers? When you look back with clarity, not blame, you can find the answers that free you to move forward without carrying the weight of unresolved doubts.

And then there's inspiration. The past can remind you of your strength, your resilience, and the moments when you overcame what felt impossible. It can inspire you to keep going, to trust that just as you've weathered storms before, you can weather the ones ahead. Sometimes, looking back shows you not just how far you've come, but how much further you can go.

The truth is, life moves forward. It doesn't wait for us to catch up, and it doesn't rewind for second takes. The gift of living is the opportunity to grow, to build, to create something new with each passing day. And while the past will always be a part of who we are, it doesn't have to define where we're going.

Let the stripes of the tiger remain. And if you choose to stay, let it be a choice rooted in clarity, not fear. Let it be a choice that honors who you are now, not who you used to be. Because rummaging through the past might help you understand where you've been, but it's only by moving forward that you'll discover where you're meant to go.

THE ETERNAL WEIGHT OF GOODBYE

There is a peculiar weight that death leaves behind—an ache that doesn't just sit in the chest but seeps into the spaces between breaths, lingering long after the funeral programs have yellowed and the flowers have dried. It's not something you ever fully prepare for.

You brace yourself for the moment, for the shock, for the tears, but no one tells you that the hardest part of grief isn't the initial wave; it's the quiet ripples that follow. The moments when life expects you to return to normal while you're still standing knee-deep in the wreckage of what was. I've been sitting with this weight for a long time now, trying to put words to something that feels beyond language. Death has been no stranger in this season of my life. It has sat at my table, uninvited but persistent, whispering truths I wasn't ready to face.

I've lost people I loved deeply, people I admired from afar, and even people I barely knew but whose absence still carved a hollow space in the world. And the thing about loss is that it's never just about the person who's gone; it's about the void they leave behind, the lives they touched, and the echoes of their presence that refuse to fade.

One of the most profound lessons death has taught me is how deeply connected we are, even to those we only know in passing.

When someone leaves this world, their absence ripples outwards, touching not just their immediate circle but everyone who ever crossed their path. It's a strange and humbling realization—to know that even the smallest interactions carry weight.

The cashier you see every week at the grocery store, the coworker you exchange polite nods with, the neighbor who waves but never speaks—their lives brush against yours in ways you don't fully grasp until they're no longer there.

But it's the losses that hit closest to home that leave the deepest scars. The kind that rearranges your world, forcing you to navigate a new normal that feels anything but normal. I remember the first time I truly understood what it meant to lose someone. It wasn't just the grief that overwhelmed me; it was the realization that their absence was permanent. That no matter how much I wanted to, I couldn't call them, couldn't hear their laugh, couldn't hold their hand. The finality of it all was a truth I couldn't outrun.

And then there's the guilt—the quiet, unspoken guilt that lingers in the background. The "I should have called more" guilt, the "I should have been there" guilt, the "Did they know how much I loved them?" guilt. It's irrational, I know.

But grief isn't rational. It's messy and unpredictable, an ocean that pulls you under just when you think you've found your footing. And yet, in the midst of that messiness, there's a strange kind of beauty—a raw, unfiltered reminder of just how deeply we can love and how much that love can hurt when it's torn away.

As I've navigated these waters, I've found myself thinking more about the people who are left behind—the spouses, the children, the friends who must find a way to live with the void. I've watched as friends and family grapple with loss, each in their own way.

Some carry their grief like a badge of honor, a testament to the depth of their love. Others bury it deep, putting on a brave face for the world while their hearts quietly break. And then there are those who get stuck, unable to move forward because the weight of the loss feels too great to bear.

One friend, in particular, comes to mind. She had been married for 25 years when her husband passed away unexpectedly. In the weeks that followed, she described feeling "uncovered," as though a part of her had been ripped away. "He was my person," she said, tears streaming down her face. "The one who knew me better than anyone else, who made me feel safe, who made life make sense. And now he's gone, and I don't know who I am without him."

Her words stayed with me, not just because of their raw honesty but because they captured something universal about loss. When you lose someone who has been a part of your life for so long, it's not just their presence you mourn; it's the life you built together, the routines, the inside jokes, the shared dreams. It's the version of yourself that existed only with them. And that kind of loss—the loss of both a person and a piece of yourself—is a weight that no one can prepare you for.

And yet, life demands that we move forward. The world doesn't stop for our grief. Bills still need to be paid, children still need to be cared for, and the dog still needs to be walked. There's a cruel irony in how life continues, indifferent to the fact that your world has been shattered. But maybe that's also the gift of it. Because in the midst of the mundane, we find a way to keep going. We find glimpses of joy in the small things—a child's laughter, a warm cup of coffee, a sunset that takes our breath away. And slowly, almost imperceptibly, we begin to rebuild.

I've come to believe that grief is not something we overcome; it's something we carry. It becomes a part of us, woven into the fabric of our lives. And while the weight of it may never fully disappear, we learn to live with it, to find strength in it, to let it shape us in ways that honor the ones we've lost. We carry their memory, their love, their lessons, and in doing so, we keep a part of them alive.

For me, this journey has been as much about learning to support others as it has been about navigating my own losses. I've learned that grief doesn't have a timeline, that healing isn't linear, and that sometimes the best thing you can do for someone who is grieving is simply to be there. To sit with them in their pain, to let them cry or rage or sit in silence without feeling the need to fix it.

Because grief isn't something that can be fixed. It's something that must be felt, honored, and given space to exist.

I've also learned the importance of staying connected. Too often, we assume that people have all the support they need in the immediate aftermath of a loss. We send flowers, attend the funeral, and offer our condolences, but as the weeks turn into months, our attention wanes. Life moves on, and we forget that for the person grieving, the pain is still fresh. The calls and texts that once flooded in become sporadic, and the silence can be deafening.

If there's one thing I've taken away from these experiences, it's this: don't underestimate the power of presence. A simple text, a phone call, a coffee date—these small acts of connection can mean the world to someone who feels like they've been left behind in their grief. They remind us that while the person we lost may be gone, we are not alone.

As I sit here, reflecting on the weight of goodbye, I'm reminded of something a dear friend once said to me: "Grief is the price we pay for love." And though the price feels steep, I've come to see it as a testament to the depth of our connections, the beauty of our shared humanity, and the enduring power of love. Because even in the face of loss, love remains. It lingers in the memories, in the stories, in the way we carry forward the lessons and the legacy of those we've lost.

So, to anyone who is grieving, I offer this: feel the weight.

Let it press against you, let it remind you of the love you shared, and let it shape you into someone who carries that love forward. And when the weight feels too heavy to bear, reach out. Because in the end, we were never meant to carry it alone.

THE LEGACY OF THE ETHER: LIFE, DEATH, AND THE CALL OF PURPOSE

There's a thought that's been weighing on my mind lately—a thought about life, death, and the space between them. It's an idea I feel compelled to capture, even if I'm not sure where it belongs in this book just yet. Perhaps it will find its place in time, but for now, I need to lay it down, to release it from the confines of my mind and give it breath.

I truly believe that the sole reason we live our earthly lives is to fulfill the unique callings and passions that are woven into the fabric of our existence. Those callings, those deep, intrinsic purposes, are not random. They are designed, intentional, and profoundly necessary. They are the means by which we contribute to the ever-expanding ethos of the universe.

And it is this ethos—a collective spirit of every dream fulfilled, every lesson learned, every joy shared—that carries the wisdom, hope, and favor of the world.

Living out our calling isn't just about personal fulfillment. It's about leaving behind something greater than ourselves. Every life, no matter how small or grand, is a piece of puzzle that extends far beyond what we can see or comprehend. When someone lives a life of purpose, their essence—what they've built, loved, taught, and shared—becomes a part of this universal ether. It doesn't end when their body is laid to rest.

It lingers, influencing the living, fueling their dreams, and giving strength to their hope.

When we mourn those who pass, what we truly grieve is the presence of that tangible expression of their calling—their laughter, their touch, their voice. Yet, their life's essence doesn't disappear.

234

It becomes part of the air we breathe, the wisdom we draw on, the quiet inspiration that stirs us when we're at our most uncertain.

The reason we remember certain people so vividly, why their names echo long after they're gone, is because they lived lives of contribution—offering themselves fully to the world's greater good. They didn't hold back their talents, their passions, or their truths. They poured them out like water into the soil of humanity, nurturing the growth of others long after their departure.

To live without pursuing your calling is to deny the world a piece of that ethos. It is to withhold a part of the energy that carries humanity forward. But to live fully, to live with intention and courage, is to leave behind something eternal. It is to ensure that, when your name is spoken in rooms you'll never enter, it will be with gratitude, admiration, and perhaps even awe.

This is why living out your calling matters—not for recognition or accolades, but because your life, when lived authentically and passionately, becomes part of the spirit that sustains the world. It is your unique thread in the endless fabric of time, a thread that ensures the universe doesn't just survive but thrives with beauty, purpose, and hope.

THE WEIGHT OF LOSS: WHEN DEATH REDEFINES FRIENDSHIP AND CONNECTION

Death, in its finality, has a way of shaking the foundation of everything we thought we knew about connection, permanence, and the way we navigate the world. It's not just the absence of the person that hurts—though that absence is palpable, heavy, and unrelenting. It's also the way their loss redefines us, shifts our perspective, and creates an invisible line between who we were before they left and who we become after.

I've often said that relationships have the power to shape us. They give us joy, teach us lessons, and sometimes even define how we see ourselves. But what happens when those relationships are severed by death? What happens when someone who held space in your life—whether as a friend, a sibling, a parent, or a partner—is suddenly no longer there? The loss isn't just external; it becomes an internal reckoning, a reconfiguration of the emotional and mental frameworks that held your identity together.

Death, especially of those we hold close, carries a kind of trauma that is hard to articulate. It isn't just about grief—though grief is a significant part of it. It's about how that grief alters the lens through which we see the world. The colors dim, the edges blur, and the once-familiar becomes unfamiliar. It's a loss of certainty, a loss of safety. And for many of us, it's a loss of innocence, the shattering of the illusion that we'll always have time to say what needs to be said, do what needs to be done, or simply exist alongside the people who matter most.

But it's not just how we see the world that changes; it's also how the world sees us. When you lose someone close to you, people begin to see you through the lens of that loss. You become "the one who lost so-and-so," a label that, while well-meaning, can feel isolating. People treat you differently. Some offer sympathy, some withdraw because they don't know what to say, and others project their own fears onto you. In their eyes, you become a reminder of their own mortality, their own fragility.

It's an unspoken shift that can feel both comforting and alienating, as though you're being seen but not fully understood.

I've experienced this shift in my own life, particularly as I've grown older and the losses have begun to accumulate. Each one leaves a mark, a scar that never quite fades. And while the world keeps turning, while life continues to demand your attention, there's a part of you that stays frozen in the moment of that loss. You replay conversations, remember laughter, and cling to the fragments of a connection that now feels both tangible and fleeting. Over time, you learn to carry the weight, but the weight never disappears.

For me, the loss of friendships to death has been particularly impactful. Friendships, especially the deep, soul-level ones, are the relationships we often take for granted. They're not bound by obligation like family, nor are they tethered by romance or shared assets. Friendships are chosen, nurtured by mutual respect, shared experiences, and a kind of love that doesn't demand but simply exists.

When you lose a friend to death, it feels like losing a piece of yourself—the part of you that only they could see, only they could understand. It's a loss that reverberates through your sense of identity, leaving you questioning not just who they were to you, but who you are without them.

And then there's the trauma. The trauma of waking up each day knowing they won't be there. The trauma of seeing their name pop up in old messages, of hearing a song that reminds you of them, of reaching for the phone to call them only to remember you can't. This kind of trauma isn't loud or explosive; it's quiet, insidious. It seeps into the cracks of your life, altering the way you move through the world. It makes you more cautious, more guarded. It teaches you to hold on a little tighter, to love a little harder, but it also teaches you to fear the inevitable loss that comes with loving.

In many ways, death forces us to confront our own humanity. It strips away the illusion of permanence and leaves us face-to-face with the truth that life is fragile, fleeting, and unpredictable. It reminds us that every relationship is both a gift and a risk, that to love is to open yourself to the possibility of loss.

And yet, it is in this confrontation that we find meaning. It is in this space of vulnerability and grief that we discover the depth of our capacity to love, to connect, to endure.

As I think about the losses I've experienced, I'm struck by how they've shaped my understanding of what it means to live fully. Losing someone doesn't just teach you about death; it teaches you about life. It teaches you to appreciate the moments you have, to say the things that need to be said, to show up for the people who matter.

It teaches you that while death may take away the physical presence of someone you love, it cannot erase the impact they've had on your life, the memories they've left behind, or the lessons they've taught you.

This is the context through which I now understand the loss of Lawrence Wilbon, a man whose life and friendship meant more to me than words can express. His passing is not just the loss of a friend; it is the loss of a brother, a confidant, a partner in this journey called life. It is a reminder of the fragility of the connections we hold dear and the importance of cherishing them while we can.

It is a reminder that grief, while painful, is also a testament to the depth of love we've experienced.In the face of such loss, we have a choice. We can let it harden us, make us fearful, close us off from the possibility of future connections. Or we can let it open us, deepen our understanding of what it means to love and be loved, and inspire us to live in a way that honors those we've lost.

For me, I choose the latter. I choose to carry Lawrence's memory not as a burden but as a beacon, a reminder of what it means to live fully, to love deeply, and to leave a legacy that endures long after we're gone.

THE DEATH OF THE L

I'm still trying to figure out how to begin this piece. It's difficult, almost impossible, to find the right words for something like this. This piece is in dedication to my good brother, my friend, my confidant, Lawrence Wilbon, who passed away on December 26, 2024. I've been sitting with this loss, trying to make sense of it, though I know that's a futile effort. Where do I begin? How do I talk about a man like Lawrence, a man who meant so much to so many, who left a mark so profound that words feel inadequate?

Maybe the best place to start is with the title: The Death of the L.

The title is rooted in a joke I used to share with Lawrence. March 23 was his birthday, and I used to tell him it was the day the letter "L" was born, a playful nod to how central he was to everything and everyone around him. That's just who he was: the letter L personified. But now, as I sit here writing this tribute, the title carries a weight I wasn't ready for. The death of Lawrence Wilbon feels like the death of a part of me, a part of us, a part of the world that was lucky enough to know him.

Lawrence wasn't just a coworker at Fathers Incorporated. He wasn't just a friend I met through mutual connections. And he wasn't just someone I called "brother" in the casual way we often use the term today. Lawrence was my brother in every sense of the word. He was my brother from another mother, bound not by blood but by a connection deeper than words can fully explain.

Our paths crossed about six years ago when he and his family moved from Louisville, Kentucky, to Atlanta, Georgia. We were introduced through mutual friends, and he came to talk to me about potential opportunities at Fathers Incorporated. I expected a brief meeting, maybe an hour or so. Instead, we sat for nearly four and a half hours, talking about everything—our lives, our goals, our families, our work. By the end of that conversation, I knew I'd met someone extraordinary.

At the time, we didn't have any positions available, but Lawrence wasn't deterred. He asked if he could volunteer, and I said yes, unsure of where or how he would fit. He showed up at the office, eager to work on whatever we needed. We started with a few small projects, but soon, he became indispensable. When an opportunity opened up under a federal contract we were renewing, I knew exactly who I wanted to hire. Lawrence became our Vice President of Business and Community Development, a role he embraced with a passion and dedication that was unmatched.

But Lawrence was so much more than his title. He was the glue that held our agency together, the one who saw gaps and filled them without hesitation. He was the plug, the catch-all, the buffer, the regulator. He caught things I couldn't, handled things I didn't have time for, and did it all with a grace and humility that made it seem effortless. He took every responsibility seriously, not because he had to, but because he wanted to. He loved this work, loved our mission, loved being part of something bigger than himself.

More than that, Lawrence loved people. He loved his family with a fierceness that was evident in everything he did. He adored his wife and children, spoke about them with a light in his eyes that made you understand they were his world. He loved his sister and nephew, always sharing stories about their bond. And he loved his extended family—the people he chose, like me and the rest of the team at Fathers Incorporated. His love was never conditional, never transactional. Once he gave it to you, it was yours, no strings attached.

Losing Lawrence at just 47 years old feels unfair. It feels like a cruel joke, like a reminder of how fragile and fleeting life is. He and I often talked about mortality, about the inevitability of death and the importance of making the most of the time we have. He'd witnessed so much loss in his own life, losing family members at young ages, enduring a level of grief that would have broken lesser men. And yet, he never let that grief define him. He lived fully, intentionally, aware of life's fragility but unafraid to embrace its beauty.

I've been reflecting on those conversations a lot these past few days. Lawrence was so aware of the weight of legacy, of what it means to leave something behind. He and I used to laugh about how we were getting older, how we needed to take better care of ourselves, eat right, exercise, take our medicine.

But beneath the humor was a shared understanding: we wanted to be here for the people who needed us. We wanted to live long enough to see our work make a difference, to see our children grow, to leave a mark on the world.

And Lawrence did leave a mark. He left a mark on me, on Fathers Incorporated, on everyone who was lucky enough to know him. He had a laugh that could break the tension in the heaviest of moments, a knack for finding humor even in the darkest times. He had a way of making people feel seen, valued, understood. He built relationships with intention, not just for the sake of networking but because he genuinely cared about people. He wanted everyone to win.

There's a phrase Lawrence once posted on Facebook that sums up who he was: "Collaboration over competition. Any day. I just want everyone to win." That was his ethos. He believed in the power of connection, the importance of working together, the value of lifting others up. It's a lesson I'll carry with me for the rest of my life.

One moment that sticks with me happened just a few weeks ago. I had wanted to bless Lawrence financially for helping me with a particular project, something outside the scope of his usual work. I added the bonus to his paycheck but forgot to tell him about it. When he saw the extra money, he immediately thought it was a mistake. Before I even realized what had happened, he was on the phone with our CFO and COO, trying to figure out who had made the error, wanting to make sure they fixed it, before I found out.

When he finally got to me, I explained that it wasn't a mistake, that it was my way of thanking him for going above and beyond. We laughed about it, and in his classic style, he replied, "Man, I was about to send that money back so fast! I ain't trying to go to jail and hell at the same time!"

That was Lawrence. He could take a serious moment and find the humor in it, lightening the mood in a way only he could. But even as I celebrate the life Lawrence lived, I can't ignore the hole his absence has left. It's a square hole on a board of round holes, a void that no one else can fill. He was my armor bearer, my protector, my shield. He took on my dreams, my responsibilities, my burdens, and carried them as if they were his own. He was my hedger of protection, the answer to a prayer I didn't even know I'd prayed. And now he's gone. His Zoom square will forever be empty in our meetings.

His laugh will no longer echo through our office. His voice will no longer be there to reassure me when I'm doubting myself, to remind me of what's possible, to make me believe in the goodness of people even when the world feels heavy.

Death is an inevitable consequence of life, but that doesn't make it any easier to bear. I miss my brother. I miss the way he showed up, not just for me but for everyone around him. I miss his heart, his humor, his unwavering commitment to love and service.

As I write this, I'm reminded of the history we carry as Black men, of the legacy of resilience and loss that has defined our existence. Slavery taught us the pain of separation, the anguish of losing family, the struggle to hold onto love and connection in a world determined to tear us apart. Lawrence understood that history, felt it deeply in the way he loved his family, the way he built relationships, the way he gave so much of himself. He knew that love was an act of defiance, a way of reclaiming what was stolen from us.

So as I mourn Lawrence, I also honor him. I honor the way he lived, the way he loved, the way he refused to let the weight of life crush his spirit. I honor the legacy he left behind, a legacy of kindness, generosity, and unwavering faith in the power of connection.

Rest in peace, my brother. You were, and always will be, the letter L personified. And though your absence is felt deeply, your presence will live on in our hearts, in our memories, and in the work we continue to do in your honor.

You will never be forgotten.

CHAPTER NINE

EMBRACING CHANGE: ADAPTING TO LIFE'S TRANSITIONS WITH GRACE

THANK YOU

First, let me take a moment to say thank you. Thank you for staying with me through the latter part of the last chapter. I know it wasn't easy—those pages were heavy, the weight of loss and the reality of love's fragility pressing down on every word. Writing it wasn't easy, either. It was a section I had been dreading for a long time, knowing that to fully honor the truth of being seasoned, I had to go there.

I had to sit in the pain, not skim over it. But pain has a way of making space for growth, and your patience through that chapter shows me you understand that. For that, I am grateful.

As I continue to evolve in the writing of this book, it feels less like a solo project and more like a shared journey. Your presence, your attention to these words, feels like having a companion on a long road. It's humbling to know that you're walking alongside me, reflecting on your own life as I unpack mine. This book is as much about you as it is about me, and together, we're peeling back the layers of what it means to live, to grow, to become.

Now, here we are, moving into a new chapter—one I've been looking forward to sharing with you. This is the part where we shake off the heaviness, loosen up, and laugh a little.

Embracing the Change. That's what it's all about. For my fellow seasoned folks, this chapter will make you chuckle, nod knowingly, and maybe even see your own reflections in my stories. And for the youngins? This is a glimpse into the mindset of the gray-haired crowd you might sometimes dismiss. I promise, there's wisdom here if you're open to it.

So let's dive in. Let's explore what it means to move from the rush of youth to the rhythm of being seasoned. Let's talk about how we've traded relevance for resonance and how we've learned to stand tall in the face of change.

I'm excited to bring you into this chapter, into this moment, and into the joy of living life at this stage. Let's embrace it together.

SEASONED: PUT SOME RESPECT ON MY NAME

There's something about seasoning that transforms the ordinary into the extraordinary. A little salt, a touch of paprika, maybe a hint of garlic, and suddenly, the bland becomes bold. That's what life feels like when you've lived long enough to collect a little seasoning of your own.

Not just the years, but the wisdom, the lessons, the hard-earned truths sprinkled over your existence like an invisible marinade. You become richer, deeper, more nuanced. And yet, there's always someone out there who mistakes your seasoning for staleness, as if the gray in your hair is an announcement of irrelevance rather than a testament to resilience.

Let me tell you something about gray hair. It's not stress. It's not the wear and tear of years grinding us down. No, it's the sparkle of wisdom. It's God's way of sprinkling a little salt on us, making sure the youngins can spot those of us who've been through some things. You don't get this kind of seasoning by accident. It's earned, and it comes at a cost. But let me tell you, it's worth it.

And I've reached a point in my life where I need you to put some respect on that. Respect on the gray, on the journey, on the battles fought, and the lessons learned.

Now, I hear you out there, especially the younger generation, saying things like, "Man, y'all were born in the 1900s. That was forever ago!" And you're right. It does sound like another century—because it was. But let me tell you something about the 1900s. That's when a lot of the seasoning got cooked up. The experiences we had back then built the very foundation of the world you're standing on now.

Just because we're not sprinting around with the energy we had in 1985 doesn't mean we don't know what we're talking about. We've earned every one of these gray hairs, every wrinkle, and every quiet smile we give when you think we don't get it. Trust me—we get it. We've been where you are. The difference is, now we don't have to run. We've mastered the art of walking with purpose.

Being seasoned is not about being old. It's about being refined, like aged wine or a well-cooked meal. It's about understanding that life, with all its ups and downs, is a process of becoming. Every mistake, every heartbreak, every victory—they're all ingredients, blending together to create the flavor of who you are. But it seems like the world has forgotten how to appreciate that kind of richness.

They call us "old timers" or "has-beens," like we've been shelved away, expired and forgotten. I'm here to tell you differently.

We are not expired. We are seasoned.

And when I say seasoned, I'm talking about the ability to hold joy and pain in the same breath, to let one inform the other. Love and pain, they're two sides of the same coin, both of them necessary to make life feel full. If you've lived long enough, you've learned that pain can be a teacher, even when you hate the lesson. Take Mary J. Blige, for example. I used to say, half-jokingly, that if I were her manager, I'd keep her in pain. Now, don't get me wrong—I'd never wish hardship on anybody. But something about her heartbreak, her struggle, brought out the kind of music that could put you in a knot.

Her My Life album? Whew. That wasn't just music; it was survival, catharsis, testimony. When she was in pain, her voice carried a depth that could reach into your own heartbreak and make you feel seen. That's the thing about pain—it sharpens the edges of your creativity, your focus, your ability to connect. And when you mix that with love, with joy, with hope? That's the seasoning of life.

We seasoned folks, we've been marinated in both love and pain, and it shows. We know the joy of falling in love, that dizzying, head-over-heels feeling where you're convinced the person you're with is your forever.

We also know the sting of falling out of it, when the forever you envisioned becomes a memory you have to learn to let go of. And that's okay.

Because every time you fall, you learn. Every heartbreak, every loss, every triumph—it all adds to the complexity of your story. And when you're seasoned, you learn to savor it all, even the parts that hurt.

Now, I'm not saying the shift into this space happens overnight. For most of us, it sneaks up on you. One moment, you're the youngest person in the room, the one with all the potential. The next, you're seasoned, standing in the back with a quiet smile, letting the younger ones take center stage while you watch. At first, it feels like a loss, like you're being pushed to the margins. But then you realize something beautiful: you've moved from the heat of the battle to the wisdom of the watchtower. You're no longer the relevant warrior. You've become the wise general.

And that comes with its own power.

But let me tell you, that power is often unrecognized. The younger generations—they're so busy sprinting toward the future, they forget to look back. They don't see the value in what's behind them because they're too busy chasing what's ahead. They call us outdated, old-school, irrelevant. But here's what they don't understand: it's the seasoning that makes the dish. Without us, the world is bland.

So to the youngins reading this, let me give you a little perspective. While you're busy swiping and scrolling, racing to keep up with the latest trend, we're sitting here with our gray hairs and our salt-and-pepper beards, watching you, remembering when we were just like you. And let me tell you—there's a freedom that comes with letting all that go.

When you've lived long enough to stop caring about who's watching, you find out what really matters. You learn how to embrace the change.

Technology? Oh, it's wild. I remember watching Dick Tracy on TV as a kid, marveling at his wristwatch communicator. We thought that kind of stuff would never happen, and here we are, talking to each other on Apple Watches. Cars drive themselves now. Food gets delivered by strangers in their own cars. It's enough to make your head spin. And don't even get me started on AI—that's a whole conversation for another chapter.

But even as the world speeds up, even as it feels like we're living in the future, there's a part of me that stays rooted in the past. Not stuck, but grounded. I think about the golden moments of life—the ones you hold onto when everything else feels uncertain. And here's what I've learned: the joy of being seasoned isn't just in reminiscing about the past; it's in embracing the present with the wisdom the past has given you.

So put some respect on our name. On the gray hairs, on the wrinkles, on the slower steps and the quieter voices. We're not just old—we're seasoned. We've been through the fire and come out richer, deeper, more alive. And one day, if you're lucky, you'll be seasoned, too.

> *And when that day comes, you'll look back and thank us for reminding you that life is more than a race. It's a recipe. And seasoning is what makes it worth tasting.*

THE OLD GUY IN THE CLUB

There are some statements you say to yourself over and over, like a personal mantra. For me, one of those lines was, "I never want to be the old guy in the club." It started out as a throwaway comment—one of those things you say for a laugh, but that sticks because it's rooted in truth. And while people may chuckle when I say it, I've always meant it. I never wanted to be the old guy in the club. Yet, the more I think about that figure—the seasoned man with his quiet two-step, his well-cut suit, and his drink in hand—the more I've come to realize how much that image represents a blend of wisdom, nostalgia, and the complexity of aging.

When I was younger, I saw him often. As a DJ spinning vinyl in New York clubs, I'd watch him from my perch above the crowd. He was always there, tucked into a corner like a secret. His presence was undeniable. He wasn't loud or flashy, but there was something about him that demanded attention. The way he moved—or didn't move. The way he smiled, a knowing grin as if he was in on a joke the rest of us didn't quite get. His drink was his prop, his buffer, his silent companion. And that little two-step? It was the punctuation mark in a sentence he'd been writing his whole life. Left, right, left, right. No more, no less.

But what stood out most about the old guy in the club was his eyes. They scanned the room not in a predatory way, but in a way that said he'd seen it all before. He wasn't searching for anything; he was taking it all in. Absorbing the energy. Watching the young men and women dance like their lives depended on it. Maybe he was remembering a time when he danced the same way. Or maybe he wasn't. Either way, he'd become a fixture in those spaces—a symbol of time passing quietly in the middle of chaos.

As a DJ, I'd think to myself, What keeps him coming back? Was it the music? The ambiance? A sense of connection to something younger, more vibrant? Or was he clinging to a piece of his youth, fighting the inevitability of aging by refusing to let go of the spaces that once defined him?

Music has a way of doing that—transporting you, rewinding the clock in ways nothing else can. It's not just sound; it's memory. One song—just four bars—can take you back decades. A love lost. A moment of triumph. The best summer of your life. Music doesn't just make you feel young; it makes you feel alive.

And maybe that's why the old guy in the club keeps showing up. Not to relive his youth, but to tap into the energy that music brings. The way it lightens the load of responsibility, even for just a few hours. The way it makes you forget. And honestly, haven't we all needed that? A place—a song, a moment—where we could shed the weight of who we've become and remember who we used to be?

When I was younger, skating rinks served the same purpose for me. Roller skating was everything. The rink wasn't just a place to skate; it was a stage. The music blared, the disco ball spun, and everyone moved in rhythm. It was exercise disguised as euphoria. Hours would pass, and I'd glide across that polished floor without a care in the world.

The energy was magnetic—a crowd of people, all in sync, propelled by the beat of a house track or the smooth croon of an R&B classic. I could skate for hours then. Now? I'd be winded after ten minutes. My calves would burn, my knees would protest, and my body would remind me that I'm no longer the kid I once was.

Have you ever felt that shift—when your body reminds you of the years you've lived? It's humbling, isn't it? But also, in a strange way, grounding. Because it forces you to ask, What do I carry from those years? What part of that young, carefree version of myself still lives inside me?

That's the thing about time. It sneaks up on you. One minute, you're in the middle of the action, and the next, you're the one watching from the sidelines. That's how I felt when I moved to

Atlanta and started attending a new church. Back in Brooklyn, the deacons were the old guys in the church—the ones who carried wisdom in their voices and strength in their postures.

They were protectors, advisors, and the pillars of the community. But in Atlanta, something shifted. I walked into that church and realized I wasn't the young guy anymore. There were no deacons older than me to look up to. I was becoming the elder, the seasoned one. And that realization hit me like a freight train.

You start to see it everywhere—those subtle reminders of your seasoning. It's in the way people address you. "Pops," they say, with a tone of respect that also holds a mirror up to your age. It's in the questions your kids ask, like the time my son stopped in front of the TV while I was watching an old Western and said, "Dad, who broke the TV? Why isn't it in color?" In his eyes, I might as well have been born in the 1800s.

And then there are the moments that sting in ways you didn't expect. Like when I attended an open house for a creative program in Atlanta. I was there to learn—to expand my skills in graphic design and filmmaking. But as the guide led us through the building, he stopped next to me and the young man I'd been standing beside. He smiled at me and asked, "Is this your son?" I didn't have the energy to be mad. I just laughed, nodded, and thought, So this is what it feels like to be the old guy in the club.

The truth is, I've spent my life avoiding that role. Not because I'm ashamed of my age, but because I never wanted to feel out of place. I didn't want to be the man who didn't realize he no longer belonged. But what I've come to understand is that the old guy in the club isn't out of place. He's just occupying a different role. He's not there to prove anything or to chase youth. He's there because he's earned the right to be. Because his presence, quiet and steady, is as much a part of the fabric of that space as the music itself.

Do you see it that way? That sometimes being present isn't about making noise, but about holding space—being a witness to the energy around you? I think we all have spaces where we've transitioned from participant to observer. How do you carry yourself in those moments? Are you comfortable being still, or does it make you restless?

I'm not the old guy in the club—not yet. But I no longer fear him. If anything, I admire him. I see him in myself, in the way I've learned to savor moments rather than rush through them. In the way I've embraced my "seasoning," the pepper in my beard and the wisdom in my words.

Being seasoned isn't about clinging to the past. It's about wearing your years with pride. It's about being the calm in the storm, the steady rhythm in a room full of chaos. It's about knowing who you are and standing in it, unapologetically.

So, to the old guy in the club, I say this: Keep dancing. Keep smiling. Keep showing up, drink in hand, suit pressed, two-stepping in your corner. You're not out of place. You're the anchor. The reminder that time doesn't take away—it adds. Adds depth. Adds wisdom. Adds presence. And when my time comes to take that spot in the corner, I'll be ready. Because I'll know that being seasoned isn't something to hide. It's something to celebrate.

THE FOUNTAIN OF YOUTH: THE BARBERSHOP AND THE BLACK MAN'S COUNTRY CLUB

There's a place where time bends, where seasoned men and wide-eyed boys exist in the same breath, sharing space, trading wisdom, measuring their lives against one another in ways both spoken and unspoken. It's a place where age is irrelevant, where the ghosts of your younger self sit beside you in the chair, nodding in approval or shaking their heads at what you've become. The barbershop. The Black man's country club.

Men go there to be seen and unseen. To speak and to listen. To belong. It is where you can both feel young and be young, a rare moment where the body's limitations bow to the mind's infinite ability to remember, to relive, to reshape. But for seasoned men, the barbershop is more than a nostalgic retreat—it is a testament to transition, a space where age is embraced, and wisdom is honored. It is where men learn to adapt to new phases of life with grace, to see the beauty in growing older, and to recognize their place in the evolving cycle of manhood.

When you step into a barbershop, the air thick with the familiar mix of talcum powder, alcohol, and the sharp scent of clippers biting through fresh hair, you are not simply entering a place to get a haircut. You are stepping into an arena, a sanctuary, a theater, a classroom. It is a place where the thug and the pastor can sit side by side, debating politics, sports, or faith, bound together not by their differences, but by the sacredness of the space. In the barbershop, titles are left at the door, and what matters is the strength of your argument, the conviction in your voice, and the rhythm of your presence in the conversation.

The air is thick with unfiltered truth, what some might call the shop's "truth serum." No matter your status outside, when you step inside, you will be challenged. You will be measured by how well you can hold your own in debate, how confidently you can express your opinions. A man's manhood is not just in his haircut, but in his ability to stand by his words, to defend his point, and to listen when wisdom is being spoken.

The young and old alike spar in verbal jousts, learning how to articulate themselves, how to think critically, and, most importantly, how to respect a man who knows more simply because he has lived more.

There are the elders—men who wear their years like a second skin, their wisdom tucked between their lips like an unlit cigar. Their presence is the foundation of the space, their words heavy, deliberate, often slow but never without meaning. When they speak, younger men lean in, not just out of respect, but out of necessity. This is where knowledge is passed down, where lessons are taught not through lectures but through storytelling, through banter, through the ritual of the lineup and the fade. They are the reminders that embracing change means accepting the wisdom that comes with it, rather than resisting it.

And then there are the young men, full of energy, bravado, ready to spar, eager to prove they have something to contribute to the conversation. They bring the music, the slang, the urgency of youth. They challenge the elders, push back against the wisdom that feels outdated, irrelevant. But they are listening. Even when they act like they aren't, even when they roll their eyes at an old man's tale about how things used to be, they are absorbing, storing these lessons for a later date when they will need them most.

Then there are the boys. Like my son that day in the barbershop, sitting at my knee, lost in his own world but surrounded by the world he will one day grow into. He was on his iPad, completely absorbed in whatever game or video had captured his attention. But in my mind, I was somewhere else.

I found myself staring at him, lost in thought. What does this moment mean to him? I wondered. Does he even know? Does he see what I see?

I never had this. I never had a father sitting beside me, never had the experience of watching my old man getting a lineup while I waited my turn. My mother took me to the shop, handed off the instructions, and left. I sat in silence, soaking up the atmosphere but never fully feeling like I belonged in the way other boys did. Now, here I was, sitting with my son in that same space. He wasn't engaged, not yet, but one day he would be.

I imagined him years from now, debating basketball with the barbers, chiming in on grown-man conversations, laughing at the same kinds of jokes I laughed at now. Will he remember this moment? Will he understand its significance? I didn't know, but I hoped. I hoped that one day, he would think back to these Saturdays, sitting in the barbershop with his father, and realize just how much it meant.

Would he see me? Would he see himself in the same chair one day, with his own son sitting at his knee? Would he recognize the importance of this space, the conversations, the rhythm of it all? Does he even know what I'm giving him right now?

I exhaled, shaking the thought from my head. One day, he will. One day.

THE LEGEND OF OLD OTIS

Every barbershop has an Old Otis. The elder statesman. The man who has seen it all, done it all, and isn't afraid to remind you of it. He sits in the same chair, day in and day out, watching, listening, occasionally chiming in with a story that you're never quite sure is true but never dare question.

Old Otis is the embodiment of embracing change with grace. He doesn't fight time; he flows with it. He tells his stories not to dwell in the past but to bridge the gap between then and now.

His presence in the barbershop serves as a reminder that wisdom is not just something to be acquired, but something to be shared.

Martin Lawrence captured the essence of this kind of man perfectly with his character Old Otis, the hilariously exaggerated security guard from Martin. There was one episode in particular that sticks out, the moment when a young man, full of swagger and arrogance, tried to dismiss Otis as just another old man past his prime.

The scene unfolded in a shoe store, where the young man attempted to cut in line, pushing past the elders waiting patiently. Otis, always ready, stepped up. "Hold on, young fella. You just gon' skip the line?"

"Move out my way, old man," the young man scoffed, his bravado on full display.

Otis tilted his head, his trademark squint tightening as he took in the disrespect. "Oh, so you callin' me old?" he asked.

The young man smirked. "Yeah, you old!"

Otis turned to the other people in line, pointing one by one.

"So he old?" "Yeah!"

"And she old?" "Yeah!"

"And he old?" "Yeah, he even older than her!"

Otis took a deep breath, squared his shoulders, and then delivered the line that would go down in sitcom history: "I think what we are having here is a failure to communicate between the young people and the old people. Whenever a young person was disrespectful to the old people, we had this thing back in the day. Ahhhh, what was it called? It was called, ahhhh. Oh, yeah—it was called whoopin ass'."

With that, Old Otis did what Old Otis does best—he handled his business. The young man, full of energy but empty of wisdom, found himself learning the hard way that experience always trumps arrogance.

That's what makes the barbershop special. It is the fountain of youth and the well of wisdom, a place where men transition through life with grace, where they embrace change rather than resist it. It is where a boy becomes a man, where a young man finds his voice, and where an elder finds his purpose in passing down what he knows.

It is where men gather, not just to groom their hair, but to sharpen their understanding of what it means to grow older with dignity, humor, and wisdom.

THE WHISPERS OF THE BODY: LISTENING TO THE LANGUAGE OF AGE

There comes a time when your body begins to speak a language you never quite learned in your youth. It doesn't whisper in the way it once did—it announces itself, declares its presence with every ache, every stiffness, every unexpected sound that wasn't there before. It's a language that demands you not just hear but listen, truly listen, because the consequences of ignoring it grow heavier with time.

When I was young, my body spoke in energy, in resilience, in bounce-back ability. A sprained ankle was a temporary inconvenience, a bruise was a badge of honor, and an all-nighter was nothing a good meal and a nap couldn't fix. There was a rhythm to it, an understanding that no matter what happened, healing was swift, recovery was certain. But that was then.

Now, the dialogue has shifted. My body no longer operates on blind faith; it expects me to participate in its well-being. And the conversation is no longer passive—it is persistent.

It asks me questions I never thought to answer before: How much water have you had today? When was the last time you stretched? Did you really think you could eat that and not pay for it later? And worst of all—the most humbling of all—Are you sure you should be doing this?

The body keeps score. Every choice, every indulgence, every missed opportunity for rest adds up. I've felt it in the way my knees hesitate before taking the stairs, in the cautious way I rise from a low chair, in the deliberate placement of my feet when stepping onto an escalator. I move differently now—not because I want to, but because I must.

A few years back, my son challenged me to a game of one-on-one basketball. He was young, quick, and full of the confidence that comes from never having known what it feels like to hesitate before running. I laced up my sneakers, feeling the old fire return, the competitive spirit whispering, Bro, you still got it.

I did not still have it.

Within minutes, my breath was a stranger to me, my legs questioning every movement. My mind remembered the agility, the footwork, the skill—but my body filed a formal protest. I left that court with a sore pride and a reminder that aging is not an invitation to stop moving; it is a command to move wisely.

And then there was the obstacle course at my church teambuilding retreat.

I remember standing at the base of that towering wooden structure, staring up at the ropes, the beams, the climbing walls that once would have felt like nothing more than a playground for my younger self. The instructor explained the course, their voice full of enthusiasm, but all I could hear was the silent negotiation happening in my head.

Can I do this? Should I do this? What happens if I fall? But pride, as it often does, nudged me forward. Not to mentioned that my wife is standing in full view of what was about to happen.

I strapped on the safety harness and took my first step onto the structure. The wooden beam beneath my feet felt narrower than it should have, the first rope I grabbed thinner, my grip less certain. I willed my legs to be steady, my arms to find their old strength, my breath to remain even. But halfway up the climb, my body started speaking louder than my willpower. My arms trembled, my thighs burned, my breath turned shallow. I was at war with myself, my younger self egging me on while my seasoned self whispered caution. And then, about three-fourths of the way up, my body made the decision for me.

My grip faltered, my legs turned to jelly, and suddenly I was hanging there, my fingers barely curled around a rope, dangling between ambition and reality. Below me, a few of my church brothers were cheering, urging me forward. But there was a different kind of silence within me now—not defeat, but an understanding. I could push forward, or I could listen. And so, with one final exhale, I signaled to the instructor that I was done.

I descended slowly, landing back on solid ground with a mix of disappointment and relief. I had wanted to conquer that course, to prove something to myself. But what I realized in that moment was that listening to my body was no failure—it was wisdom. There was no shame in acknowledging my limits, no disgrace in knowing when to let go. My body had spoken, and this time, I had listened.

And so, I embrace it. I listen when my body speaks, I respond when my mind whispers. I move with intention, I rest when needed, I cherish the days of feeling good and accept the ones when I do not. Because this is the season I am in, and I have earned every ache, every wrinkle, every silver strand. They are not signs of decline—they are evidence of life well-lived.

And then there's the part that nobody really wants to talk about— the shift in intimacy, the way sex itself changes as you age. It's funny, because when you're younger, you assume that passion is infinite, that your body will always respond the way it once did, that desire and performance will always go hand in hand. But then life comes along with its humbling lessons.

I used to think that aging in this regard was something that happened to other people. That loss of stamina, slower recovery, and shifting desire were things that belonged to men much older than me. And yet, here I am, experiencing a new reality. It's not that the fire is gone—it's that it burns differently. What used to be spontaneous now requires intention. What used to be effortless now demands a little more patience, a little more care. And what I've come to understand is that this isn't a loss—it's a transformation.

The introduction of the little blue pill into cultural conversation was a revelation to many men. The idea that there was a quick fix, a shortcut back to youth, was both a relief and a reckoning. Because the truth is, every man wants to feel virile, to feel capable, to still command the presence in the bedroom that he once did. But for all the solutions that exist, the real battle is in the mind.

It's in learning to accept that intimacy isn't just about physicality—it's about connection, communication, and trust.

It's also about adjusting expectations. The reality is, you don't recover the same way. You don't move the same way. And while there's a part of you that resists admitting it, there's another part that is learning to appreciate what's still possible, what's still good, what's still worth celebrating. And in some ways, this new level of intimacy is richer, deeper, more meaningful. It's not just about proving something—it's about experiencing something.

This is one of those conversations that doesn't happen often enough among men. We joke about it, we make passing remarks, but we don't really talk about it. We don't admit to the frustration, the adjustments, the small losses that we don't quite know how to grieve. But what if we did? What if we made space to share, to normalize, to support each other in the understanding that aging isn't the enemy—it's just another stage of the journey?

And then, of course, there's the little pill compartment. The one I swore I'd never need. I remember walking into the pharmacy, strolling past the aisles like I always had, until my eyes landed on that section—the one I had always associated with old people. The little clear box with compartments labeled Sunday through Saturday, the same ones I used to tease my mother about when I was young. I remember laughing then, thinking, That'll never be me.

And yet, here I am.

It started with just one pill, something small, easy to remember. But then another was added, and then another. Vitamins, blood pressure medication, allergy pills—all of them now a daily routine. It became too much to keep track of, too easy to forget. And so, one day, I found myself standing in that pharmacy aisle, reaching for the very thing I swore I would never need. I brought it home, set it up, and placed it on my nightstand, where it now sits as a daily reminder that my body requires more attention than it once did.

At first, I resented it. That little box felt like an admission of something I wasn't quite ready to say out loud. But over time, I began to see it differently. It wasn't a symbol of decline—it was a tool of care, a simple act of self-preservation. Each compartment isn't just a space for medication; it's a commitment to showing up for myself, to doing what's necessary to maintain my health, to respecting the body that has carried me this far.

This is the conversation of the seasoned. This is the language of age. And I am finally fluent.

THE WEIGHT OF VALIDATION: SEEKING WORTH IN A SEASONED LIFE

I've been thinking a lot about validation lately. The ways we search for it, the ways we need it, and the ways it shapes us. When we're young, affirmation is everything—parents, teachers, peers, even the world at large.

We look outward for confirmation that we belong, that we are enough, that we are seen. But as we grow older, particularly as we become more seasoned, the question shifts. It's no longer just about affirmation; it becomes about validation. Not just being seen, but being deemed worthy of what we bring to the world.

There comes a point when you start asking yourself: Am I still useful? That's the quiet, persistent question that lingers in the mind of anyone stepping into the latter half of life.

And as much as we like to believe we don't need external validation, that we've done enough, that our contributions speak for themselves—the truth is, we still seek it. Consciously or subconsciously, we look for the world to tell us that we matter. That our presence is still necessary. That we are still a force.

I've found that one of the strongest validations we receive as we age comes from our children. We look at them as proof that our time wasn't wasted, that our sacrifices bore fruit. Their successes become intertwined with our own sense of accomplishment. And it makes sense—after all, we spend years pouring into them, molding them, preparing them for the world. But it's also where the danger lies.

Because what happens when their path doesn't unfold as we envisioned? What happens when they take a turn we didn't expect, or worse, when they reject the lessons we tried to teach?

I've seen fathers, especially, wrestle with this. The ones who obsess over their children's achievements, who hover, who discipline with an iron fist because they see their child's success as a direct reflection of their own worth. There's a term for it: helicopter parenting. Always circling, always watching, always ensuring their child doesn't falter. Because if they fail, what does that say about us? Did we fail too?

The truth is, our validation cannot be solely tied to our children. Yes, they are a testament to our efforts, but they are also their own people, navigating a world that is different from the one we prepared them for. Their journey is not our report card. And if we place all our validation in their hands, we risk losing ourselves when they no longer need us in the ways we were accustomed to.

Which brings me to another source of validation: availability. Someone once asked me what the greatest gift a father can give his child is, and my answer was simple—availability. Not money. Not status. Not the illusion of perfection. Just being there. Because no lesson, no legacy, no discipline holds weight if we are not present in their lives. And as we age, that same availability extends beyond just our children—it becomes the measure of our usefulness to the world. The ability to still show up, still contribute, still offer something of value. That is validation in its purest form.

Yet, as an example, in this world of responsibilities and obligations, I see something troubling in my work with Fathers Incorporated as it relates to the way some dads express the value of their financial contributions to their child—dads who celebrate not having to pay child support anymore, as if their financial obligation marks the end of their responsibility as a parent. It's a loud, misguided celebration that speaks to a fundamental misunderstanding of what fatherhood truly means. To believe that support ends at 18, or that the conclusion of a court-ordered financial obligation releases one from their role as a parent, is to fundamentally misunderstand the essence of availability.

Fatherhood is not measured in dollars. It is measured in presence. In time spent listening, guiding, supporting, and simply being there. The idea that a man can wash his hands of responsibility simply because the law no longer requires a financial contribution is not just flawed—it's tragic. Because real fatherhood extends far beyond a paycheck. It extends into adulthood, into mentorship, into legacy. To celebrate the end of child support as if it were a personal victory is to announce to the world that you never understood the role of a father in the first place.

But we live in a time where validation has been reduced to likes, shares, comments. We watch people chase it, posting everything from profound thoughts to the mundane details of their day, hoping for acknowledgment. And while it's easy to judge, the truth is, we all crave it in some form. Who doesn't want to be seen? Who doesn't want to know that their voice matters? The problem isn't in seeking validation—it's in letting it define you. In believing that its absence means you are not enough.

I've spent years collecting validations in tangible forms—awards, plaques, proclamations. Boxes filled with certificates that tell a story of a man who has achieved. And yet, there are days when I look at those boxes and wonder if they are enough. Because validation, no matter how much we receive, can still leave us empty if we don't believe it ourselves.

That's the tricky part about validation. It's not always about how much you receive; sometimes, it's about who you receive it from. We've all been there—received praise from a hundred people, but fixated on the one person who withheld it. Sat at a funeral and listened to someone be eulogized with such reverence that we wonder if our own legacy will be spoken of the same way. Wondered if the people closest to us, the ones who truly know us, see us the way the world does.

And so, in those quiet, introspective moments, I found myself praying. Not just any prayer, but a prayer that I have whispered in my most uncertain times: Lord, please keep me useful. It was never a prayer for wealth, or power, or even success. It was a plea for purpose. I would sit in the silence, hands clasped, eyes closed, and say, God, if I still have something to give, if I still have work left to do, let me know. Keep me sharp. Keep me present. Keep me useful.

As I sit in this season of my life, I am learning to redefine validation. To see it not just in awards or words, but in the lives I have touched, the spaces I have occupied, the moments I have made count. To find it in my presence, not just my achievements. To recognize that validation is not about proving I am useful, but knowing I still have something to give.

Because at the end of the day, the question isn't just Am I still useful? It's Do I still believe that I am? And that is a question only we can answer for ourselves.

THE WEIGHT OF UNFORGIVENESS: A CAGE WITHOUT A KEY

It was the most unexpected question—the kind of question that made the air feel heavier, thick with something unseen but suffocating. We were deep into filming Spit'in Anger, a documentary that, for all intents and purposes, was supposed to be a lens into the lives of children impacted by father absence.

But as the cameras rolled and the questions dug deeper into my own wounds, I realized it was becoming something else. It wasn't just about absent fathers anymore. It wasn't just about the statistics or the sociological impact of men who disappear from their children's lives. It was about me.

And that was something I hadn't fully prepared for. I wanted to tell the story; not be the story.

The producer—persistent, almost relentless—kept circling back to the same question. Would you forgive your father? He asked it like he already knew the answer, like he was waiting for me to reach an inevitable conclusion that I was nowhere near accepting. And so, I answered the only way I knew how.

"I don't know."

But that wasn't the truth.

The truth was that I did know. I just wasn't ready to say it. I didn't want to forgive him. The thought of releasing him from the weight of his absence made me feel like I was betraying myself—betraying the boy who had spent too many nights wondering why his father never came. Betraying the young man who carried that absence like a badge of honor and a chip on his shoulder. Forgiving him would mean letting go of something that, for so long, had been the fuel behind everything I did. And I wasn't ready for that. Not then.

I felt the heat rising in my chest as the producer pushed. I wanted to tell him to stop, to cut the cameras, to leave it alone. But he knew that this—this tension, this raw, unfiltered emotion—was exactly what the film needed. And so forced me to play out, even as my hands clenched into fists and my jaw locked with the force of every unsaid word.

What does it mean to forgive a ghost?

Because that's what my father was to me—a ghost. A shadow in the corners of my life. A name without a face. A presence felt only in the places where he should have been but never was. And ghosts don't ask for forgiveness. They don't come back seeking redemption. They don't apologize. So why should I give it to him? Why should I grant him peace when his absence had stolen so much of mine?

But then life, as it always does, reminded me in front of someone who would shake me to my core. Someone who knew more about forgiveness than I ever could. Darryl Green, CEO of Deep Forgiveness, recently sat across from me on my I Am Dad podcast and told me the story of how he forgave the man who murdered his brother. The man who murdered his brother. I listened, silent and still, as he spoke about the weight of holding onto pain, about how resentment isn't just a burden—it's a cage. A prison where you hold the key but refuse to use it.

And then he said something that settled into my bones like an unshakable truth: Unforgiveness blocks change.

It was that moment—the moment when his words struck something deep within me—that I started to see my own chains. Even though I forgave my father years ago during the filming of Spit'in Anger; I can still remember the anger, the bitterness, the walls I had built brick by brick to keep people from getting too close, to protect myself from ever feeling the sting of betrayal again.

Over time I have realized that I had spent so much of my life guarding against pain that I had also locked myself away from love, from trust, from the possibility of something better.

Because here's the thing about betrayal—it rewires you. It makes you suspicious. It makes you hesitant to believe in anything that feels too good, too stable, too secure. And trust? Trust becomes a myth, an illusion you once believed in before reality snatched it away. Whether it's a father who never showed up, a friend who turned their back on you, a lover who shattered promises, betrayal and broken trust leave scars. Deep ones. Ones that don't fade just because time passes.

I know this because I've lived it. And I know that for years, I let that pain dictate the way I moved through the world.

I called men my brothers, only to watch them disappear when I needed them most. I gave my loyalty to people who used it as a weapon against me. I learned, over and over again, that people leave. That they lie. That they betray. And so I carried that knowledge with me like armor, convinced that as long as I never let anyone in too deep, they could never hurt me the way my father did.

But what I failed to see was that the armor was also a cage. It kept the pain out, but it also kept the love out. It kept me safe, but it also kept me alone.

And so the question of forgiveness haunted me. Not just in that moment with the producer, but in the quiet spaces of my life. Could I do it? Did I even want to? And if I did, what would that mean? Would it make me weak? Would it mean I was excusing what he did—or rather, what he didn't do?

Then came the second realization—the one that truly set me free. Forgiveness wasn't about him. It was never about him. It was about me.

Luke 23:34 echoed in my mind, the words of Jesus on the cross piercing through my resistance: Father, forgive them, for they know not what they do. He wasn't speaking in comfort, not removed from pain. He was in agony, nailed to a cross, betrayed, abandoned, humiliated. And yet, in the midst of that suffering, he still chose forgiveness. He still released those who had wronged him. He still let go.

And so, I made a choice.I chose to forgive.
Not because he deserved it. Not because he asked for it. But because I deserved it.
The cage isn't locked.
It never was.

Because here's what life teaches you if you're paying attention: everything has a season. People, places, and even pieces of yourself are not meant to be held onto forever. Some things come to teach, to guide, to shape, and then they must be released. Holding on doesn't keep things as they were—it keeps you from becoming who you are meant to be.

> *Letting go is not just about release; it is about celebrating life, finding joy and fulfillment in the present, and making space for new growth and happiness.*

So today, ask yourself: What are you still holding onto that's holding you back? What are you afraid to release, not because it's good, but because it's familiar? And then, when you're ready—or maybe even before—let it go.

The new season of your life is waiting, and with it, the opportunity to celebrate life and truly find joy in the present.

CHAPTER TEN

CELEBRATING LIFE: FINDING JOY AND FULFILLMENT IN THE PRESENT

THE WEIGHT OF WISDOM, THE LIGHTNESS OF JOY

I'm here. We're here. We have arrived at the place where life doesn't just happen to us anymore—we stand at the threshold of understanding, of embracing, of fully absorbing what it means to be seasoned. This isn't just about age; this is about life slowed down enough for us to finally see its every crack, every crevice, every beautiful imperfection.

There's a shift that happens when you step into this seasoned space. It's not a sudden moment, not a grand announcement that tells you, "You are now officially seasoned." It's more subtle than that. It's the first AARP letter that shows up in your mailbox and makes you pause like—how the hell did they find me? It's the moment when the waitress at a restaurant asks, almost too casually, "Do you qualify for the senior discount?" and you hesitate—not because you don't appreciate a good deal, but because accepting it feels like admitting something you're still figuring out how to embrace.

It's when someone younger calls you 'sir' or 'ma'am' with a respect that carries just a hint of distance, as if they see something in you that you haven't fully acknowledged yet.

The funny thing about aging is that it comes with contradictions. We live in a world that tells us to work hard, save up, plan for the future—but when we get to this future, it doesn't always look like we imagined. Retirement? That's a fading concept. Some of us are still grinding, still pushing, not necessarily because we have to, but because stopping doesn't feel like an option. And for some, stopping isn't even a luxury we can afford. The economy has shifted, life costs more than it used to, and for a lot of folks, retirement isn't a reality—it's a myth. But even for those who could stop working, the idea of just sitting, just existing without purpose, feels unnatural. The body might slow, but the mind, the spirit, the hunger for something meaningful—that remains.

And here's the thing—there's power in this season of life. There's a freedom that comes with knowing who you are, with not apologizing for the wisdom you carry. There's clarity, the kind that only comes from having lived enough life to see through the nonsense. It's why we can look at a young person and recognize their struggle before they even speak it aloud. It's why we don't just listen to the words they say, but to the spaces in between—the silence, the hesitations, the tones.

We've learned to read between the lines, to see what isn't being said. We can sense when a friend is pretending to be okay, when a child is carrying a weight they don't know how to name, when the energy in a room shifts before anyone else notices. That's what wisdom gives us. It's a sharper vision, a heightened awareness that makes us not just observers of life, but interpreters of it.

But wisdom doesn't come without its price. There's weight to it. The weight of knowing too much. The weight of memories that refuse to fade. The weight of looking in the mirror and seeing a face that holds every triumph, every heartbreak, every sleepless night. And yet, alongside that weight, there is also lightness. There's the joy of finally knowing what matters and what doesn't. There's the release that comes with letting go of caring so much about what other people think. We've done the proving, the striving, the endless climb. Now, we get to just be.

And being seasoned comes with some unexpected perks. There's a small, private thrill when someone asks for your ID at a bar, like they're questioning whether you've really been walking this earth for six-plus decades. For a moment, it feels like a nod to the youth that still flickers inside. And yet, the moment you hand over that ID, reality settles back in. They'll see the numbers. They'll know. And you'll laugh at the irony of it all—how youth is both behind you and still pulsing through you in ways no ID card could ever capture.

And then, there's the physical reality of being seasoned—the body reminding you in small but insistent ways that time has been here. Waking up with a stiff back, knees that creak louder than the floorboards, needing just a little more time to stretch, to move, to feel fully present in your own skin.

And yet, with all of that, there's also gratitude. Gratitude for still being able to move, to dance if you want to, to get up without help, to still recognize your own reflection and remember your own name. Because we've seen what it looks like when the mind betrays the body, when memories slip away like water through fingers. And if we're still here, still sharp, still aware—then that in itself is a gift worth holding onto.

But the greatest revelation of being seasoned is the realization that the game of life is both faster and slower at the same time. It moves at a relentless speed, yet for those of us who've been in it long enough, we've learned the secret—how to slow it down in our minds. Like a veteran athlete who's mastered their craft, we can see the plays before they happen, anticipate the moves, understand the rhythm of it all in ways that the younger players can't yet grasp. And that's the advantage. Not moving faster, but seeing clearer. Not reacting impulsively, but responding with intention.

There's an urgency that comes with this stage of life, a fire that says, If not now, then when? We chase experiences, not things. We crave connections, not validation. We travel, we love, we invest in the moments that make the heart feel full, because we know—deeply, intimately—that time is the only currency that truly matters. And so we spend it wisely. On people who bring us joy. On experiences that leave us breathless. On conversations that linger long after they've ended.

And if we're lucky, if we're truly lucky, we become wells of wisdom for those who come after us. We tell our stories—not just because we want to be heard, but because we want others to learn without having to make all the same mistakes.

We give our guidance, our hard-earned lessons, our quiet knowing. We stand as living proof that life isn't about reaching some arbitrary peak, but about learning how to dance through every stage of it with grace, with laughter, with unwavering authenticity.

Because at the end of the day, being seasoned isn't about just being older. It's about being richer—in knowledge, in experience, in love.

It's about knowing that every scar, every lesson, every triumph, and every loss has led to this moment. And this moment? This moment is ours to savor.

So we stand here, seasoned and unshaken, ready to pour every last drop of wisdom into the world before our time is done. Not because we fear the end, but because we've learned that every ending is just another beginning. And what a gift it is to still be here, to still be living, to still be learning, to still be becoming.

THE CROWN'S BURDEN: THE LINE BETWEEN CONFIDENCE AND ARROGANCE

There comes a moment in a man's life when he looks around at the sum total of everything he has built, everything he has earned, and everything he has survived, and he sees proof of his journey reflected back at him. It's a quiet moment, one that carries weight. Not the weight of doubt, nor the burden of regret, but the undeniable weight of arrival.

I have arrived.

The air around me carries an echo of the voices that once whispered, once doubted, once questioned. I can hear them still, those ghosts of uncertainty, those murmurs of inadequacy that tried to convince me I wasn't meant for this, that I was reaching too high, dreaming too big. But standing here now, feeling the solid ground beneath my feet, I know better. I know that every step was earned. Every sacrifice was necessary. And every battle, whether won or lost, was part of the journey to this very place.

There is a song—"Look Ma, I Made It"—a song about a man stepping into his own greatness, longing for his mother to witness it, to validate it. That moment of saying, See? I told you I would. It is the anthem of many who have walked this road, who have fought against doubt, not just from the world but from within themselves. I think about Tony Montana in Scarface, standing before his mother, money in hand, telling her that her son had made it. And yet, there is an unease in that moment—a tension between triumph and the sharp edges of arrogance.

Because there is a difference. A thin, razor-sharp line between confidence and arrogance. And that line is respect. Confidence stands firm in its own truth without needing to diminish anyone else's. Arrogance, however, thrives on comparison. Arrogance looks outward, measuring its own success by the shortcomings of others. Confidence is internal, personal, rooted in self-awareness and gratitude.

I've thought about this a lot, especially now. Especially in this season of my life where the evidence of my labor is undeniable. There are certain luxuries I allow myself, things that bring me joy, things that feel like the natural rewards of years of unrelenting effort. Travel, for instance. It is the one area where I am bougie, where I do not compromise. When I can, I love the comfort of traveling in first class. I want to be in my seat before the masses shuffle in, before the flight attendants bark at overhead bins that won't close. I want to move through the airport without feeling herded, without feeling like just another body in transit. I want the comfort, the space, the calm. And I do not feel guilty for it.

I have stood in lines before. I have fought for space before. I have carried my share of heavy luggage, both literal and figurative. But now, I allow myself ease, and that ease is not arrogance. It is not entitlement. It is the quiet assurance that I have done what was required of me, and I have earned the right to enjoy the fruit of that labor. That is confidence.

But arrogance would be different. Arrogance would be looking at someone struggling with their baggage and feeling superior instead of remembering when that was me. Arrogance would be scoffing at the man trying to board his flight in Zone 5 instead of remembering when I was praying for an upgrade I couldn't afford. Confidence does not erase the past; arrogance pretends the past never existed.

It's a conversation I've had with my daughter. She has watched me move through life, through challenges, through triumphs. She has seen the effort, the discipline, the long nights, the quiet sacrifices that no one else witnessed. And in a moment that I will carry with me always, she looked at me and said, Dad, I watch you.

Four words. Simple, unembellished, yet brimming with meaning. She sees it. She sees me. She understands that what I have was not handed to me. That it was not easy. That it was not guaranteed. And more importantly, she understands that my accomplishments are mine—not weapons, not shields, not excuses to look down on others, but markers of a life lived with intention.

And still, there is one thing left. One more mountain to climb. One more goal that lingers on the horizon, waiting to be reached.

I want to make my first million.

Not for vanity. Not for proof. Not for status. But because I can. Because I believe in my ability to do it. Because I have moved past the conditioning that once told me to dream small, to be content with just enough. Because I want to create legacy, not just for my children, but for their children.

It is not arrogance to say that I will do it. It is confidence.

Because confidence is knowing what you are capable of and stepping boldly into that truth. Confidence is recognizing that every tool, every lesson, every failure, every victory has prepared you for this very moment.

Confidence is faith—not just in yourself, but in the divine hand that has guided you this far and will carry you even further.

My wife, in her wisdom, tells me, You've already made your million. And in some ways, she is right. I have built an empire that has garnered millions in funding, that has impacted countless lives, that has created ripples that extend far beyond what I will ever fully see. But I am not speaking of those millions. I am speaking of personal wealth. Of creating something that is not just for the mission but for the man.

Because even men who serve must also build. Even men who give must also receive. Even men who lead must also secure. So I will do it. I will claim it. I will step into it. Not with arrogance, not with ego, but with the unwavering confidence of a man who has spent his life walking in faith, in purpose, in passion.

And when it is done, when I stand at the summit of this goal, when I have marked this milestone, I will not shout it from the rooftops to belittle those who are still climbing. I will not wield it as a weapon. Instead, I will turn to those I love, to those who have walked this path with me, to those who have watched and supported and believed, and I will simply say: I told you I could.

And one day, when the sum total of my life is finally clear, when my grand total is tallied, I will listen for the only validation that truly matters. The only words that will confirm that every step, every choice, every moment was worth it.

And I will hear:
Job well done, my good and faithful servant.

THE LITTLE DRUMMER BOY INSIDE US

There are moments in life that whisper to us so softly, we mistake them for passing thoughts. But every so often, a whisper becomes an echo, and an echo becomes a calling. It's in those moments—those inexplicable, soul-stirring moments—that we realize something has always been speaking to us. Something ancient, something small, something childlike.

For me, that something is an eight-year-old boy.

It has always been strange to me that I can't remember much about my childhood before the age of eight. It's like a fog exists over the early years, a veil that keeps me from recalling details, faces, laughter, or even pain. But eight—that's where my memory starts.

That's where my awareness of the world first took shape. That's where I first remember Mrs. Pendergrass, my third-grade teacher, the only thing I can recall from those days that brings warmth to my spirit. Why her? Why is she a glow in the darkness? I don't have an answer, but I know the feeling is there.

What I do know is that my memory, or lack thereof, intrigues me. What am I blocking? What don't I want to remember? And maybe the more important question: is that normal? Or is there a reason why certain memories never solidified into my consciousness? At some point, I might have to sit with a professional, dig deeper, and try to understand why my mind is a locked room with missing keys. But what I do know is this—the little boy inside me remembers.

And I hear him.

He's not a voice of logic or structure. He's not a scholar or a preacher or a sage. He doesn't analyze or articulate.

He only feels. He feels with every fiber of his small body, and he pulses those feelings through my heart, into my spirit. He is the seat of my emotions. He is the keeper of my joy, my pain, my wounds, my wonder. And every now and then, he makes himself known, reminding me that though I've grown, he has not.

I've come to believe that everything we cannot remember from childhood still exists within us, like an unfinished song whose melody hums softly beneath our daily rhythms. And sometimes, that song plays so quietly, we don't even notice. But it shapes us nonetheless. It moves us, influences us, draws us to certain people, repels us from others. That little boy inside me is the keeper of those melodies, the guardian of emotions I haven't fully unpacked. And no matter how old I get, he will always be there.

That's why, when I work with fathers, I tell them: there is no such thing as a fatherless child. Every child has a father—it's just a matter of where he exists. Some are present, some are absent, some are ghostlike memories, hovering in the margins of our lives. But all fathers exist in one form or another. And the absence of their presence does not erase the presence of their absence. It lingers. It carves holes in hearts, questions in minds, and longings in souls. And the little boy inside us? He feels that absence like an ache that never quite heals.

That's why, as we grow into adulthood, the echoes of our inner child don't ask questions like an adult would. They don't ask about responsibilities, choices, or circumstances. No, the child inside us only has one question: Why? Why didn't you come for me? Why didn't you love me? Why wasn't I enough?

And when we finally come face to face with the parents who left those holes inside of us, we think we're speaking as grown men, but we're not. We're speaking as that eight-year-old boy, that wounded little child who never received an answer.

And no matter how old we get, that voice does not age. That wound does not time-stamp itself and fade away.

I think about Will Smith's book, where he spoke about his deep-seated need to protect women. That drive wasn't born from adulthood—it was a direct response to the little boy inside him, the one who couldn't protect his mother from his father's abuse. His adult self was answering a call that had been crying out from his childhood. And so, he became the protector, the savior, the knight in shining armor. He built a life around making sure no woman he loved would ever suffer again.

That's what we do, isn't it? We spend our lives responding to the needs of our inner child, often without even realizing it. The anger we feel, the fears we carry, the relationships we chase or avoid—they are all shaped by the silent conversations we have with the child inside us. And when we don't listen, when we ignore that voice, the child inside us doesn't disappear. He just finds another way to make himself heard.

"I have no gift to bring, pa rum pum pum pum, that's fit to give our king."The little drummer boy inside us does not speak in words. He speaks in feelings, in beats, in rhythms of pain and joy. He beats his drum, over and over, trying to get our attention. And if we don't listen? He doesn't stop. The drum just gets louder, the rhythm more chaotic, until we are forced to face him, to sit with him, to hold his small hands and finally say, "I hear you."

"Shall I play for you, pa rum pum pum pum, on my drum?"
So today, I ask you—when was the last time you listened? When was the last time you acknowledged the boy or girl inside you who never got the answers they needed? And more importantly, when was the last time you gave them the love they've been waiting for all these years?

Because the truth is, that little child inside you? He still believes in you. He's been waiting for you to come back, to sit with him, to answer his questions, to heal his wounds. And when you do—when you finally hear his drum, meet his gaze, and tell him he is seen, he is loved, he is enough—that's when the echoes of your past begin to transform into the rhythm of your future.

Pa rum pum pum pum.

THE QUIET FLOOD OF HUMANITY

There are moments in life that move through you like quiet floods, filling every crevice of your soul with an understanding so profound that it demands to be felt, not just acknowledged. Moments that drape themselves over your heart, making it impossible to retreat from the depth of their touch. I have always been emotional. But now, in this seasoned space of my life, everything finds its way into me with an intensity that is at once overwhelming and divine.

In the early years of my career, when I took to the stage to speak about fatherhood—particularly my own experiences with my biological father—I knew only one way to communicate: through the raw, unfiltered narrative of my life. My voice was never just words. It carried my story, the stories of the men I encountered, the wounds left by absence, the echoes of longing, and the desperate hope of redemption. And inevitably, there came a moment in every speech where my emotions overtook me, and I would cry.

Not a strategic pause. Not a single dignified tear. No, I would cry.

Sometimes it was quiet, a welling up that I could barely contain, my voice catching, my body tightening against the flood. Other times, it was a breaking—my spirit cracking open in front of strangers, allowing them to see, to feel, to witness the full measure of my vulnerability. And after, they would come. They would approach me with eyes full of their own stories, with hands extended, telling me how my words had moved them. They saw inspiration in my openness. But at home, alone with my thoughts, I hated it.

Hated the surrender to emotion. Hated that I couldn't master my feelings the way others seemed to. I had seen men deliver speeches about unimaginable pain, about histories of oppression and suffering, and they stood firm. They were steel. Their voices carried the weight of experience without cracking under its force.

I envied that.

I envied their composure, their ability to deliver devastation with steady hands. And so, one night, I prayed. I prayed for God to take away my tears, to allow me to speak without drowning in the depth of my own feelings. I asked Him to give me the strength to stand without breaking.

> ***And in response, He did not take away my tears. Instead, He gave me an answer: When you are speaking, it is Me speaking through you. When you are crying, it is Me speaking to you.***

That was the moment I understood. My tears were not a weakness. They were my testimony. They were the evidence of my connection to the very thing I was speaking about. When I cried, it was because my spirit had been touched, because God was pressing His hand against my heart, telling me that what I was saying mattered.

Now, when I speak and I cry, I welcome it. I recognize it for what it is—a divine signal that I am aligned, that I am exactly where I am meant to be, saying exactly what I am meant to say.

And if you've ever seen me speak, you know God must be talking to me all the time.

But my sensitivity doesn't end at my own words. It seeps into every part of my being. I can't watch a sports injury replay without feeling the ghost of pain in my own body. I can't stomach certain scenes of violence on television because something in me absorbs it. It's not just sympathy—it's presence. My body, my mind, my heart feels the suffering of others as if it were my own.

This sensitivity extends beyond reality and into fiction. Movies, books, commercials—anything with a deep emotional under-current can undo me. There are films I cannot watch without breaking down, not because of their plot but because of the depth of emotion they evoke in me. King Kong, for instance—the 1933 version—reduces me to tears every single time. That moment when he stands atop the Empire State Building, the King of the Jungle now a hunted beast, and Carl Denham says, It wasn't the planes that killed the beast; it was beauty that killed the beast. That line wrecks me. It speaks to something primal, something deeply human—the idea that sometimes, what destroys us is not our enemies, but our longing, our love, our inability to exist in a world that does not understand us.

The Wizard of Oz does it to me, too. The moment Dorothy real-izes she always had the power to go home, that she never truly lost what she was searching for—that moment carries a truth so universal that it pierces me every time. And Forrest Gump—his love for Jenny, unwavering and undying, no matter how many times she leaves him, no matter how the world changes around him—that kind of love, that kind of loyalty, is something I feel in my soul. Even The Godfather moves me—not for its violence, but for its portrayal of family, of legacy, of a man who, in the end, dies not in battle, not in glory, but in a garden, playing with his grandson.

And I've come to realize that this depth of emotion, this constant pull toward feeling, is not a burden. It is a gift. It is the very thing that keeps me tethered to humanity. Because humanity requires care. Humanity demands that we feel. And in a world that is increasingly loud, increasingly fast, increasingly disconnected, it is far too easy to stop caring.

I see it every day in my work. The ways in which we have divided ourselves, pulled so far apart from one another in our narratives that we have forgotten that at our core, we all ache for the same things. I see it in the conversations around gender—how in the quest to empower women, we have left men uncertain of their worth. How the pendulum swings so far in one direction that it no longer seeks balance but replacement. And I understand. I understand the history, the correction needed, the long-overdue recognition of a group long ignored. But humanity doesn't work on a trade system. It does not ask for one to be sacrificed for another. Humanity requires that we rise together.

But we don't.

And much of that has to do with the Law of Belief. Brian Tracy once said, whatever we believe with feeling becomes our reality. If we believe in scarcity, we act as if there is not enough to go around. If we believe in division, we create walls between us. But the opposite is also true. If we believe in our collective strength, if we believe that humanity can be an expansive, abundant force— then we act in ways that make it real. The danger, however, is that our beliefs do not always stem from truth. They are shaped by the narratives we consume, by the words spoken into our hearts, by the limits we place upon ourselves.

I am older now. More seasoned. And if there is one thing that has become crystal clear to me, it is that humanity and selfishness cannot coexist. To be truly humane, to truly care, is to recognize that the tide must lift all boats—not just some. And that begins with feeling. It begins with the quiet flood that moves through us when we allow ourselves to truly see and connect with the world around us.

So yes, I cry.
Because I care.
And I will never pray for that to change again.

THE UNSHACKLING OF A SEASONED SOUL

I don't want to finish this book. That's the truth of it. Not because I don't have the words. No, the words are still flowing. They come faster than my hands can shape them, cascading like a waterfall that's been held back for years, like they've been waiting for this very moment to spill out, to drench these pages with the last bits of my reflections. But still, there's something about the end that makes me hesitate.

A small, nagging voice whispers, What if this is the crescendo?

What if this is where the symphony of my wisdom, my teaching, my evolving, reaches its peak? What if there is nothing left to say beyond this? What if I wake up tomorrow and the thoughts I've been gathering my whole life suddenly dissipate, leaving me with only the empty echoes of words I've already spoken?

I know that's not true. But knowing and feeling are two different things, and right now, I'm sitting in the feeling. I'm letting myself marinate in this strange, unshakable sensation that finishing means something deeper than just putting a period at the end of a final sentence. I am not merely closing out a book; I am facing the realization that I am becoming exactly what I set out to become, and there is something terrifying about standing in the fullness of my own becoming.

And so, I sit. I linger in this moment, stretching it as far as it will go, because I want to be honest with you. I want to tell you about the things I still care about, even in this state of not caring. I want to bring you into the beauty of this paradox—the art of caring deeply while refusing to be owned by the weight of others' perceptions. I want to show you what freedom tastes like, seasoned with all the flavors of a life lived fully.

And here's where we begin—where we always begin—with the things that truly matter. The things that make up the marrow of who I am, the things I hold close, the things that bring me joy, the things I still care about. And in a peculiar twist of fate, they all start with the letter C. Perhaps that's the universe playing some poetic joke on me, or maybe it's just how my mind has chosen to frame them, but nonetheless, they stand as pillars in this moment of reflection.

Children.

God, there is no joy like watching your children grow into themselves. It's the closest thing to time travel—to see yourself in them, to hear echoes of your younger self in their laughter, to recognize the fire in their eyes, the way they move through the world, their little habits, their stubbornness, their kindness, their hunger for life. It's surreal, this feeling of knowing that you have not just lived, but you have given life. That something of you will stretch beyond the years you are given.

I sit back sometimes and watch them, trying not to hover but always observing, always studying, always taking mental notes of the tiny evolutions they go through daily. The way their minds expand, their perspectives shift, their choices carve them into something new. And in those moments, I feel the weight of legacy—not as an obligation, but as a privilege. To have been able to plant

seeds in them, to have watered them with wisdom, to see them
bloom in their own unique ways.

There is something divine about that. Something unspeakably
beautiful about knowing that your hands have shaped the future in
ways you will never fully grasp. And so, I care. I care about what
kind of people they become, I care about the world they are inher-
iting, I care about whether they have the tools to navigate it with
strength, grace, and wisdom.

Control.

Not in the way you might think. Not the kind of control that
dictates and dominates, but the kind that steadies. The kind that
lets me wake up in the morning and know, with certainty, that my
life belongs to me. That I am not subject to the chaos of someone
else's expectations. That I have earned the right to make choices
with full agency over my mind, my spirit, my body, my destiny.

There were times when life felt like a storm, and I was just a
man trying to keep his feet planted in the wind. Times when my
circumstances dictated my movements, when survival overrode
desire, when I had to bend and break just to stay standing.

But not anymore. Now, I am the architect of my days. I decide
what I will engage in, who I will give my energy to, where I will
invest my heart. And there is a peace in that—an unshakable joy in
knowing that I am no longer at the mercy of anything that does not
serve me.

Clarity.

Ah, this is the sweetest one. The ability to see life for what it truly
is, without the distortions of ego, fear, or insecurity. To be able to
step back and see the grand design, to understand why things had

to unfold the way they did, to connect the dots that once felt scattered and chaotic. There is an ease that comes with clarity, a relief that settles in the bones.

Clarity is what allows me to move forward without regret. To embrace every moment—good or bad—as a necessary piece of the puzzle. To sit in my truth without needing validation. To let go of what no longer fits and make room for what truly matters.

Comfort.

Not complacency. Not stagnation. But the kind of comfort that comes with knowing that I am exactly where I am meant to be. The kind that allows me to exhale fully, to sit in my own skin without restlessness. To wake up in the morning without the weight of proving, without the burden of performance.

It is a rare and beautiful thing to reach a point in life where you are comfortable being exactly who you are. No more masks, no more pretending, no more bending to fit into spaces that were never meant for you. Just you, in all your fullness, existing unapologetically.

Curiosity.

Even now, with all the answers I've gathered, I am still hungry for more. I still want to know. I still ask questions. I still explore. I still seek.

Because life is vast, and understanding is infinite. Because there will always be something new to learn, a perspective I have not considered, a mystery yet to be unraveled. And that excites me. That keeps me moving. That reminds me that, no matter how seasoned I become, I am still a student in this grand classroom of existence.

CELEBRATING LIFE: FINDING JOY AND FULFILLMENT IN THE PRESENT

The truth is, I have spent years thinking about how we care and, just as importantly, how we stop caring. And yet, as I reach this moment, I realize that not caring has never been the point. The goal was never to shut off the world or move through it untethered. The goal has always been to release—to let go of the unnecessary weight, to care about what deserves my care, to cherish the things that bring fulfillment without the burden of external validation.

I celebrate differently now. Not just the milestones, but the small moments. The mornings when the air is crisp, and the taste of my fresh; cold orange juice is just right. The nights when the laughter of family fills the house.

The quiet moments of reflection when I can feel the presence of all the versions of myself that led me here. I used to wait for reasons to celebrate. Now, I find them everywhere. I create them. I wake up every day knowing that this, this right here, is a gift, and I refuse to let it go unappreciated.

This is the essence of what I have learned. This is the truth I want you to walk away with. It is not about whether you care or don't care. It is about knowing what to care about. It is about reclaiming your time, your energy, your heart. It is about refusing to be controlled by anything that does not serve your spirit.

I do not want to be viewed. I want to be seen. And I want you to be seen, too. So as I bring this book to its close, I ask you—what do you still care about? What is worth your attention, your passion, your love?

And what, my friend, are you finally ready to let go?

Because there is freedom waiting on the other side. And I hope—no, I know—that you will embrace it.

And so, as I near the end of this book, I realize that it is not an ending at all. It is simply another unfolding. Another moment of clarity. Another step in a journey that does not stop until the last breath is drawn.

CHAPTER ELEVEN

LETTERS TO MY YOUNGER SELVES

THE CONVERSATION ACROSS TIME

You don't realize how much a moment means until you revisit it years later, standing in the doorway of your own past, watching yourself fumble through life's lessons like a child walking barefoot through an unlit room, hoping not to step on something sharp.

You were just living then—surviving, adjusting, figuring things out as best you could. It never occurred to you that one day, an older, more seasoned version of yourself would peer back through time with an aching awareness, seeing the small details, the missed warnings, the moments of quiet bravery, and the ones you let slip through your fingers.

It hit me somewhere in the middle of writing this book, some-where between the words and the memories, that life doesn't move forward in a straight line. It shifts, it loops, it circles back to remind you of what you missed the first time.

I started thinking about the different ages at which things happened to me—the milestones, the losses, the decisions made with the wisdom I had at the time, which was always, in hindsight, just a fraction of what I needed. And it was then that I knew I needed to write this chapter, not for the sake of nostalgia, but because there are things I would say to myself if I had the chance.

I started thinking about this theory I had read somewhere, about life moving in cycles of seven years. Scientists got hold of it, tangled it in jargon, and diluted its meaning. But at its core, it still rang true. Every seven years, you are a different person. Not just older, but changed—physically, emotionally, spiritually. Who I was at seven was not who I was at fourteen. Who I was at twenty-one was a completely different being than the boy I had been at fourteen. And by the time I reached twenty-eight, I had already become a stranger to my twenty-one-year-old self. So, if I were to write one letter to my younger self, who exactly would I be addressing? Which version of me would truly understand the words I would spill onto the page?

That's when the thought evolved. One letter wouldn't be enough. Because at each stage, I wasn't just older—I was someone else entirely. And so, I have chosen to write these letters not to one younger self, but to all of them, at the critical junctures where life turned, where my understanding shifted, where I unknowingly stepped through a doorway into the next version of me.

Seven. Fourteen. Twenty-one. Twenty-eight. Thirty-five. Forty-two. Forty-nine.

Each of them deserves a conversation. Each of them deserves my voice, now filled with years of knowing, calling back through time to offer a hand, a word, a whisper of understanding. Not to prevent them from making mistakes—because mistakes are necessary—but to give them something more valuable: perspective. The kind of perspective that allows you to walk into the fire, knowing you will come out on the other side changed, but not destroyed.

I think about my seven-year-old self first. A boy still fresh with wonder, whose world was shaped by the warmth of his mother's voice and the unpredictable, distant presence of his father. He didn't yet understand the concept of absence, only that sometimes people were there, and sometimes they weren't. He didn't yet know that love could be complicated, that sometimes the people you adore are the same ones who leave you with questions you'll spend a lifetime answering. To him, the world was still big and possible.

Then I think of my fourteen-year-old self, caught in that awkward purgatory between childhood and manhood, trying to measure himself against boys who seemed older, tougher, more certain. The weight of expectations starting to press against his shoulders, but still too young to fully understand what they meant. He was just beginning to see the fractures in the world around him—learning that fairness was a myth and that being good didn't always mean being safe. He was starting to question things he once accepted as truth. He was angry sometimes, though he didn't always know why.

At twenty-one, the world felt like an open road, stretching endlessly ahead. I was a man in theory, but still figuring out what that meant in practice. Responsibility had started to make itself known, tapping insistently at the edges of my consciousness. I made choices then that would ripple through my life in ways I couldn't yet see. I chased dreams with reckless confidence, unburdened by the knowledge of how dreams can shift, how they can demand sacrifices I wasn't prepared for.

By twenty-eight, the fire had touched me. I had learned that love wasn't always enough to hold things together. That hard work didn't always yield success. That some of the friendships I thought were forever had expiration dates I hadn't noticed. But I had also learned resilience. I had started to understand that growth wasn't comfortable, that becoming the person you are meant to be requires breaking apart the person you used to be.

At thirty-five, I had begun to settle into my own skin. The insecurities of my youth weren't as loud, though they still whispered now and then. I had experienced loss in ways that reshaped me. I had tasted success, but I had also seen its price. I had children looking up to me, their eyes filled with a trust that both humbled and terrified me. Fatherhood had changed me more than I ever expected—it had softened me, but also sharpened my sense of purpose.

Forty-two. The age of reckoning. The past no longer felt like a distant thing—it was present, woven into every choice I made, every interaction, every lesson I passed down. I had made peace with some things, but others still haunted me in quiet moments. I had become more reflective, more willing to admit what I didn't know. I had also begun to realize the limits of time, that the years were moving faster now, that every moment spent unwisely was a moment lost forever.

And then, forty-nine. Standing on the edge of fifty, looking back at all the versions of myself that had come before. If I could sit with them, if I could look them in the eye, what would I say? Would they even recognize me? Would they understand the choices I had made, the regrets I carried, the wisdom I had gathered along the way?

This chapter is a conversation across time. It is my voice, reaching back through the years, speaking to the boy, the young man, the struggling dreamer, the exhausted father, the reflective mentor. It is an exercise in understanding—not just for myself, but for anyone who has ever wished they could whisper wisdom into their own past.

Because if we cannot change what was, at least we can honor it. At least we can give it voice.

And perhaps, in doing so, we can learn to speak more gently to ourselves in the present, knowing that the person we are today is simply another stepping stone toward the one we are still becoming.

THE WORLD IS BIG, BUT YOU ARE ENOUGH

Dear KV.7 (my seven-year-old self),

I see you. Standing there with those big, curious eyes, watching the world shift around you, trying to understand what it means when love no longer belongs to just you. It must feel strange, unsettling even, to go from being the center of your mother's universe to sharing space with two tiny beings who don't yet know their own names. But hear me when I say this—you are enough.

I am you, but older, wiser, weathered by years that will shape you in ways you can't yet comprehend. I have walked the roads you're just beginning to discover, and I write to you now not to change your path but to whisper reassurance into the ears of the boy who still lives inside me. Because, KV.7, there are things you will not be told. There are moments that will make you question your worth, times when the world will seem too big, too loud, too uncertain. But through it all, I want you to remember: You are enough.

I know what you're thinking. How can you be enough when the attention that once wrapped around you like a warm blanket is now stretched thin? How can you be enough when the space that felt like yours alone is now crowded with the sounds of a brother's cry and a sister's laughter? I wish I could tell you that it will be easy, that you won't feel lost in the shuffle of it all. But I won't lie to you, young king. You will feel the sting of change. You will wonder if you've been forgotten. You will sit in silence, listening to the world move around you, and wonder where you fit in it.

But let me tell you what I know now, what I didn't know then—love does not shrink; it stretches. It bends, it expands, it finds new corners to fill. Your mother does not love you any less because she loves them too. She has simply learned how to love in more directions, and so will you. That feeling of being unseen? It is a trick of the mind, a shadow cast by doubt. Step into the light, KV.7. You are not forgotten.

And oh, little brother, you are special. You don't see it yet, but I promise you, the world does. Your family sees it. Your Uncle Eddie sees it. Even those who don't know what to do with you—they see it too. There is something in you, something different, something extraordinary. But the weight of being special is that not everyone knows how to handle it.

People will look at you and sense something they cannot name, and because of that, they will not always know how to love you. They will misunderstand you. Some will try to mold you into what makes sense to them. Others will dismiss you because they cannot categorize you. But do not shrink to fit their understanding. Do not dim your light so they feel comfortable in your presence. You are not meant to be easily defined.

At seven, you are beginning to notice the world beyond your mother's arms. School is a new beast, a place where you must learn the unspoken rules of friendship, of belonging, of navigating spaces where love is not guaranteed. You will feel awkward. Your body will feel foreign to you, your face unfamiliar in the mirror.

You will wonder if you are too much—too round, too light-skinned, too quiet, too something. And the world, in its casual cruelty, will confirm those fears in small, cutting ways. The way a teacher overlooks your raised hand. The way a kid snickers when you run. The way you are told, subtly and explicitly, that you do not fit.

But listen to me—none of that defines you. You are more than the sum of their opinions. You are more than the weight of their words. You will grow into your body, into your voice, into the rhythm of your own existence. You are enough.

I wish I could hold you in those moments when you feel small. I wish I could stand beside you in that classroom, whisper in your ear every time you hesitate, every time you feel uncertain. I wish I could shield you from the moments that will bruise you.

But I can't. And truth be told, I shouldn't. Because it is in those moments that you will learn the most important lesson of all—that even when the world makes you feel invisible, you are still here. You still matter.

You are still enough.

So be seven, KV.7. Run without worrying about how you look. Laugh without questioning if you're too loud. Be awkward, be uncertain, be exactly who you are. The world will try to tell you who to be soon enough. Hold onto yourself for as long as you can.

And when the years stretch ahead and you become me, remember this letter. Remember this moment. And when you hear the whispers of self-doubt, when you stand in rooms that make you question your place, when you feel the weight of being unseen, know that I am here, speaking through time to remind you.

You are enough.
Always.
KV.63 (Our 63 Year-Old Self)

YOU WON'T ALWAYS FEEL THIS LOST

Dear KV.14 (my fourteen-year-old self),

Listen to me, young man. You're fourteen now, standing at the intersection of who you've been and who you are trying to become, and I need you to know something—you won't always feel this lost.

I know you're thinking about eighteen. I know that number feels like a finish line, a ticket to freedom, a way out. You want to be independent, to take care of yourself, to write your own story without anyone dictating the pages. But the truth is, you don't even know what that looks like yet. You're still figuring it out, still feeling your way through the dark, still searching for pieces of yourself in a world that doesn't always feel like it belongs to you. And that's okay.

Over the last seven years, life has introduced you to things that have left their mark on you. You've learned the value of a dollar, the urgency of needing your own, because you know that resources don't always stretch as far as you wish they did. You're being the best son you know how to be, and even when things don't seem fair, you love your mother fiercely. She's doing the best she can, and even though she can't always tell you, she sees you. She sees your efforts, your sacrifices, the way you try to carry more than a child should. She sees you, and she loves you.

You are stepping into a space where your independence is becoming a necessity, not just a desire. Being the oldest, you don't have the same kind of sibling friendship that others do. Your little brother and sister will always love you, but they can't yet walk beside you in the way you need. So you've built your family in the streets, in the school hallways, in the corners of Brooklyn where laughter is loud and friendships feel like lifelines. Those friends, the ones who feel like brothers now, they will shape you, but hear me—most of them won't walk this whole road with you. They are seasonal. They are meant to teach you, to leave their imprint on your heart, to be a part of your story, but they are not your forever. And that's not a loss, KV.14. That's just life.

And then there are the girls. You're going to be introduced to love in ways you never imagined. You'll chase it, stumble over it, and some days, you'll wonder if it was ever real at all. You will meet young women who will change you, who will show you parts of yourself that you didn't know existed. Some of them will be kind. Some of them will be careless with your heart. And some will leave echoes in you that will shape the way you love forever. But you will also see something else—you will see that they are searching, too.

They are learning the language of love the same way you are, through trial and error, through tenderness and heartbreak. And even when love leaves you aching, don't close yourself off to it. Love will teach you, and one day, it will find you in the right way, at the right time.

But there will be dangers, KV.14. The streets will whisper your name. You will be offered things that promise escape, things that promise to make you feel invincible. There will be moments where you will have to choose—between following and leading, between belonging and standing alone. And I want you to remember something: you were born to lead. People will follow you, not because you demand it, but because there is something in you that draws them in. You will be the kind of man who others look to for guidance, for wisdom, for direction.

But to be that man, you must first learn to lead yourself. That means knowing when to walk away. That means knowing when the thrill isn't worth the consequence. That means standing firm when the world tries to pull you into its currents.

You are not meant to be just another face in the crowd. You are meant for more.

And there's something else—you are brilliant. But the problem with brilliance is that it can be isolating. You will get bored, KV.14. School won't always challenge you. People won't always see the depth of your mind, and so they won't push you. You will coast, not because you aren't capable, but because the world around you doesn't always demand more. And that is the greatest danger—you, settling into a life that doesn't stretch you. I need you to want more. I need you to demand more of yourself, even when no one else does. Your mind is a gift. Do not let it go to waste.

Finding your tribe will not come easily. You will spend years searching for where you belong, for people who feel like home. There will be days when you feel unanchored, drifting between identities, trying to find the one that feels right. You will try on different versions of yourself, some that fit, some that don't. And that is okay. Growth is messy. Finding your place is not a straight road. But do not lose yourself in the search. Do not shrink yourself to fit into places that were never meant for you. Your tribe will come. And when they do, you will know it.

But there is one thing that will change you more than anything else—you will become a father. And in doing so, you will confront the ghost that has haunted you since you were old enough to understand what was missing. Your father's absence has been a wound you have carried without knowing how deep it ran. And when your daughter is born, that wound will ache in ways you cannot yet understand. You will ask yourself questions that have no answers.

How do you father when you were never fathered? How do you give what you never received? And you will not know. But I will tell you what I wish someone had told me then—your presence is enough. You don't have to have all the answers. You don't have to be perfect. You just have to be there.

Because the one thing you always longed for was not a perfect father, but a present one. And that is what you must be.

Life is going to move fast, KV.14. These next seven years will feel like a lifetime. You will travel, you will grow, you will stumble, you will rise. You will have experiences that set you apart from your peers, and they will see something in you that they cannot name, but they will know it is special. And they will be right.

So, KV.14—embrace these years. They will shape you. They will test you. They will prepare you for the man you are becoming. And in the moments when you feel lost, when the road ahead seems unclear, remember this:

The world is big. But you are enough. And you won't always feel this lost.

Love You More.
KV.63

A LETTER TO MY YOUNGER SELF: DREAM BIGGER, LOVE DEEPER, ASK MORE QUESTIONS

Hey, KV.21 (my twenty-one-year-old self),

You still feeling lost? You should be. I know that in the last letter I sent you, I told you that you'd feel a little out of place, and I wasn't lying. That's going to continue for the next few years as you keep trying to define yourself in this thing called young adulthood.

You're going to wrestle with where you belong, what your future holds, and how in the hell you're going to obtain the things you want. But here's the thing—feeling lost isn't a curse; it's a sign that you're moving. It means you haven't settled, and that's a good thing.

You lived a lot of life as KV.14. You saw things, learned things, and carried the weight of moments that should have belonged to grown men. And now, as KV.21, you're about to live even more. You're fresh out of the military, and that in itself is a transition most don't talk about. You've seen the world outside of Brooklyn, but what they don't tell you is that even freedom can feel like a cage when you don't know what to do with it. And on top of that—you're married. And divorced. Already. That's a whole different level of experience that's going to shape how you see love, commitment, and yourself.

I need you to hear this: dream bigger. Looking back at you, I recognize that we dreamed too small. I know why we did. Nobody in our world expected big things. They taught us to survive, not to soar. Big dreams felt like a luxury reserved for people who didn't look like us.

So we dreamed in bite-sized pieces, enough to keep us moving but never enough to press against the walls of our limits. You need to press against those walls. Push them so hard they crack. You can be more than you ever imagined, but first, you have to imagine it.

Something huge is about to happen in your life. You're about to meet the ghost that's been haunting you since birth—your father. In the flesh. It's going to be surreal, and it's going to open up doors to a past you never got to live. You'll meet a whole new family, and you're going to try to reconcile who you are with where you came from. And let me tell you this—ask questions. Don't assume you'll have time to ask them later, because one day you'll be me, sitting here at 63, still holding unanswered questions for people who ain't here to answer them anymore. Ask now. Demand the truth.

And while we're talking about fathers—don't become the ghost that haunted you. Right now, you're making choices that will leave a hole in your daughter's heart. I know, it doesn't feel like that now. You think you're doing the best you can, balancing the wreckage of a failed marriage and figuring out how to move forward. But hear me, she didn't ask to be here. She didn't choose to be a part of your love, your mistakes, or your lessons. She just needs you. And she needs you to fight like hell to be present. Don't let your pain create her absence. Make her your priority, no matter what.

There's a woman you're about to meet who will change everything for you. She will love you in a way that challenges you, pulls you into new spaces, and exposes you to a life beyond what you thought possible. She will unearth pieces of you that you didn't know existed, and for a while, you'll believe she's your forever.

Maybe she could have been. Maybe she should have been. But remember this—it's your choice whether she's for a season or for a reason. I chose the season. You still have time to decide.

Your whole environment is about to shift. You're going to leave the concrete jungle of Brooklyn for the rolling hills of upstate New York.

Life is going to slow down, and it's going to force you to sit with yourself in ways you never have before.

This new home? It's the place that's going to help you grow. Embrace it. It's going to feel foreign at first, but don't fight the stillness. Use it. Let it be the soil where you plant new dreams.

You're going to start learning—really learning. Not just school learning, but learning yourself. You'll uncover new talents, explore new skills, and meet people who will challenge you to be better. Some of these people will be passing through, but some? Some will be in your life forever. Pay attention to who stays.

Even with all this growth, you're still going to feel lost at times. That's okay. Enjoy the exploration. Enjoy the jobs that don't make sense. Enjoy the relationships that teach you what you don't want. Enjoy the random experiences that seem disconnected, because I promise you—nothing is random.

One day, all of these threads will weave into a story that makes sense.

You're also going to start feeling the weight of your purpose, but it's not going to be clear yet. That's normal. Most people don't find their purpose at 21. Hell, most don't find it at 31. You're going to stumble into it, piece by piece, without even realizing it. Just keep moving.

Keep pushing forward, even when life doesn't make sense. Especially when life doesn't make sense.

And listen—some friendships will change. Some relationships will shift. Let them. Some people are in your life for a reason, others for a season. Don't fight the transitions.

And don't burn bridges unless you have to, because some of the people who leave your life as lovers will return as lifelong friends. That's one of your gifts, Kenny—you know how to keep people in your orbit without holding them hostage. Use that gift wisely.

Finally, I need you to hear me on this—you are enough. Even when you feel like you aren't, even when the world tells you you're not, you are. Life is going to stretch you, challenge you, and make you question everything. But through it all, you're still here. You're still breathing. And as long as you have breath, you have purpose.

Now go. Live. Dream bigger. Love deeper. Ask the hard questions. And when the road gets tough, just remember—you are me, and I am proof that you make it through.

With all the wisdom time has given me,
KV.63

LOVE HARD, BUT LOVE YOURSELF FIRST

Dear KV.28 (my twenty-eight-year-old self),

I see you standing there, caught between where you've been and where you think you're going, straddling the line between confidence and uncertainty. You've learned a lot already, but you're still trying to figure out what matters. You've loved hard, worked even harder, and yet, there's this lingering question pressing against your chest—Am I enough?

I know that question keeps you up at night. You don't say it out loud, but it's there in the way you move, in the way you overthink every decision, in the way you chase validation like it's something you can catch and hold onto forever. But let me tell you something, and I need you to hear me clearly—you don't have to prove yourself to anyone. Not through work, not through success, not through the applause of strangers who won't remember your name in a decade.

I wish I could tell you that the pressure eases as you get older, but it doesn't—not in the way you think. The expectations shift, the stakes get higher, and the weight of responsibility grows heavier. But the difference—the thing that will change everything—is you. You will learn to stop living for the nods of approval. You will learn that your worth isn't tied to what you can do, but who you are when no one is watching. And more importantly, you will learn how to rest in that truth without feeling like you have to justify it.

But right now, at 28, I know you're running. Running from stillness, running from doubt, running toward something you can't quite name. You've finally stepped into work that feels meaningful, and you can see a glimpse of the bigger picture. But the moment you start to feel settled, you hear another voice in your head whispering, What if this isn't enough? What if I should be doing more?

What if I lose all of this?

I want you to stop for a second and breathe.

You are not an accident. Every skill you are developing, every door that opens and every one that closes, every late night spent figuring out how to make this all work—it all matters. Every piece of it is building something you can't yet see. Right now, you feel like a jack of all trades, a man stretched thin by many talents and unsure which one will carry you furthest. But let me tell you, there is nothing wrong with being good at many things. People will tell you to pick one lane, to narrow your focus, to stop stretching yourself so wide.

Ignore them. There is a way to move with focus while embracing the fullness of your abilities. One day, you will understand that you were never meant to fit neatly into a single box. You were always meant to build something bigger than that.I know you're also carrying another kind of weight—the one that love has left behind. She was everything to you, wasn't she? The way she saw you, the way she made you feel like more than just your ambition. And now, she's gone, and you don't know what to do with that. It feels like losing a part of yourself, like you are unraveling in slow motion.

Let me save you some time: you will love again. You will love better. And one day, you will understand that her leaving wasn't an ending—it was a redirection. She gave you what she was meant to give, and you gave her what you were meant to give. And now? Now, you get to learn how to love yourself without needing someone else to affirm that you are worth loving.

And about your father—his absence, his loss, the confusion of not knowing how to grieve a man who was both there and not there? That grief will teach you more about yourself than you can imagine. One day, you will find the language for the things you couldn't

310

say to him. One day, you will stop searching for him in the work you do, in the wisdom of other men, in the echoes of memories you barely remember. One day, you will release him—not in anger, not in pain, but in peace.

But right now, you are in the in-between. And the in-between is messy. You are standing at the threshold of becoming, holding pieces of your younger self while trying to grow into the man you are meant to be. You don't have all the answers. And let me tell you something else—you never will. But that's the beauty of it.

You don't have to have it all figured out to move forward. You just have to trust that the road will rise to meet you when you step.

Here's what I want you to hold onto:

- You are already enough. You don't have to earn that. You don't have to prove that.
- You are allowed to rest. You don't have to run yourself into the ground to be worthy.
- Love will find you again, but first, you have to learn how to be whole by yourself.
- Not everyone will understand your vision, and that's okay. Keep building anyway.
- Your father's absence does not define you. You will make peace with it in your own time.

And most importantly—you don't have to chase the applause. The people who truly see you, the people who truly value you, will never require you to perform for their approval. So walk with your head high, KV.28. You are becoming. And becoming is the most powerful thing you will ever do.

With love and wisdom,
KV.63

THE FIRE WILL REFINE YOU, NOT BURN YOU

Dear KV.35 (my thirty-five-year-old self),

Thirty-five, huh? Wow. You made it here. And let me tell you, what a journey it's been. Seven years ago, you were a different man, standing on the edge of your dreams, reaching for something you couldn't quite name yet. But now? Now, life is filling you up—sometimes like a cup overflowing with abundance, and other times like a storm drowning you in the flood. And I know you're wondering what all of this means.

Why the highest of highs feel like they exist in the same breath as the lowest of lows. Why success and failure feel like two hands around your neck, wrestling for dominance, leaving you breathless in the middle of it all.

Let me start by saying this: it will all be worth it.

Yes, every moment of triumph, every agonizing defeat, every lesson wrapped in the fire of hardship. Because that's the thing, Kenny—the fire will refine you, not burn you. And you will feel the heat, oh my God, you will feel it. There will be moments when you are on the edge of yourself, questioning whether the fire will consume you or purify you. And I need you to believe me when I tell you that you will not be destroyed. You will be reborn.

You're in the middle of something right now, aren't you? You've got one foot in the world you built—the one laced with entertainment, radio broadcasting, and the fast-moving current of a career that has given you access to people and places you once only imagined. And yet, the other foot is planted in something deeper, something that feels like service, like purpose, like a calling you didn't expect. You've walked into rooms you never thought you'd enter. You've been part of organizations that hold history in their hands.

You've been trusted to lead, to shape, to influence. And you keep asking yourself, "Why me? Why now?"

Because you are supposed to be here.

I know you don't always feel like you belong in the spaces you're stepping into, but hear me clearly—you do. You've been equipped for this. Every setback you've endured, every mistake you've made, every victory that felt just out of reach—those were your lessons, your preparation. The moments you thought broke you were actually carving you into the man you needed to be.

And yet, even as you rise, there will be places where you fall. Businesses you poured your heart into will fail. Relationships that you thought were safe will crumble. You will stand in the wreckage of things you once held dear, and you will wonder if you are cursed to repeat the same cycles. You will wonder if you are doomed to lose what you love. And I won't sugarcoat it for you—some of it will hurt like hell.

But Kenny, listen to me. Every loss is not a defeat. Some losses are releases. Some losses are the universe making room for something greater. You will learn this in the most profound way when you hold your second child in your arms. She will be the catalyst for change in ways you never saw coming. She will redefine love for you, and in her, you will find a fire that refuses to let you repeat the past. The pain of separation from her mother will cut deep, reopening wounds you thought had closed.

It will feel like a cruel joke, the same chapter playing again with different characters. But this time, you will write a different ending. You will fight for fatherhood in a way you never have before. And that fight will birth the work that will define the rest of your life.

And then, there will be that other relationship—the one that will gut you. The one that will shake your self-worth, leave you questioning who you are and what you deserve. It will leave scars, ones that whisper to you in the dark, ones that make you hesitate before loving again. But I need you to know, that pain will not be for nothing. That pain will lead you to a calling you never imagined. That pain will be the very thing that pushes you into purpose.

In the ashes of that heartbreak, you will make a decision. A decision to step fully into the work of fatherhood, of advocacy, of healing. And it will not be easy. The weight of it will feel unbearable some days. But Kenny, you will be okay. More than okay—you will thrive.

You will stand in rooms filled with men searching for the same answers you once sought. You will speak words that feel like water in the desert to fathers who have felt forgotten. You will build something that outlives you. And one day, you will look back and realize that every tear, every sleepless night, every unanswered question was leading you here.

So, breathe. Take it all in. The good, the bad, the joy, the sorrow. Live in it. Learn from it. Let it shape you but never break you. Because the fire will refine you, not burn you. Keep going.

Your best is yet to come.

With love and wisdom, Your Future Self
KV.63

PROTECT THE DREAM, PROTECT THE BRAND

KV.42 (my forty-two-year-old self),

Goodness. I have waited seven years to write you this letter. Not because I didn't have the words before, but because I needed you to be ready to hear them. And I can feel it now—you are. I can feel that something in you has shifted, that the ground beneath your feet has steadied, that life no longer feels like a reckless sprint toward an unknown destination.

You are standing in a place where pain has burned away the excess, leaving behind only what is real, only what is necessary. And from that fire, something unshakable is emerging. This letter isn't here to tell you anything you don't already know. It's here to remind you of what you already feel in your bones.

This fire inside you, the one that pain has forged, is the thing that will define the rest of your life. It's the calling you have tried to name for years, the reason why every road you've walked has led you here. You are stepping into something now—something bigger than ambition, bigger than validation, bigger than anything you ever thought would define you. You are beginning to build your life around the only thing that ever truly mattered: speaking to the hearts of men.

Everything is clicking into place now, isn't it? The pieces of you that once felt scattered and disconnected are aligning in ways that finally make sense. The way radio taught you how to communicate, how to hold an audience in your hand like a delicate, sacred thing. The way your years in agencies taught you about systems and structures, how to build something that lasts.

The way your failed businesses weren't failures at all, but class-rooms—teaching you about resilience, about sacrifice, about the

315

weight of responsibility. Even the chapters of your life that seemed like detours were always part of the plan. You see it now, don't you? Every thread was woven with intention, pulling you toward this moment.

And now, you are moving differently. There's a confidence in you that wasn't there before—not the loud, performative kind, but the quiet kind. The kind that doesn't need applause, that doesn't need permission. The kind that stands in a room and shifts the air simply by existing. You are beginning to own your worth. You are beginning to see yourself the way others have seen you all along.

You have traveled. My God, you have traveled. You have stood in places where your language didn't belong, and yet, your presence spoke louder than words. You have walked into rooms where leaders gathered, where men and women shaping nations have listened to you, not because of your title, but because of your truth. You have carried the mission of responsible fatherhood across oceans, across borders, across barriers that should have kept you out. And yet, here you are.

But let's talk about the things you didn't expect. The ones that blindsided you.

The ones that changed you in ways you never saw coming. Like love. The kind you didn't chase. The kind that didn't chase you. The kind that simply arrived, settled, and stayed. The woman who walks beside you now, she isn't like the others. She didn't ask you to shrink, didn't ask you to perform. She saw you—really saw you—and chose you anyway. This love is different because you are different. Because you came into it whole. Because you finally understood that love was never about being completed; it was about being complemented.

And then, there's him. The son you never thought you'd have. The boy who carries your name, your fire, your light. This child, he will stretch you. He will challenge you. He will show you what it means to love beyond your limits. He will give you what you never had—a chance to father a son, to shape a man, to build a legacy that isn't about your work, but about your blood.

KV.42, you are entering a season where things will settle. Not in a stagnant way, not in a way that dulls you. But in a way that allows you to focus. In a way that clears the distractions and leaves only what is essential. And here's what I need you to know: you will not want for anything. You will not have to beg, borrow, or steal to fulfill the mission you have been given. Every resource, every tool, every person you need will be sent to you in due time. And because of that, you will not be owned.

No one will control you. No one will claim your success. Because what is for you will be for you.

But make no mistake—this is not the end of your battles. There will be storms. There will be moments where you doubt, where you wonder if you have enough left to keep going. But when those moments come, remember this: you were never carrying this alone. You have been carried. You have been covered. And you will continue to be.

So go forth and be great. Not because the world is watching, but because you were made for this. Because you have earned this. Because this fire inside you, the one that pain tried to extinguish, is the very thing that will light the path for others.

KV.42, this is only the beginning.

With love and certainty,
KV.63

SEASONING AIN'T AGING, IT'S BECOMING

KV.49 (my forty-nine-year-old self),

This is the last letter I will send to you, not because I don't want to continue writing, but because I know you no longer need these letters. You've arrived. You've become. You are exactly where God intended you to be, precisely when He intended you to be there. You are seasoned. Not aging, not deteriorating, not fading— seasoned. Refined. Sharpened. Steeped in wisdom that only experience, hardship, and growth could cultivate.

And so, as I write these final words, I write them with the weight of knowing you are settled in your spirit, that you are no longer searching for your voice but rather strengthening it, amplifying it. The whispers of self-doubt have been replaced by the quiet confidence of knowing. You have long moved past asking for permission to exist fully, and now you simply do.

I look over the span of our life—yes, our life—and I marvel. The chapters we have written, the moments we have endured, the lessons we have carried with us, the wisdom we have gathered. From the boy who once craved approval to the man who now moves with intention, knowing his worth. From the dreamer who wondered if he was good enough to the architect of a legacy that will outlive him. You, sir, have done well. Take a bow. Stand in the fullness of that truth and let it hold you steady.

This phase of your life, KV.49, will be different. You will find yourself in spaces of influence, not just absorbing but shaping the very nature of those spaces. People will seek you out—not just for what you have done but for who you have become. Your voice will carry weight, not because it is loud, but because it is undeniable. You have built a foundation that allows you to stand, unwavering, while others take notice and draw near.

You are now the head of a national project, overseeing the work of Responsible Fatherhood for a major federal agency. That is no small feat. And you will be that person for as long as you desire to be that person. The brilliance they recognized in you long ago, when you were KV.7, KV.14, KV.21, is now evident to all. They see your works. They see your commitment. They see the influence you carry—not as a gimmick, not as an act, but as a result of decades of dedication and purpose. They admire you, even when they don't know how to say it. Some are unsure of how to place their adoration, unsure of where to direct their gratitude.

And while there will be times when you feel unseen, unrecognized, know this: God has not overlooked you. Your work is being honored in ways you cannot yet perceive.

But here's the truth, KV.49—you will not be the award recipient standing in the center of grand stages, receiving accolades and public praise. That is not the path carved out for you. Your rewards come in the quiet moments, in the spaces where real impact is made, where lives are changed not with spotlights but with substance. Do not mourn this reality; embrace it. You are not meant for fleeting applause. You are meant for enduring legacy.

I told you back in KV.42—God will continue to provide. And He has. And He will. Your sources will never run dry. Your opportunities will continue to expand. And that vision you once whispered into the night, the wish you carried deep within you, it will manifest. I know you have always dreamed of Fathers Incorporated becoming an institution, spoken of in the same breath as the YMCA, Boys & Girls Club, Big Brothers Big Sisters. That day is coming. Your work is laying the foundation for that reality. One day, when people speak of transformative non-profits that have shaped families and communities, Fathers Incorporated will be mentioned among the greats. Mark my words.

But before that day, you will take another leap of faith. You've taken many before, and they have always led you to greater heights. This time, the leap will not be about validation, but about expansion. You will move to a new location—not out of fear, not out of escape, but out of necessity. The ceiling in your current environment is too low, and your spirit knows it. Where you are going, there will be no ceiling. Your influence will be as vast as you dare to dream. Do not shrink your vision. Allow it to stretch beyond what feels possible.

And in the midst of all this change, God will surprise you once more. You will learn of another daughter, one you never expected but will embrace wholeheartedly. She will enter your life in a way that is both beautiful and complex, and though you may struggle with the how, trust in the why. Love will lead the way. Keep the lines of communication open, and let patience guide you. What is meant to be will unfold as it should.

Lastly, as you step into your fiftieth year, know this: You are widely loved. You are deeply appreciated. Your presence in this world matters more than you know. You have shaped lives, inspired movements, built bridges where there were once walls. And now, as you enter this next chapter, I leave you with a final blessing: Enjoy the ride. Let go of any lingering fear. Walk with confidence, with grace, with the unwavering knowing that you are exactly who you were always meant to be.

I love you. And there is absolutely nothing you can do about it.

With all the wisdom and love of the years we have traveled together,

Your Older Self.
KV.63

CHAPTER TWELVE

THE NEXT HORIZON - WALKING FORWARD WITH GRACE

And here we are.

At the end of this road, not at a conclusion, but at a place of clarity—a space where the weight of expectation, judgment, and unnecessary burdens can be set down for good. If you've made it this far, I hope you feel what I feel: lighter, freer, seasoned but not worn, wise but still willing to learn.

This journey we've taken together wasn't about finding the perfect answer or reaching some final state of enlightenment. It was about peeling back layers, unlearning what no longer serves us, and standing firm in who we are without needing permission or approval. It was about embracing the evolution of self—the mistakes, the lessons, the moments of doubt, and the undeniable victories of simply making it this far.

If there is one thing I want you to take away from this book, it is this: You are enough. Not in the way that the world defines worth—not by titles, accolades, or external validation—but in the deep, undeniable way that says, I am here. I am whole. I am worthy just as I am.

For too long, we have measured ourselves against unrealistic expectations. We've carried the weight of past missteps, allowed fear to dictate our choices, and let the whispers of others drown out the voice inside of us. But here, in this seasoned stage of life, the only thing that truly matters is whether or not you can look in the mirror and love the person staring back at you.

Not tolerate. Not critique. Not wish they were different. But love—fully, unapologetically, without condition.

I didn't arrive at this mindset overnight. It took years of trials, years of wrestling with my own insecurities, years of trying to be everything to everyone before realizing that the most important person I needed to be was myself. And once I accepted that, the world opened up in a way I had never experienced before.

There is a peace in not caring—not in the sense of detachment or indifference, but in the powerful release of things that do not serve your joy, your purpose, or your soul. It's in choosing authenticity over performance. It's in setting boundaries without guilt. It's in knowing that your worth isn't up for negotiation.

So, as you close this book, my hope is that you walk away with a renewed sense of self. That you give yourself the grace to grow without apology, to step into spaces without shrinking, to take up the room you deserve without hesitation.

That you recognize the beauty of your own seasoning—that every hardship, every joy, every lesson has made you into the person you are today.

You are too seasoned to care about the noise. You are too seasoned to care about pleasing everyone at the cost of yourself. You are too seasoned to care about fitting into a mold that was never meant for you.

Instead, care about what matters. Care about the life you're building, the love you're giving, the peace you're protecting. Care about being present in the time you have left. Care about the freedom to just be.

Because at the end of the day, that is the greatest gift we can give ourselves.

DEDICATION: WHAT REMAINS WHEN EVERYTHING ELSE FALLS AWAY

I stand here at the edge of this book, at the edge of this moment, looking back at the road I have traveled. I didn't think I would get here—not because I lacked the endurance, but because I didn't know how much I had left to say. Turns out, I had more in me than I thought. Writing this has been a journey, one that forced me to sit with my past, wrestle with my present, and embrace the unknown future.

And now, as I close this chapter, I find myself reflecting on the people who carried me, the lessons that built me, and the truths I have come to hold dear.

This book is dedicated to those who shaped my soul and fueled my spirit, each leaving fingerprints on the man I have become.

To Mr. Art Mitchell, the Renaissance man who taught me what it meant to serve, to build, and to give selflessly to our community. He showed me how to stretch beyond my limits, navigate adversity, and figure it out when the path wasn't clear.

To Diana Jones Ritter, whose quiet strength and wisdom about strategic patience taught me to tackle life's challenges one step at a time, and whose leadership remains a guiding light in how I move through obstacles today.

To Dr. Jack Conway, the red-headed Irish professor who carried more of my history than I knew myself, challenging me to know, to love, and to fight for my people—and in doing so, helped me find a deeper version of myself.

To Greg Owens, my brother-in-arms in the fatherhood movement. Together, we planted seeds across New York State—seeds that may still bloom long after our season has passed.

To my mother, complicated, resilient, and strong—who survived so I could thrive. Though much was left unsaid, her sacrifices have become the soil from which I grew.

To Javid, Rodney, Charles, Patrick, James, David, Eugene, Bishop, and Ferguson—my accountability circle, my iron sharpeners. Brothers who have kept me grounded, honest, and pushing toward my best self.

To Lawrence Wilbon, my dear friend whose life and legacy continue to inspire and whose absence has left a space that will never be filled but always be honored.

To Dr. Ronald Stewart, who arrived in Albany unafraid, challenged the establishment, fell, rose again, and taught me that true leadership is measured not by how you stand when praised, but how you rebuild after you fall.

To the mothers of my children, whose journeys intertwined with mine. Though our paths evolved, I honor the love, the lessons, and most of all, the beautiful lives we created together.

To the fathers everywhere who show up—especially when it's hard. Your resilience, your love, and your fight are the heartbeat of hope.

And to my living legacy, the pulse that drives my overwhelming desire for excellence:

To Monica, Tiarrah, Amber, Nzinga, and KJ—my children. You have taught me more about love, purpose, and pride than any accolade ever could. You are my why.

To Andrew, my nephew, who has walked beside me as a son, carrying the honor and dreams of our family on his shoulders.

To my grandchildren, Neveah, Max, and Naila—the joy of my seasoned years. Your laughter is my light. Your future is my promise. Your dreams are the new chapters I long to see written.

As I close this book, I think about what remains when everything else falls away. The accolades, the titles, the battles won and lost— none of that matters as much as the people who shaped you, the love that carried you, and the wisdom you leave behind.

So here's my final lesson: Stop agonizing over distractions.

Stop letting the voices of doubt and criticism take up space in your mind. Stop replaying old wounds like a broken record that skips on the same lyric. Life is too short to live for the approval of others.

The moral of my story is this—live with intention, move with purpose, and leave no words unsaid.

Heal when you can. Forgive when you must. But never stop moving forward.

I've spent too much of my life caring about what people think. But now? Now, I am too damn seasoned to care about distractions. Too seasoned to waste time on things that do not serve me. Too seasoned to let someone else define my worth.

Whatever title this book ends up with, whatever subtitle graces its cover, know this: At this point in my life, I don't give a fuck about what you think about me.

And that, my friends, is the freest I have ever been.

THE SEASONED COLLECTIVE

RESOURCES OF THE SEASONED COMMUNITY

Where experience becomes wisdom, and wisdom becomes impact.

The Seasoned Collective is a purpose-driven space for experienced professionals ready to align their life, leadership, and legacy with clarity and intention.

Contact Information
Email: admin@seasonedcollective.com
Telephone: 404-477-4471

Visit our digital home to explore the mission, engage with featured resources, and learn how to take the next step in your Seasoned journey. Whether you're seeking clarity, connection, or content, everything starts here.

The Official Website
https://www.theseasonedcollective.com

Tune in to real, reflective, and relatable conversations with voices that understand what it means to grow, lead, and evolve in your seasoned years. Each episode offers perspective, truth, and tools to help you navigate life's next chapter.

Seasoned Conversations

The Podcast
seasonedconversations.podbean.com

Follow, connect, and contribute across our digital platforms as we build a vibrant, intentional community of seasoned leaders. From shared wisdom to community engagement, your voice belongs here.

Social Media Community

Facebook:
www.facebook.com/theseasonedcollective

LinkedIn:
linkedin.com/company/the-seasoned-collective

YouTube:
www.youtube.com/@TheSeasonedCollective

Instagram:
www.instagram.com/seasonedcollective

Continue the Journey with The Seasoned Collective

You've read the story. Now join the movement.

The Seasoned Collective is a private, purpose-driven community for those who have lived enough to know that peace matters more than performance—and who are ready to live, lead, and love from a place of alignment.

Inside the Collective, you'll find resources, real conversations, and people who understand the weight you've carried and the wisdom you've earned. From live sessions and training to reflective content and connection, this is the space where experience becomes elevation.

Because you're not behind. You're not broken. You're seasoned—and that changes everything.

YOUR COMMUNITY AWAITS

www.theseasonedcollective.com

Deepen Your Journey with the Too Seasoned to Care Journal Workbook

Reflection transforms insight into lasting wisdom. Accompany your reading experience with the Too Seasoned to Care Journal Workbook, a thoughtful companion designed to guide you deeper into personal growth, authenticity, and liberation.

Filled with powerful journaling prompts, self-reflective exercises, and insightful questions, this workbook encourages you to explore your own seasoned story. Gain clarity, celebrate your truths, and uncover the courage to live boldly and unapologetically.

Perfect for personal introspection, group discussion, or guided workshops, the Too Seasoned to Care Journal Workbook is your invitation to turn lessons into lasting change, reflection into empowerment, and wisdom into liberation.

Embrace your seasoned wisdom—
start your journaling journey today.

AVAILABLE NOW

www.theseasonedcollective.com

Made in the USA
Monee, IL
14 September 2025

24561699R00194